A Genealogical Record of the Descendants of Thomas Carhart of Cornwall, England

Mary E. (Carhart) Dusenbury

Alpha Editions

This edition published in 2020

ISBN : 9789354026089

Design and Setting By
Alpha Editions
email - alphaedis@gmail.com

As per information held with us this book is in Public Domain.
This book is a reproduction of an important historical work. Alpha Editions uses the best technology to reproduce historical work in the same manner it was first published to preserve its original nature. Any marks or number seen are left intentionally to preserve its true form.

A

GENEALOGICAL RECORD

OF THE DESCENDANTS OF

𝕿𝖍𝖔𝖒𝖆𝖘 𝕮𝖆𝖗𝖍𝖆𝖗𝖙,

OF CORNWALL, ENGLAND.

COMPILED FROM OFFICIAL RECORDS AND PRIVATE MSS.

WITH AN APPENDIX OF NOTES.

BY

MARY E. (CARHART) DUSENBURY.

"OUR DEAD ARE NEVER DEAD TO US UNTIL WE HAVE FORGOTTEN THEM."
George Elliot.

A. S. BARNES & COMPANY,
NEW YORK, CHICAGO, AND NEW ORLEANS.
1880.

PREFACE.

This Memorial, commenced in 1873, has grown out of an effort to arrange the fragments of fact and tradition found floating in memory, and to add to them such information as might be obtained from other sources, for the purpose of answering the question: "What is known of the early ancestors of the Carhart family?"

The desire to know something more concerning these early ancestors had often arisen in my own mind, but not with sufficient force to lead me to make the necessary research, until this request was presented, when I took the matter in hand, without any intention beyond that of giving a simple sketch.

In the beginning of my investigations I found that the desire to collect and compile the records and traditions of the past, in relation to their ancestors, was active also in three other branches of the family.

Charles Carhart, of Perryville, Hunterdon Co., N. J., had already collected valuable information, and Elwood Carhart, of Oxford, Chester Co., Pa., proposed to visit the families of his native State, New Jersey, and subsequently did so, and collected such records and traditions as could be obtained. He also spent some time at Trenton in searching for and copying documents from "East Jersey Records," which have been arranged in the order of their dates.

For nine years previous to 1879, George Beavers Carhart, of Macon, Ga., and at present of Brooklyn, N. Y., had been residing with his family in Europe, mainly in France, and during this period, his son, Amory Sibley Carhart, had visited at times the native land of his early ancestor, and obtained the Coat of Arms at the Herald's Office, in London, and extracts from records of the family in Co. Cornwall, which will be found in their appropriate place.

Previous to the commencement of these researches, neither the New Jersey branches, nor those of Rye, Westchester Co., N. Y., were aware that they were descendants of a common ancestor. When this was made known, it became a source of great encouragement to all interested, to find the desire aroused in each branch to trace the pedigree of the family. It was then proposed to place the matter as collected, in my hands, for the purpose of being arranged in the orderly form of a Genealogical Record.

The task of collecting my own branch, John,[1] of Rye, together with the principal part of the Appendix, has devolved upon me, with one exception, that of Daniel, of Coeymans, Albany Co., N.Y., which was furnished through the patient efforts of Mrs. Margaret A. Hauxhurst, of that town.

The labor of collecting these materials has exceeded the expectations of all. In my own case, about three hundred letters have been received, and treble that number written, to gather up the names of descendants, and such items of interest as could be reached.

It is not claimed that all of the name of Carhart have been found and recorded. The family of Thomas,[3] of Bethlehem, Albany Co., New York—grandson of John,[1] of Rye—is fragmentary. His living descendants are unable to give any account of those of his sons, Thomas,[4] and Peter Carhart, or his daughters, Clorinia=Durie and Annie=Cregier.

There are also, in the New Jersey branches, some names whose families cannot be traced. The search for these missing ones has been thorough, but thus far unsuccessful.

It is worthy of notice that the various families have been located in their appropriate places in the regular line of descent, and the simplest form of designation by numbers has been adopted. To avoid confusion by breaking the line of descent, by generations, these have been marked simply at the left of the page.

More extended lists of the female branches have been given than is usual in works of this kind. In every instance, where the records could be obtained, the descent has been carried to the second generation,

An Appendix of Notes has been added, giving sketches of the pedigrees of many of those who have intermarried with the Carhart family, and notices of some of the descendants. Those who find themselves unmentioned here, must refer the omission to their own neglect.

The sketch of the family of Major William Phillips has been collected from various historical authorities, at an expense of much time and labor, and will be found to contain many interesting facts.

The most grateful acknowledgments are tendered to those who gave a ready response to calls for private family records and documents, and for kind words of encouragement from various branches who seemed to appreciate my feeling and motives.

Perfection, however, in such a work, cannot be expected. In some instances no dates can be found, in which case only an approximation to accuracy is attempted, and in every such instance it is so stated.

The entire manuscript has been rewritten twice, and parts of it three and four times, to admit of additional families, and different arrangement.

The author has endeavored to make the record as full and accurate as faithful effort can render it. She assures the living descendants of Thomas Carhart, that she has spared no pains to make it a repository of facts that will interest the members of the family ; and to her, at least, the object has appeared to justify this bestowal of time and attention.

To preserve the memory of a heroic life, or noble name, among one's ancestors, should be an honorable pride. Such a name, or life, is a stimulus to higher and nobler living—not food for vanity.

To do this, as a duty, lovingly and conscientiously performed, one should feel that the work is private, and, in a sense, done in the sanctity of family life.

"The love of kindred underlies true patriotism."

With these explanations and remarks, the work is submitted to the members of the family, in the hope that it will be acceptable.

M. E. C. D.

SEA VIEW PLACE, HOBOKEN, N. J., *January*, 1880.

Carhurta.

ARMS: ar. two bars, sa. in chief, a demi-Griffin, issuant of the last.

CREST: a demi-man, naked, ar. a wreath about his head, sa. in right hand an oaken branch, vt. acorns, or.

Carhurta.

ARMS: ar. two bars, sa. in chief, a demi-Griffin, issuant of the last.
CREST: a stag, ermined, attired, or.

CONTENTS.

	PAGES
COATS OF ARMS,	7, 9
INTRODUCTION,	11
EXTRACTS FROM PUBLIC DOCUMENTS,	15
GENEALOGY OF NEW YORK BRANCH,	23
CHART OF FAMILY OF JOHN,	24
GENEALOGY OF NEW JERSEY BRANCHES,	59
CHART OF FAMILY OF ROBERT,	60
CHART OF FAMILY OF WILLIAM,	78
APPENDIX — NOTES,	85
INDEXES — DESCENDANTS OF JOHN,	117
DESCENDANTS OF ROBERT,	125
DESCENDANTS OF WILLIAM,	130
DESCENDANTS FROM FEMALE BRANCHES,	134
INTERMARRIED NAMES,	138

INTRODUCTION.

THOMAS CARHART, the progenitor of the Carhart family in America, arrived at New York, August 25, 1683, holding the appointment of private Secretary to Col. Thomas Dongan, English Governor to the Colonies in America, at that date.

He was the son of Anthony Carhart, of Co. Cornwall, Gentleman. The exact place and date of his birth, have not been ascertained. He was probably born about 1650, and was unmarried when he came to America.

I am informed by Mr. Stephen Carhart, of Nevada, Story Co., Iowa (who was born in Cornwall, and has resided in America for several years) that, "A valuable Pedigree, from 1550, to the present time, is in the possession of a clergyman, connected with the family, now living in Cornwall." Repeated efforts have been made to obtain extracts from this Pedigree, but they have been unsuccessful. "The Bible of Anthony Carhart—more than two hundred years old—containing the name of Thomas Carhart, his son, who came to America in 1683—is said to be in the possession of a Mr. Hunt, of Treslothian, Co. Cornwall."

The following historical facts, obtained in England, were furnished by Amory Sibley Carhart, of Brooklyn, N. Y.

While in London, in January, 1876, he engaged the services of a Herald, who was most highly recommended to him, as the best in the city, and a person of undoubted honesty. He, after having had the books of the various Visitations in the British Museum, thoroughly searched, and after consultation with other persons, whose authority in such matters could be vouched for, informed Mr. A. S. Carhart that, "At the earliest mention of the family, 1420, in the Herald's office, and British Museum, London; the name is found to have been *Carhurta*, and *Carharta*, and the arms:

Shield. Ar. two bars, sa. in chief, a demi-griffin, issuant of the last.
Crest. A demi-man, naked, ar. a wreath about his head, sa. in right hand, an oaken branch, vt. acorns, or.

"The Griffin was most probably instituted by Richard II.," who reigned from 1376 to 1399, "as his signet ring bore that emblem, denoting strength and swiftness, and was afterwards introduced into Heraldry."—*Edmondston's Heraldry.*

From this statement, taken in connection with the date of record at the Herald's office, it may be inferred that these arms were achieved and granted, either during the reign of Richard II., or soon after.

Edmondston also says, that by systematizing the recording of arms, Richard II. established the order out of which has grown the Herald's College: thus banishing the confusion and irregularity which had previously rendered the tracing of arms almost impossible.

The Carhurta arms are also found quartered with those of Cottell, Malherb, and Godfrey: surmounted by the Cottell crest. Quartering became usual in the time of Richard II.

Cottell, of Yoembridge, Devonshire:
    Arms. Or. on a bend gu. a crescent for difference.
    Crest. Out of a ducal coronet. or, a leopard sequant proper. charged with a crest. or. for a difference.

Malherb, of Devonshire:
    Arms. Or. a chev. between three nettle leaves proper.

Godfrey, of Bodgood, Cornwall:
    Arms. Az. a Griffin sequant. sa.

For the purpose of preventing the unlawful assumption of arms, it was ordered in the 16th century, that a Herald should be sent every thirty years, throughout England, to ascertain whether all families bearing arms had the right to do so. The records of one of these Heralds, named Harl, are received as standard authority on all questions pertaining to Heraldry, from that time.

In Harl's MSS. of Visitations of Devonshire, in 1565, (to be found in the British Museum), p. 5871, he says: " The Carhurta family have the right to bear arms," and describes those before mentioned.

Also, in Harl's Visitations, is found the marriage of Thomas Carhurta, with Margery, daughter and heir of Richard Malherb, of Thorne. Issue of this marriage, Roger Carhurta.

In the parochial and family history of the Deanery of Trigg-minor, in the Co. of Cornwall, by John McCleon, Esq., F. S. R. in the Parish of Minster, is found the family name of Cottell, Cotel, Cotele, and Cottle. John Cottell, of Yoembridge, Co. Devonshire (who lived about 1420, and was probably the representative of the house of Cotele), heads the pedigree recorded at the Herald's Office. He married Sarah, daughter and heir of Roger Carhurta, of Devonshire; whose mother was Margery, daughter and heir of Richard Malherb.

The name of Malherb is found in the Roll of Battle Abbey, among those who came to England with William the Conqueror.

The names of Carharta and Carhurta, are apparently of Saxon and Danish origin, from

    Carr. Anglo Saxon, a rock, or *Caer*, a town or city.
    Heorte. A. S. and *herta*, Old Saxon, from which is derived the word, *heart*.
    Heort. A. S. *hert*, Danish, from which is derived, *hart*, a stag.

Mark Antony Lowers, in his dictionary of family names, says: "*Car, Carr, Caer*, was the initial syllable of many local names, which have become surnames, especially in Scotland and Cornwall. It is a Celtic word, signifying an artificial military strength, whether fort or castle."

Wm. Smith, L.L.D., author and classical examiner, in the University of London, says: " As to memorials of the Saxons, preserved in the names of men, families, or places, they are so numerous that there is hardly a locality in the whole extent of England where a majority of the names is not pure and unadulterated Saxon. They have in many cases been converted into English, by contracting, or otherwise modifying the pronunciation and orthography."

For example,—In a record of the Cornish Gentry, the name is found spelt, *Carrheart*—Mr. Hicks Carrheart spelling it thus, leaving the Saxon, *herta* or *hurta*, and taking the derivative, *heart*.

In Burke's Landed Gentry, is recorded the marriage of Peter Symonds, an eminent merchant and Alderman of Plymouth, who died in 1787, son of Rev. Wm. Symonds, of Chadderwood, to Elizabeth, daughter of *Hicks Carhart*, Esq., of *Carhart*, Co. Cornwall, in 1764. It will be observed that this is the same gentleman, whose name is spelt *Carrheart*, showing a second change in the orthography.

"The family of Symonds is of great antiquity in Cornwall; is stated to have come over with William the Conqueror, and the descent is deduced from the Counts of Avranches, in Normandy, and is entitled in point of antiquity, and its alliances, to rank with the highest in the Co. of Cornwall."—*Burke's Heraldry*.

Arms. Per fesse. dancette gu. and ar. a pale counter charged. three tripods. one and two clipped of the first.
Crest. On a mount vt. in front of a saltire, gu. an ermine holding in mouth a fern branch. ppr.

Lyson records, in his history of Cornwall, that the elder branch of the family, that of Thomas Carhurta, became extinct, but does not give the date. We may infer, from the last record of the family—given by Harl, in 1565, that it was subsequent to this date, or during the latter part of the 16th century.

In the event of the elder branch becoming extinct, the younger were granted the privilege, on petition, to adopt the arms of the elder, and as appears, a younger branch, on the adoption of the Carhurta arms, chose, as was their right, a new crest, which is recorded in both Edmondston's and Berry's Heraldries thus :

Carhurta, *Arms*. ar. two bars. sa. in chief a demi Griffin issuant of the last.
Crest. a stag. ermined. attired. or.

As the last syllable of the name, is apparently derived from the Saxon and Danish words ; *herta, heort*, and *hert*, the roots of the two English words, *heart* and *hart*, there is, evidently, a connection between the latter syllable of the modern name, and the second crest.

Sir George McKenzie says, "Some have taken their surnames from their arms, or their arms to suit their names."

A parochial history of Cornwall states, that the beginning of the use of the English language in Cornwall, dates from the latter part of the reign of Henry VIII,—who died in 1547—and that in 1640, the Cornish language was banished from the churches, and the English substituted.

Probably, names began to be changed at the same time, from the Saxon, to the English orthography.

It is not improbable that these arms were brought to America ; as the tradition exists in the family of John of Rye, that the Carhart arms contained a *hart*, or stag.

Mr. A. S. Carhart, while residing in France, held correspondence with Col. Armand Constantine Cahart, a retired officer of the French army, residing at present in Paris, 20 Rue Mozart, who was able to trace his family to England ; they having left that country between 1648 and 1688, in consequence of their religious tenets, just before the revocation of the Edict of Nantes.

This gentleman's family resided for a while in Normandy, passed thence into Ardennes and Lorraine at the revocation of the Edict of Nantes. His father was master of the Poste at Steney, department of the Meuse. A brother of Col. Cahart, is landed proprietor and mayor of the town of Fresnes en Woerve, near the city of Verdun, department of the Meuse.

There have been found attached to public documents, wills, etc, in Cornwall, the following names ; which seem to prove that the name became permanently changed, during the 17th century.

William Carhart, of Luxulian, in 1707. Eliza Carhart, of Lanivet, 1717. Philip Carhart, of Blissland, 1723. Robert Carhart, of Roach, 1773. William Carhart, of Bodmin, 1778. Richard Carhart of St. Minever, Wadebridge, 1875. John Carhart, Miller of Crockapit Mills, Broad Oak, Lostwithiel, 1875, who married a cousin of F. E. Gurney, of Buckingham Villa, Aylesbury, Bucks Co. William Carhart, of Lostwithiel, 1876.

Stephen Carhart, of Nevada, Story Co., Iowa, is brother of William, of Lostwithiel.

Descendants of Thomas Carhart have been found settled in the states of Maine, Vermont, Massachusetts, Connecticut, New York, New Jersey, Pennsylvania, Maryland, Dis. Col., Virginia, N. Carolina, Georgia, Michigan, Ohio, Kentucky, Tennessee, Illinois, Missouri, Wisconsin, Iowa, Minnesota, Nebraska, Utah, Texas, Louisiana, California.

William S. Carhart, of New Orleans, in 1852, cannot be assigned to his family.

In Rye, W. C., Co. N. Y., which became the place of residence of John, oldest son of Thomas of Cornwall, the name is found spelled in three different ways, Carhartt, Carehartt, and lastly, Carhart. In some parts of the country, the name is still spelt, Carhartt.

EXTRACTS FROM PUBLIC DOCUMENTS.

MAY, 1691. The first record found in America, referring to THOMAS CARHART, is, of a joint petition with William Britton; for lands on the south side of Staten Island, at a place called Great Hill, dated May, 1691. —*See vol. 39, p. 211, N. Y. Col. Mss.*

"Thomas Carhart was clerk of Richmond Co., 1691."—*Clute's Annals of Staten Island.*

"May 4th, 1691, ordered Thomas Stilwell, sheriff of Richmond Co., Staten Island, to summon the widow of Richard Stilwell, to appear before the council, and set forth her title to a tract of land applied for by Thomas Carhart and William Britton of Staten Island."—*Land Calendars of N. Y.*

Nov. 22, 1691. "In the same year, Nov. 22d, "A marriage license was granted to THOMAS CARHART of Staten Island, in the Co. of Richmond, Gentleman, and MARY LORD."—(*See vol. 4, Records of Wills, Surrogate's Office, Marriage Licenses of N. Y. State.*)

[The date and place of marriage have not been found.] "A grant from the British Crown, to Thomas Carhart, of Staten Island, Gentleman, for 165 acres, on the south side of Staten Island, at a place called Great Hill, dated April 16th, 1692," is recorded in the *Old Field book at Albany, N. Y.*

Nov. 14, 1694. "A deed of conveyance from Anthony Brockholtz, of the city of N. Y., Gentleman, and Susanna his wife, to Thomas Carhart, for land and premises in the within Patent," (Location not designated). Witnesses, Edward Taylor, English Smith, city of New York. Stephen Van Courtlandt, Justice of Peace.—(*Liber E. East Jersey Records, page 172, Trenton.*)

[Previous to this date Thomas had removed to Woodbridge, N. J.]

May 24, 1695. "A deed of Thomas Carhart, of Woodbridge, Middlesex Co., N. J., Gentleman, and Mary his wife, to John Loofburrow, of Woodbridge, for one acre of upland, on the south side of Crane Creek, to frame and erect a Grist Mill, with right of way, through the land of Thomas Carhart."

THOMAS CARHART [L. S.]
MARY CARHART. [L. S.]

Witnessed by
 ROBERT VANQUILLIAN.
 JOHN CARRINGTON.   *Book E, p. 445, E. J. Records, Trenton.*

[The death of Thomas Carhart seems to have occurred between these dates.]

Feb. 19, 1686. "A lease by Mary Carhart of Woodbridge, N. J., to Thomas Bills, of Burlington in West Jersey, of house and plantation on Crane Creek, in the town of Woodbridge, N. J. containing one hundred and twenty acres, during the term of three years, after the first of May next, at a yearly sum of five pounds, N. Y. money," etc, etc, etc.

          MARY CARHART. [L. S.]
Witnessed by   THOMAS BILLS. [L. S.]
 BENJ. GRIFFITH.
 RICHARD ALLINGHAM
 JOHN BARCLAY.

(*Recorded in Book F of Deeds, p.* 219, *Trenton.*)

WILL OF THOMAS CARHART.

IN THE NAME OF GOD. AMEN.

 I, Thomas Carhartt, of Woodbridge, in the Co. of Middlesex, in the Province of East New Jersey, being sick of body, but of sound and perfect memory, praised be Almighty God ; do make, and ordain, this, my last will and testament in manner and form following, hereby revoking all former wills made by me.

 Imprimis. I will that my funeral charges and debts be well and truly paid, in some convenient time after my decease, by my executrix, hereafter named, and as to my real estate, my will is, and I do hereby, will, devise, and bequeath, in manner and form following, *viz.:* That my wife, Mary Carhart, shall have, hold possession and enjoy, all my lands, tenements, and hereditaments, whatsoever, for, and during her natural life, for the maintenance, and bringing up of our children.

 But if she shall happen to marry, then my will and meaning is : that the one-half of my lands and tenements shall be to her, for and during, her natural life, and after her decease, all my lands and tenements, shall descend and come unto my three sons, John, Robert and William, to be equally divided between them.

 But if it shall happen, that my said wife shall be inclined to go for Auld England, with her children, that then I do, hereby give full power and authority, by and with the assent of my overseers, hereafter named, to sell, alien and dispose of all my lands and tenements whatsoever, one-third part of the real value thereof to be to her, the said Mary, my wife, her heirs, and assigns forever, the remainder to be equally divided between my three sons, above mentioned, to be paid to them, when they come to the age of one and twenty years. And I do hereby nominate, constitute and appoint, my trusty and well beloved friends, Mr. English Smith, Mr. Thomas Hamerdan, both of N. Y., to be my trustees, to council and advise my said executrix. And I do hereby nominate and appoint my loving, and dear wife, Mary Carhartt, to be my sole executrix of this my last will and testament.

 In witness whereof, I have hereunto set my hand and seal, this sixteenth day of March, Anno Domini, one thousand, six hundred and ninety-five.   THOMAS CARHARTT. [SEAL.]

 Signed, sealed, published, and delivered by the testator, to be his last will and testament, in the presence of
              JOHN LOOFBURROW.
              JOHNATHAN DENHAM.
              WILLIAM FROST.
              BENJAMIN GRIFFITH.

Mar. 26th, 1696. "By the Governor. Perth Amboy, Mar. 26th, 1696. Then appeared before me, Benjamin Griffith, John Loofburrow, William Frost, three of the witnesses to the aforesaid last will and testament, and did solemnly declare, in the presence of God, that they did see the said Thomas Carhartt sign, seal, publish, and declare, this to be his last will and testament, and that at the time thereof, he was of a perfect and sound mind and understanding."

ANDREW HAMILTON.

April 6, 1696. "To all Christian people, and others, * * * * * the Governor and Proprietors of the Province of East Jersey, send greeting. Know ye, that the last will and testament of Thomas Carhartt, late of Woodbridge, in the Co. of Middlesex, deceased, and hereunto annexed, was rendered, proved, and approved, before us, and the said Thomas Carhartt, having, whilst he lived, divers goods and chattels to be administered of, within the said Province, and the right of disposing thereof. Now further know ye, that we have admitted the administration, &c., &c., unto Mary Carhartt, widow, and sole executrix, &c., &c., of the said will, to administer of the same, &c., &c., according to law, and further to make a true and just acct. of her administration, on or before the seventeenth of April one thousand, six hundred and ninety-seven."

ANDREW HAMILTON.

Given, &c., &c., Apr. 6th, 1696.

"State of New Jersey. I, Henry C. Welsey, Register of the Prerogative Court, of said State, do hereby certify that the foregoing is a true copy of the will of Thomas Carhartt, &c., &c., taken from, and compared with the original Record, in *Book E. of Deeds, page* 458, now in my office.

Witness my hand and seal, of the Prerogative Court, at Trenton, Dec. 24th, 1875."

HENRY WELSEY.

AN INVENTORY of the goods and chattels of Mr. Thomas Carhart, deceased, taken and apprised by us, whose names are underwritten, this 21st day of May, 1696:

Imprimis.	£	s.	d.
To wearing clothes	06	00	00
" a rapier sword, and belt, shot pouch, and bagenet	01	10	00
" a pair of pistols, broken and out of order	00	10	00
" 6 silver spoons and salt, a small tumbler, plates	03	12	00
" white earthenware, and drinking glasses	00	09	00
" eight glass bottles	00	02	00
" a ould warming pan	00	06	00
" a paire of andirons	00	12	00
" a small round table, ould	00	06	00
" a case of drawers, ould and decayed	00	15	00
" a trunk and chest	01	00	00
" a looking-glass	00	12	00
" a flock bed, three pillows and bolster, two ould blankets and a rug	01	05	00
" 5 leather chairs and one cane chair, and 6 turned chairs, ould	01	04	00

	£	s.	d.
To a ould round table	00	09	00
" a square table	00	12	00
" a bedstead and ould hangings	00	03	00
" pair of andirons	01	00	00
" a pair of tongs and ould fire shovel	00	02	06
" 24 lbs. of bar iron	00	09	00
" a pott and pott hooks, two trunks	01	00	00
" a pair of salt sellers	00	15	00
" 4 pewter platters and one pie plate	2	09	06
" 6 good pewter plates, and 12 ould ones	1	01	00
" 2 candlesticks	0	06	00
" a pewter basin and ewer, one salt	0	06	06
" a tankard, and pint pot, a brass candlestick		07	03
" pewter pie pan		03	00
" 3 tin pans, 1 funnell, 1 fish pan		12	00
" a brass kettle, small skillet and skimmer		14	09
" copper pot, wooden pestle and mortar		06	00
" a forcing pan, chaffing dish, gridiron		06	00
" 3 earthen basins, 3 plates		05	00
" a spit and jade, 3 trays, ould iron	2	06	06
" ould lumber		07	00
" one cow, 3 one yr. ould colts, 2 two yrs. ould	13	10	00
" 3 yearlings, 28 sheep, 3 goats, 4 swine	23	05	00
" an ould waggon	1	10	00

SAMUEL JAMES.
JOHN BISHOP.

[It may be reasonably inferred, from the fact that no farm implements are mentioned in this inventory, that Thomas Carhart did not resume farming operations after his removal to Woodbridge.]

The Estate of Thomas Carhart, late of Woodbridge, in the Countie of Midsx., Gentleman, deceased, Dr.

	£	s.	£	s.	d.
To Wm. Loveridge, payd him towards the funeral charges	2	7			
" Widow Carrington for funeral charges	4	18			
			7	5	
For ditto payd her on a bill and accpt. as per receipt			11	10	10½
" John Barclay for letters of administration, &c			2	3	9
" Richard Powell			3	18	6
" Benjamin Griffith for bill			9		
" "Sarah Smith" of New York			9	19	6
" John Ireland			1	10	
" Thomas Hawardsen's accpt. for moving			6	17	6
" David Hewitt			2	3	1
" Edward Iwans			1		
" John Robinson			1	3	10
" Hannah Vanhock			1	5	6
" John Leland			2	17	3

	£	s.	d.
To John Pallog...	1	2	10½
" Wm. Frost...	2	8	9
" Henry Coleman.......................................	1	16	9
" Samuel Moore...	4		
" Cattle and sheepe dead since the apprisement (viz., 2 sheepe, one cow, and two hogs, lost)................	4	16	
	£75	00	

Contra.

	£	s.	d.
By an inventory of his goods and chattels taken and apprised, amounting to, in all................................	69	18	00
" James Armour received...............................	3	04	00
" Thomas Coddington "		15	00
" Jacob Corbill...		11	00
" Thomas Dundas......................................		12	00
	£75	00	

Apr. 2, 1697. "Perth Amboy. A true and just account of the administration of Marie Carhart, widow, and executor of Thomas Carhart, deceased.

In right of her executorship upon the goods and chattels of the estate of the sayd Thomas Carhart, made up and adjusted, and taken the day and year aforesaid, and before me."

JAMES DUNDAS, *Com.*

Dated in the Office, 2nd Apr., 1697.

Apr. 20th, 1697. Date of quietus to Marie Carhart, as executor of last will and testament of Thos. Carhart. *Book F, p. 219, East Jersey Records, Trenton.*.

Aug. 28, 1699. "The land on Staten Island comprised in the Grant of April 16th, 1692, was sold to Catharine Vandeventer, and Annie Jacobson, Aug. 28th, 1699."—*2nd Vol. Johnson's Reports, p. 170.*

May 20th, 1700. [Previous to this date, Mary Lord Carhart had married Thomas Warne, probably about 1698, as her last signature of Mary Carhart bears date 1697, and first as Mary Warne 1700.]

"Thomas Warne, Sen., of Dublin, merchant, was one of the twenty-four Proprietary Governors of East Jersey, which was purchased by them from the Duke of York, March 14th, 1682. He sold two-thirds of his interest, and the remaining third descended to his sons, Stephen and Thomas Warne, Jr., who came with eleven persons to the Province of East Jersey, March, 1683, and are recorded as becoming owners of several lots at Amboy."—*Whitehead's History of N. J.*

In Burke's Landed Gentry, the Warne family is recorded as seated at St. Colomb and Padstow, Co. Cornwall.

Arms. Sa. a cross or. in the first and fourth quarters a martlet of the second, in the second and third a chaplet, ar.
Crest. A horse shoe or. between two wings ppr.

June 15th, 1713. "Land was laid out for Thomas Carhart, in the right of Henry Lessenbee, * * * * containing six acres, bounded on the north side by a highway, west, by Francis Walker's lot, north, by Timothy Bloomfield's lot, and east, by Peter Codriche's lot, lying on the north side of the southerly branch of Rahway river."—*Woodbridge Records, Liber A, p. 299.*

"This land lies between Six Road Tavern and the Second Presbyterian Church of to-day. Sept. 12th, 1875."—*Town Clerk of Woodbridge.*

DEED OF THOMAS WARNE TO THE BROTHERS CARHART.

"To all whom these presents witness shall come, I, Thomas Warne, do send greeting :

"Know ye, that I, Thomas Warne, of the Co. of Middlesex, in the Province of N. J., for and in consideration of the love, good will, and affection which I bear towards my loving sons-in-law (step-sons), John, Robert and William Carhart, their heirs, executors, and administrators, of the said Co. and Province, have given and granted, and by these presents do freely, clearly and absolutely give and grant unto the said John, Robert and William Carhart, their heirs, executors and administrators :

"Six hundred acres of land, being a share of my property not yet taken up, equally to be divided and shared between the said, John, Robert and William, etc, etc, etc, as their own proper land forever, giving and paying my proportion of the chief, or Quit-rent, etc, etc unto our new Sovereign.

"In witness whereof, I have hereunto set my hand and seal, the twenty-seventh day of Sept. A. D. 1714, in the 13th year of our Lord,—Anne, of Great Britain, Queen."

THOMAS WARNE. [L.S.]

"Signed, sealed and delivered, in the presence of JACOB ARENTS, THOMAS ELAN, SETH ELAN."

[From the fact that he signs alone, it may be inferred that his wife Mary was dead.]

April 8th 1717. "Memorandum—That on the 8th day of April 1717, the above named Thomas Warne, came before me, Thomas Gordon, of his Magisty's council of the Province of East Jersey, and did acknowledge the above written instrument to be his Will and Deed to the within mentioned."

THOMAS GORDON.
Book A, 2, p. 94.

Oct. 22nd, 1716. "Memorandum—This 22nd, day of Oct. 1716, I, John Carhart, one of the within mentioned, have assigned and conveyed unto Dr. Jacob Arents, my share, or part of the within mentioned Deed of Gift," etc., etc., etc.

JOHN CARHART. [L. S.]

Witness, RICHARD HIGGINS, JOHN HENDRICKSEN.

[As near as can be ascertained, the southern part of the city of Newark, is situated on this land.]

March 30th, 1717,—"A third lot was layed out for Robert and William Carhart, in the right of Henry Lessenbee, containing ten acres, with allowance for waste land, adjoining the land which formerly belonged to their father, Thomas Carhart."

THOMAS FISKE. Lot layer.
GEORGE BOWN and WM. ILSLEE, comtt.
MOSES ROLPH, clerk.   JOHN LOOFBURROW, Free Holder.
Freeholder's Book, folio 61.

May 8th, 1717. "A fourth lot was drawn by Robert Carhart, in the right of Henry Lessenbee, containing 8 acres, being No. 39, bounded etc." *Folio 71.*   MOSES ROLF, *clerk.*

Mr. Dally, author of History of Woodbridge, and town clerk, 1876, says: "Thomas Carhart, was admitted a freeholder, in right of Henry Lessenbee, 1695, Carhart, taking all his rights, then Carhart's heirs taking up these lands ;" and he locates the fourth division, in the favor of Robert, as laying, at what is now the depot at Woodbridge, on the N. Y. and Long Branch R.R.

June 1st, 1717. "*Indenture* made between John Carhart of Woodbridge, etc., etc., and Robert and William, of Amboy N. J., Gentlemen.

"Whereas Thomas Carhart lately deceased, stood lawfully vested etc, etc, of several tracts of land lying in the town of Woodbridge, N. J. and in the year 1695, did make his Will, etc, etc, wherein he gave all his lands whatsoever, etc, etc, to Mary, his wife, Executrix of his Will, and his three sons, John, Robert, and William to be equally divided. as by his Will, etc.

"Now this *Indenture* witnesseth that the said John Carhart, by and with the consent of his good wife Anne, etc, etc, for a consideration of the sum of seventy £s. etc, etc, to be paid by the said Robert and William Carhart, etc, etc, etc, all that tract of land being, and lying in Woodbridge, on the south side of Vanquilleis Creek, otherwise called Crane Creek, containing twenty five acres, etc, etc, etc, also ten acres of meadow, etc, etc, bounded on the east corner by John Adams, west, upon Hugh Dun's meadow, also four acres, being on the small brook, at the north end of the Lord Proprietor's land, running N. E. along the land of Henry Lessenbee, etc, etc, etc. Also, all that tract of land, etc, etc, (boundaries) etc, adjoining the Lord Proprietor's, containing sixty acres, also fifteen acres of meadow in the Raritan meadows, etc, etc. (boundaries) etc, etc, also, all the said John's right of common in the town of Woodbridge. (boundaries).

"In witness thereof, the above said parties to these presents etc, etc, etc, have set their hands and seals."

JOHN CARHART. [L. S.]
ANNE CARHART. [L. S]
Witnessed by
THOMAS GLEAUES.
ANDREW LAW.

Book 17, or B. 2, page 257, East Jersey Records.

1717 and 18. "Robert and William, selling land, balance of Thomas' tract on Crane Creek, and others bought of John."—*Book 17, B, page 259.*

ROBERT CARHART.
WILLIAM CARHART.
Witnessed by
ISAAC PIERSON.
WM. FROST.   Jan. 16th, 1718.

Acknowledged before THOMAS GORDON, Esq., Councilor for his Majesty.—*Book 2 of Deeds, p. 261.*

Jan. 31st, 1720. "Thomas Warne sells land to Dr. Arents, lying at Perth Amboy, Jan. 31st, 1720."

Aug. 23, 1722. "Letters of administration were granted his son Stephen Warne, on the estate of his father, Aug. 23, 1722."

"The inventory of personal estate and account, amounting to £348.0.6, was returned by Stephen Warne, dated Apr. 19, 1723."

[His wife is supposed to have died about 1714.]

Mar. 19, 1723. "William Carhart purchased lands of Thomas Ellison at Perth Amboy, ninety acres."—*Book* 18 *or* C. 2, *p*. 570.

July 11th, 1723. "Stephen Warne willed to Thomas Warne 3rd, his brother, 350 acres in Middlesex Co., on Matawan Creek, near Monmouth Co. line."—*Book* 20, *or* K., *p*. 297.

Witnessed by

WILLIAM CARHART, and others.

[The prosperous town of Matawan is opposite this old plantation of Thomas Warne, 2nd son of Thomas and Mary L. C. Warne.]

"A. D. 1732, July 19th. AFFIDAVIT of John Johnston, Sen., and John Matthies:

"Before Andrew Johnston, Esq., Mayor of the City of Perth Amboy, appeared Dr. John Johnston, of said city, aged about seventy years, and also John Matthies, of same city, turner, aged about sixty years, who being duly sworn, did declare that *Sarah*, the wife of *English Smith*, deceased, after the death of her said husband, inhabited in the said city, and there died, leaving no issue, by her said husband, or any other. That the said Sarah had a sister named Mary, who was first married to Thomas Carhart, of the town of Woodbridge, in the Co. of Middlesex, N. J., and that she had issue by the said Thomas, three sons, named John, Robert and William, and that after the said Thomas Carhart deceased, she married again unto Thomas Warne, of the said city, and that she, the said Mary, had issue by him, five sons and one daughter, to wit: Stephen, Thomas, Samuel, Joshua, George and Sarah, Stephen being the oldest, as they do believe, and are assured, from their long and intimate acquaintance with the several persons aforesaid; and the said John Johnston doth further say, that he knew the said Mary before her marriage with the said Thomas Carhart, as *Mary Lord*, and further the above deponents saith not.

"Sworn before me, ANDREW JOHNSTON."

Signed, JOHN JOHNSTON, M. D.
JOHN MATTHIES.

Book E. of Deeds, p. 230.

July 20th, 1732. "Andrew Johnston, Esq., Mayor of Perth Amboy, doth hereby certify that John Johnston and John Matthies, deponents, are men of undoubted good character, and that faith and credit are to be given to what they have deposed, and that John Hamilton, Esq., before whom the Power of Attorney annexed is made, is one of his Majesty's council for the Province of N. J., &c., &c.

"In testimony whereof, I have set my hand and seal, July 20th, 1732."

ANDREW JOHNSTON.

GENEALOGY

OF THE

Carhart Family.

NEW YORK BRANCH.

1.—CHART OF JOHN¹.

THOMAS CARHART $\overset{1691}{=}$ MARY LORD

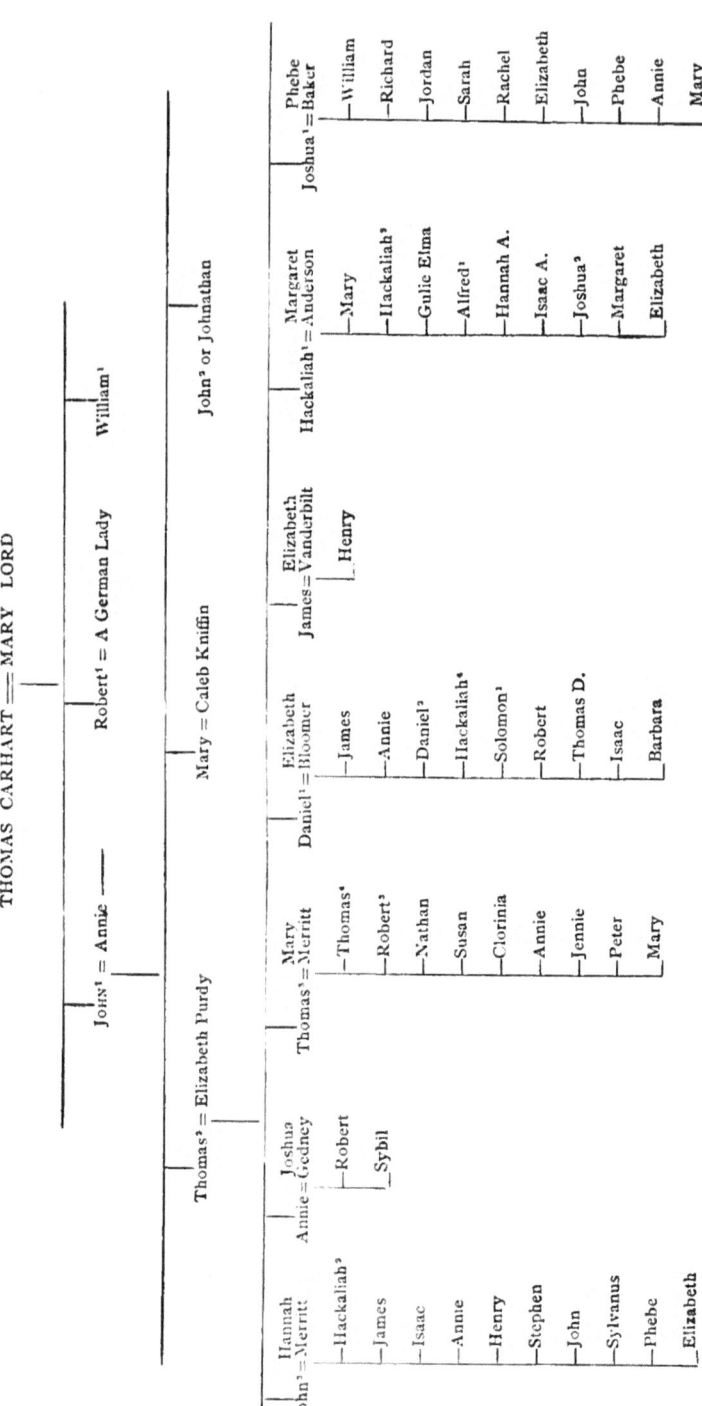

GENEALOGY

OF THE

CARHART FAMILY.

THOMAS,¹

THOMAS,¹ b. about 1650, in Cornwall, Eng., m. in Nov., 1691, MARY LORD, b. at Cambridge, Mass., July 13, 1668, (dau. of Robert Lord, (Note 1) of Cambridge, and Rebecca Phillips, of Boston, and grand dau. of Major Wm. Phillips, (Note 2) of Saco, Me., and Boston, Mass.)

THOMAS, and MARY LORD CARHART, resided on Staten Island, until the spring of 1695, when they removed to Woodbridge, N. J., where the former died, sometime between March 16, 1695,—the date of his will—and, April 6, 1696, the date at which it was admitted to probate. He had three sons, JOHN,¹ ROBERT,¹ WILLIAM.¹

[These sons of THOMAS CARHART, were reared under the care of their stepfather, THOMAS WARNE, of Woodbridge, N. J., to which place he had removed from Monmouth Co., at the time of his marriage with their mother, about 1698. When the Carhart brothers became of age, he gave them a deed for 600 acres of land in Middlesex Co., as will be found recorded.]

NEW YORK BRANCH.

JOHN,¹ *Son of* THOMAS.¹

2 Generation.—JOHN¹ was born on Staten Island, in 1692. He married between Oct. 22, 1716,—when he signs alone to a deed—and June 1, 1717, when he signs with *Anne,* his wife. [The surname of his wife has not been found, and the place of her birth is not known.]

JOHN removed from Woodbridge, to Rye, Westchester Co., N. Y., before 1717, as his name is found in a list of religious teachers at Rye, at that date. Later, he became Clerk of the Vestry of Grace Church, Rye, and held the office for many years. He was a lawyer, and practiced in his profession at Rye, from 1717 to 1750. He was living in 1764. The date of his death is not known.

"Until 1737, he lived opposite the present Episcopal Church. This property he held, in the right of George Lane. The house, with two acres of land, was afterwards sold to the Rev. James Wetmore."—*Baird's History of Rye.*

[The old house was removed a few years since, and the site is now occupied by the Episcopal Parsonage.]

June 4. 1722, "The Wardens of Grace Episcopal Church at Rye, addressed a petition to London, for a Pastor."

Signed by order, JOHN CARHART, *Clerk.*

In 1745, he signs a deed, with *Jane,* his second wife. 1762. "John Carhart, and Abraham Lane, applied in 1762, for twenty acres of land, additional in Richmond Co., S. I., by certificate."—*Baird's History of Rye.*

[It thus appears, that Thomas Carhart, did not claim his twenty acres of meadow land, in addition to the 165 acres of upland, which was allowed to those receiving grants from the Crown ; but that his son John did afterwards.]

Dec. 19, 1764. "Application was made by the members of Grace Episcopal Church, of Rye Parish, for charter of the same." Among the signers, JOHN CARHART.

JOHN, and ANNE his first wife, had, THOMAS,[2] MARY, JOHN,[2] or Jonathan, and perhaps others, but they have not been found [Joseph, Andrew and Matthew, are mentioned in Rye records, but cannot be proved to have been his children ; nor have any descendants of theirs been found. They may have been nephews from New Jersey, or have come from England, and returned.]

But little is known of his dau. Mary, except that she married Caleb Kniflin, (son of Nathan, who was son of George Kniflin, of Stratford, Conn., in 1666.) A daughter named Mary Kniflin, m. James Wetmore, and removed to Kortright, Sullivan Co., N. Y., where descendants of hers are living at this date. For further history of the Kniflin family, see *Baird's History of Rye.*

Of JOHN,[2] or Johnathan, no descendants have been found.

FAMILY OF THOMAS,[2] of *Rye, Son of* JOHN.[1]

3 G.—THOMAS,[2] of Rye, b. about 1718, m. Elizabeth Purdy (dau. of Daniel, and Annie Brown—(*Note* 3) Purdy (*Note* 4), b. 1714, as her death is recorded, "Nov. 26, 1798, a few weeks over her 84th year." Thomas died in 1761, of typhus fever. Chil.:

I. JOHN,[3] II. ANNIE, III. THOMAS,[3] IV. DANIEL,[1] V. JAMES, VI. HACKALIAH,[1] VII. JOSHUA.[1]

FAMILY OF JOHN,[3] *of Oxford, Chenango Co., N. Y.*
Son of THOMAS,[2] *of Rye, Westchester Co., N. Y.*

The name of JOHN[3] CARHART is found in 1775, subscribed to a Protest "Against the late most cruel, unjust, and unwarrantable Act for blockading the Port of Boston," also that of ANDREW CARHART.

4 G.—JOHN CARHART,[3] b. about 1740, at Rye, m. Hannah Merritt, dau. of Sylvanus Merritt, (*Note* 5). He removed about 1800, to Shawangunk, Orange Co., N. Y., and subsequently to Oxford, Chenango Co.,

N. Y., where he died Jan. 2. 1836, aged 96 years. Hannah d. May, 1844. John was a farmer. Chil.:

I. HACKALIAH². II. JAMES². III. ISAAC. IV. ANNIE. V. HENRY. VI. STEPHEN. VII. JOHN.⁴ VIII. SYLVANUS. IX. PHEBE. X. ELIZABETH.

5 G.—I. HACKALIAH² CARHART, b. about 1764. m. Mrs. Mary Ellison—born Beek—in 1801. Hackaliah d. in 1847, aged 83 years, Mary d. in 1823. Res. Oxford, Chenango Co., N. Y., and N. Y. city. Chil.:

6 G.—1. JOHN WEED CARHART. b. Nov. 3, 1805. m. April 27, 1824, Margaret Ann Reynolds, b. Aug. 7, 1807, (dau. of Sands Reynolds, of N. Y. city). Margaret d. Feb. 7, 1879. J. W. C. is a commission merchant at Chicago, Ill. Chil.:

7 G.—1. CAROLINE CARHART. b. July 12, 1826, m., Sept. 22, 1847, William S. Post, of N. Y. city. Caroline d. July 4. 1858. Res. Sparta, Wis. Chil.:

8 G.—1. WILLIAM FREDERICK POST, 2. JOHN CARHART POST.

7 G.—2. DAVID WOOD CARHART. b. June 23, 1828. in N. Y. city, m. Sept., 1853, Harriet Wright. David is proprietor of Golden Sheaf Flour Mills, at Berlin, Wis. Chil.:

8 G.—1. GERTRUDE CARHART. 2. ANNIE CARHART.

7 G.—3. JOHN WEED CARHART, Jr., b. Jan. 6. 1831, in N. Y. city, m. April, 1852, Jane Brady, of N. Y. Res. Appleton, Wis. Chil.:

8 G.—1. MARGARET M. CARHART, m. Mr. Butler. Died leaving one child. MAGGIE CARHART BUTLER.

2. GRACE CARHART.

7 G.—4. AMANDA CARHART, b. Aug. 15, 1833. in N. Y. city. m. Nathan H. Strong, of Berlin, Wis. Nathan d. Oct., 1854. Amanda m. 2nd husband, James B. Davids, of Berlin, Wis. Res. Chicago. Chil.:

8 G.—1 NATHAN STRONG, 2. JENNIE DAVIDS, 3. JAMES B. DAVIDS.

7 G.—5. HENRIETTA CARHART, b. Dec. 3, 1835, in N. Y. city, m. 1859, John T. Smith, M. D., of Fox Lake. Dodge Co., Wis., brother of Wm. E. Smith, Gov. of Wis., 1878. Henrietta d. 1869. Res. Fox Lake. Chil.:

8 G.—1. REGINA SMITH. 2. HENRIETTA SMITH.

7 G.—6. ALFRED CARHART. b. Oct. 16, 1838, m. Sept. 12, 1861, Jennie L. Brown, of Berlin, Wis. Res. Milwaukee; firm of Pride & Carhart. Chil.:

8 G.—GEORGE ARTHUR CARHART, b. 1872.

7 G.—7. GEORGE WHITFIELD CARHART. b. Aug. 8, 1841. m. 1870, Minnie Ballard. G. W. C. is agent of the North Atlantic Freight Co., Broadway, N. Y. Res. Bath, L. I. Chil.:

8 G.—GEORGE ESCOTT CARHART.

7 G.—8. MARGARET CARHART, b. June 22, 1844, in N. Y. city. was killed by an explosion on a steamboat on Fox River, Wis., July 16, 1857, while on her way from Appleton Seminary, Wis. to her home in Chicago.

6 G.—2. HANNAH MERRITT CARHART, (dau. of Hackaliah.²) b. Feb. 1, 1814. m. July 5, 1832, William Hovey, of Lowell, Mass. Chil.:

7 G.—1. Frances R. Hovey, b. July 26, 1833, m. Oct. 23, 1856, Avery T. Webb, of Waterborough. Me. Frances d. June 22. 1861.

2. HENRIETTA FAILING HOVEY. b. April 26, 1836, m. June 8, 1858, William T. Shapleigh, of Boston. Chil.:

8 G.—FRANCES HOVEY SHAPLEIGH, b. Jan. 27, 1869.

7 G.—3. HARRIET CAROLINE HOVEY, b. Aug. 23, 1838, is Prof. of Greek, Latin, and German, in the High School at Lowell, Mass.

5 G.—II. JAMES CARHART m. Mary Bush. Chil.:
6 G.—1 GEORGE B. CARHART, 2. ELLEN D. CARHART, 3. HANNAH A. CARHART.

5 G.—III. ISAAC CARHART, m. Elizabeth Bowers, at the Reformed Church of Bergen, Hudson Co., N. J., Dec. 1, 1806. Chil.:
6 G.—1. SYLVIA CARHART, who was killed on a western steamboat, date unknown. 2. HARRISON CARHART, who lived at Alton, Ill., where he left a family.
3. JEREMIAH CARHART, (*Note 6*) b. at Poughkeepsie, N. Y., Sept., 1813. He m. 1st wife, Miss Jerrold, of Niagara Falls, and had two sons, who died in infancy. Mrs. C. died in 1846. Jeremiah m. 2nd wife, Lydia E. Van Brunt, of Troy, N. Y., and died in N. Y. city, in 1868. Chil.:
7 G.—1. ALICE ELIZABETH CARHART, m. Edward Ferro, of Colombia, S. A., (brother of Señor Joaquin Ferro, the Colombian Consul at New York, and also of Señor Antonio Ferro, the Commissioner appointed by the Colombian Government, to receive, at Aspinwall, M. De Lesseps, the projector of the Panama Canal). Res. N. Y. city. 2. KATE CARHART, m. Charles Balmer. Res. Jefferson, Powhattan Co., Va. 3. JERETTA CARHART. Res. Jefferson, Va.

J. C., adopted a son, whose name is Wm. H. Carhart. Res. Jefferson, Powhattan Co., Va.

Mrs. Lydia E. Carhart, m. 2nd husband, May 15, 1873, Major Charles W. Wakeley, of Fairfield, Conn., who died soon after. Mrs. W. resides at Elmington Plantation, Jefferson, Powhattan Co., Va.

5 G.—IV. ANNIE CARHART, b. Oct. 18, 1770, m. 1805, Abner Owens. Annie d. Feb. 12, 1864, aged 94 years. Chil.:
6 G.—1. AMBROSE OWENS, 2. EUNICE, 3. JAMES OWENS, living in Chatauqua Co., N. Y., 4. ISAAC OWENS, living at Telley Creek, Chemung Co., N. Y., 5. PHEBE, m. Mr. Leonard, and lives at Norwich, Chenango Co., N. Y., 6. ALANSON, 7. HANNAH, 8. SYLVANUS OWENS.

5 G.—V. HENRY CARHART, b. Sept. 10, 1781, at White Plains, N. Y., m. 1811, Clara Everett, b. 1793. Henry d. March 11, 1871, aged 90 years. Buried at Macon city, Mo. His wife d. Sept., 1863, Del. Co., Ohio. Chil.:
1. ISAAC. 2. ELIZA. 3. LEWIS. 4. MARY. 5. STEPHEN. 6. DARIUS. 7. ELLIOTT. 8. MARIA.

6 G.—1. ISAAC CARHART, b. Aug. 12, 1813, at Oxford, Chenango Co., N. Y., m. Roxanna Peckham. Res. Del. Co., O. Chil.:
7 G.—1. GEORGE WILLIAMS CARHART, b. Nov. 24, 1837, m. Elmira Benedict, and m. 2nd wife, Anna Elizabeth Marchant. Res. Marion, Ohio. Chil.:
8 G.—1. ELLA ALMEDA CARHART, b. Mar. 4, 1863. 2. ADA R. CARHART, b. Sept. 25, 1864, at Marion, O.

7 G.—2. LUCIUS ALFRED CARHART, b. Mar. 15, 1843, in Del. Co., O., m. Amanda Torrey.

7 G.—3. ALMEDA MATILDA CARHART, b. Sept. 17, 1848, Del. Co., O., m. George Brown. Res. Marion, O. Chil.: EFFIE BROWN, d. young.
7 G.—4. HERBERT CARHART, b. Apr. 26. 1852, d. Aug. 14, 1853.
7 G.—5. ORVILLE EUGENE CARHART, b. Nov. 9, 1855. Res. Del. Co., O.

6 G.—2. ELIZA CARHART, b. Jan. 5, 1815, m. Jared Osgood, of Troy, N. Y., and d. Dec. 4, 1848; had Priscilla, Clara, and Ralph.
6 G.—3. LEWIS CARHART, b. Dec. 20, 1817, in Otsego Co., N. Y., m. Nancy Pierson. Chil.:
7 G.—1. ELIZABETH ANN. 2. HENRY. 3. HARRISON. 4. LEWIS, 5. HARVEY. 6. CLARA CARHART. Res. near Dubuque, Iowa.
6 G.—4. MARY CARHART, b. Mar. 5, 1820, in Otsego Co., N. Y., m. first husband, Henderson Hall; second husband, Wilson Cunningham; third husband, Thomas Scott. Res. Del. Co., O.
6 G.—5. STEPHEN CARHART, b. Feb. 5, 1822, m. Fanny Webster. Res. near Columbus, O. Chil.:
7 G.—1. ELENOR. 2. RALPH. 3. FANNY. 4. CLARA. 5. IDA CARHART.
6 G.—6. DARIUS CARHART, b. May 31, 1824, m. Adelia How.

6 G.—7. ELLIOTT CARHART, b. Mar. 22, 1828, m. Sept. 29, 1850, Margaret Pettit, of Zanesville, O., b. Jan. 21, 1830 (dau. of Bartholomew Pettit and Sarah Butts, of Va.) Res. Marion City, Mo. Chil.:
7 G.—1. IDA MAY CARHART, b. Apr. 16, 1852, at Eden, Del. Co., O. Ida, is Professor of Botany and Drawing, in the State Normal School at Warrensburg, Mo.
7 G.—2. ARLINGTON CARHART, b. Mar. 11, 1854, m. May 19, 1878, Lizzie Landis, of Phil. A. C. was graduated at Commercial College, Macon City, Mo. Res. Manchester, Iowa. Chil.:
8 G.—JOHN BURTON CARHART, b. July 6, 1879.
7 G.—3. CARRINGTON ELLIOTT CARHART, b. Apr. 1, 1861, was graduated at the State Normal School, Warrensburg, Mo., June, 1880.
7 G.—4. ARTHUR L. CARHART, b. Feb. 24, 1867.
7 G.—5. ROSE ELLA CARHART, b. Nov. 30, 1869.
7 G.—6. LENA BELL CARHART. b. Mar. 22, 1871.
7 G.—7. EDITH ADELAIDE CARHART, b. Nov., 1873.

6 G.—8. MARIA CARHART (dau. of Henry), b. Apr. 4, 1830, m. Sept. 1863, Dr. Mercer. Res. Lewis Centre. Del. Co., O.

5 G.—VI. STEPHEN CARHART (son of John³), b. at Rye, N. Y., Feb. 28, 1789, m. Mar. 6, 1816, Sarah Everett, b. Mar. 16, 1797. Stephen d. Jan. 20, 1852. Sarah d. Mar. 28, 1871. Res. Oxford, N. Y. Chil.:
1. PHEBE A. 2. GEORGE N. 3. HANNAH M. 4. AMBROSE. 5. OSCAR. 6. HARRIET. 7. LAURA A.
6 G.—1. PHEBE A. CARHART, b. Jan. 29, 1817, m. Oct. 12, 1835, James Walker (son of James and Jane Walker, of Oxford, N. Y.) James d. Oct. 4, 1853. Chil.:
7 G.—1. CHRISTINA V. WALKER, b. Mar. 19, 1838, m. Dec. 29, 1864, R. M. Turner. Chil.:
8 G.—1. EVERETT P. TURNER, b. June 9, 1867. 2. RICHARD TURNER, b. Aug. 2, 1877.

7 G.—2. JAMES L. WALKER, b. Apr. 2, 1840, m. Mar. 28, 1869, Julia Anderson, of Guilford, N. Y. Res. Oxford, N. Y. Chil.:
8 G.—FREDERICK L. WALKER, b. Mar. 6, 1871.
7 G.—3. CLARENCE D. WALKER, b. Feb. 7, 1842, m. Sept. 17, 1867, Cordelia Riley, of Coventry, N. Y. Res. Coventry, N. Y.
7 G.—4. SARAH E. WALKER, b. Jan. 11, 1844, m. Sept. 16, 1866, Reed Francisco. Res. Oxford, N. Y.
7 G.—5. FREDERICK C. WALKER, b. July 28, 1846, m. Sept. 13, 1876, Marion G. Anderson. Res. Fremont, Dodge Co., Neb.
7 G.—6. LAURA A. WALKER, b. Dec. 6, 1848. Res. Fremont, Neb.

6 G.—2. GEORGE N. CARHART, b. Aug. 23, 1818, m. 1846, Ann E. Foot, of Oxford, N. Y. Ann d. 1851. G. N. C. m. 2nd wife, Abigail Fish, 1868, who d. 1874. Res. Oxford, N. Y. He edited and published the *Bainbridge Freeman*, in 1849, at Bainbridge, Chenango Co., N. Y., and in 1853, he published the *Oxford Transcript*, at Oxford, N. Y. Chil.:
7 G.—1. GEORGIANNA CARHART, b. Dec. 6, 1848, d. Jan. 6, 1851.
2. SARAH G. CARHART, b. 1851, d. 1852. 3. MARY E. CARHART, b. July 15, 1853.

6 G.—3. HANNAH M. CARHART, b. May 8, 1820, m. Feb. 27, 1840, Andrew Mowrey, b. Aug. 4, 1816. Andrew, is a farmer at Oxford, Chenango Co., N. Y. Chil.:
7 G.—1. LYDIA M. MOWREY, b. Jan. 30, 1841, d. June 7, 1842.
7 G.—2. NARISSA MOWREY, b. May 7, 1842, m. Feb. 26, 1862, Julius Wheeler, b. Sept. 28, 1839. Chil.:
8 G.—ELENOR MAY WHEELER, b. Jan. 12, 1863.
7 G.—3. ANDREW FRANKLIN MOWREY, b. Feb. 16, 1847, m. Sept. 27, 1869, Jennie M. Bloomer, b. Feb. 1, 1852. Chil.:
8 G.—1. LAURA H. MOWREY, b. Aug. 22, 1870. 2. IRA A. MOWREY, b. May 16, 1874.
7 G.—4. PHILA A. MOWREY, b. May 30, 1851, m. June 21, 1868, Adelbert Seeley, b. Oct. 15, 1848. Chil.:
8 G.—1. ANNIE BELL SEELEY, b. Dec. 5, 1870. 2. HATTIE MAY SEELEY, b. June 19, 1874. 3. GEORGE RAY SEELEY, b. May 30, 1877.
7 G.—5. WASHINGTON EVERETT MOWREY, b. Aug. 15, 1859.

6 G.—4. AMBROSE CARHART, b. July 16, 1822, m. Mar. 2, 1847, Mary Gordon (dau. of John Gordon, of Oxford). Mary d. Mar., 1864. Res. Oxford, N. Y. Chil.:
7 G.—1. ALFRED CARHART, b. Dec. 9, 1851. 2. MARY ELIZABETH CARHART, b. Nov. 25, 1855, m. Dec. 17, 1872, Reuben Rounds. Res. Coventry, Chenango Co., N. Y. Chil.: MINNIE ROUNDS, b. July 31, 1875.
7 G.—3. CHARLES CARHART, b. Oct. 3, 1860. Res. Oxford, N. Y.
7 G.—4. OSCAR CARHART, b. Sept. 2, 1862.

6 G.—5. OSCAR CARHART, b. Aug. 6, 1829, m. Oct. 9, 1857, Julia A. Russell of Oxford, N. Y. (dau. of Bishop Russell). Chil.:
7 G.—IDA C. CARHART, b. July 15, 1858, m. June 19, 1878, RAY GIFFORD. Res. Oxford, N. Y.
6 G.—6. HARRIET N. CARHART, b. Nov. 30, 1832. Res. Oxford, N.Y.
6 G.—7. LAURA A. CARHART, b. Sept. 8, 1835, d. Feb. 11, 1874.

5 G.—VII. JOHN[4] CARHART (son of John,[3] of Oxford, N.Y.) b. Dec. 10, 1794, at Oxford, m. Dec., 1816, Miriam Wright, (dau. of Daniel and Polly Wright, of Fishkill, N. Y.). Miriam d. Jan. 10, 1858. John was living in 1880. Chil. :

6 G.—1. SYLVANUS[2] CARHART. b. Dec. 16, 1817, m. Jan. 21, 1847, Hannah Wheeler, (dau. of Ezekiel and Sally Deming Wheeler, and granddau. of Ezekiel Wheeler, Sen., of Coos Co., N. H., who made the first settlement in Guilford, Chenango Co., N. Y., in 1787). S. C. is a farmer at Guilford, and also Justice of the town. [To him I am indebted for the records of the family of John[3].] Chil. :

7 G.—1. ERVIETTA CARHART. b. Nov. 30, 1849, 2. JOHN MELVIN CARHART, b. Mar. 13, 1859, 3. LUCINDA CARHART, b. June 29, 1861.

6 G.—2. DANIEL CARHART, b. Nov. 21, 1820, unm.

3. ERASTUS CARHART, b. Mar. 6, 1823, m. Dec. 22, 1852, Margaret Lane, (dau. of Francis and Elizabeth Lane) of N. Y. city. Res. Guilford, N. Y. A farmer. Chil. :

7 G.—FRANCIS MATILDA CARHART, b. Nov. 1, 1855, m. Sept. 19, 1877, Samuel A. Ives, of Guilford. N. Y.

6 G.—4. FREDERICK CARHART. b. Nov. 7. 1826, m. Oct. 13, 1868, Eliza M. Smith, (dau. of Joseph and Abigail Hyer Smith, pioneers in the settlement of Guilford). Frederick is a farmer at Guilford, N. Y. No chil.

6 G.—5. MATILDA CARHART, b. Apr. 7, 1831, m. Sept. 19, 1855, Alanson Ferris. Chil. :

7 G.—CLARENCE D. FERRIS, b. Aug. 27, 1868.

5 G.—VIII. SYLVANUS[1] CARHART, d. at the age of 17 years.

IX. PHEBE CARHART, d. in 1820, unm.

X. ELIZABETH CARHART, m. 1865, Wm. Tucker.

FAMILY OF ANNIE, *only daughter of* THOMAS[2], *of Rye, Westchester Co., N. Y.*

4 G.—ANNIE CARHART, b. May 5, 1742, m. Joshua Gedney (Note 7) of Rye. b. Feb. 11, 1742. d. Aug. 28, 1786. Res. N. Y. City. Chil. :

5 G.—I. ROBERT GEDNEY. b. Jan. 19, 1773, m. Sarah Burrows, (dau. of William Burrows. and Sarah Wilcox). "He was a man of great personal beauty—six feet in height, and of noble and graceful figure ;—exceedingly polite and attractive in manner. His kind heart made him a favorite with young and old. He possessed great originality of thought and expression—was a brilliant talker—a man of unbounded energy and perseverance ; being at seventy more active than most men at fifty."

He resided in N. Y. city, for many years, and I am informed by his daughter, that, "He had seen, at the City Hall, N. Y., public documents in the hand-writing of Thomas Carhart, Sec. to Gov. Thomas

Dongan." [If I am rightly informed, these documents have been removed to Albany, N. Y.] His children were:

6 G.—1. SARAH ANN GEDNEY, who married Andrew Williams, of N. Y., a lawyer.

2. EMELINE AMANDA GEDNEY, who married Robert Rutherford, (son of Alien Rutherford, Barrister of Sligo, Ireland, and of the Scottish family of Rutherford—Episcopalian). Robert Rutherford died in a few years after his marriage. Mrs. R. resides at Sing Sing, N. Y. Chil.:

7 G.—1. ALLEN RUTHERFORD, m. Emma Albertson, born near Manchester, Eng., who died Aug. 20, 1876 at Sing Sing, N. Y. Buried at Wilmington, N. C.

"ALLEN RUTHERFORD was one of the first to volunteer for the entire term of the War of the Rebellion. He raised his own company, (F) in the Ninth N. Y. Regt., and left the city for Washington, May 1861. He rose to the rank of Major, Colonel, General, and was brevetted Brigadier General, for gallant conduct. He also held several positions of great responsibility and trust. After the war he was appointed, by Gen. Grant, Third Auditor of the Treasury; which position he filled with ability and honor, for over three years, when he resigned. He is at present practising law in Washington, D. C."

7 G.—2. ROBERT GEDNEY RUTHERFORD, m. Lizzie McK. King, (dau. of William W. King Esq., of Washington, D. C.). "He also volunteered for the term of the war, and held the rank of Lieutenant in his brother's Regiment, and was promoted to that of Colonel, on his brother's promotion. He received a severe wound in his knee, which nearly cost him his life, and during the time he was unable to do duty in the field, he was in command of the Old Capitol Prison in Washington. After the war he was appointed Quartermaster, at Governor's Island, and held the position about seven years. In 1878, he was retired on half pay for life. The brothers were admitted into the Regular Army before the conclusion of the war."

6 G.—3. MARY ELIZA GEDNEY, (dau. of Robert) has charge of the "Department of Art," in the Young Ladies' Seminary at Sing Sing. Unmarried.

4. PAULINE GEDNEY, who married James Thompson, of N. Y., piano manufacturer.

ROBERT GEDNEY had two sons, GEORGE W. BROWNE GEDNEY, now dead; and ROBERT LAWRENCE GEDNEY, living at Nyack, on the Hudson. I am unable to place these in the order of their birth.

5 G.—11. SYBELLA GEDNEY (the sister of Robert), b. May 9, 1776, married Thomas Browne, of Phil. Chil.:

6 G.—1. GEORGE W. BROWNE, who married Eliza Post, of N. Y. Chil.:

7 G.—1. LOUISE BROWNE, m. Oscar Coles, of N. Y., 2. CHARLOTTE BROWNE, m. Joseph Hutchings. 3. RICHARD DOMINICK BROWNE, who is dead. 4. SARAH A. GEDNEY BROWNE.

6. G.—2. ANN ELIZA BROWNE (sister of George W. Browne) died unmarried, about 1870-1.

FAMILY OF THOMAS³, *of Bethlehem, Albany Co., N. Y., son of* THOMAS², *of Rye, Westchester Co. N. Y.*

4 G.—THOMAS³ CARHART, b. about 1744, m. Mary Merritt, of Rye. He removed from Rye to New Marlborough, on the Hudson; and afterwards to Bethlehem, Albany Co., where he died. No dates. He was a farmer. Chil. :
I. THOMAS,⁴ II. ROBERT. III. NATHAN. IV. SUSAN. V. CLORINIA. VI. ANNIE. VII. JENNIE. VIII. PETER. IX. MARY.

5 G.—I. THOMAS⁴ CARHART was married, and lived at Troy. N. Y., in 1810. Nothing can be collected of his family.
II. ROBERT CARHART, b. June 7, 1767, at Rye, m. Oct. 5, 1803, Mary Brakeman of Germany, b. Oct. 3, 1781. Res. Whitestown, Oneida Co., N. Y. Chil. :
1. THOMAS⁵. 2. MARIA. 3. ROBERT B.. 4. ELIZABETH ANN. 5. HIRAM. 6. JAMES. 7. LUCRETIA. 8. ANNIE. 9. GEORGE W., 10. LAFAYETTE.

6 G.—1 THOMAS⁵ CARHART, b. Jan. 27, 1804, d. Aug. 26, 1825.
2. MARIA CARHART, b. Feb. 11, 1806, m. Nov. 28, 1835, William Stickney, of Bennington, Vt., b. May 30, 1807. William d. Sept. 9, 1851, at Bloomfield, Mich.
3. ROBERT B. CARHART, b. Dec. 10, 1807, m. Feb. 16, 1829, Catharine Potter, of Floyd, N. Y., b. Mar. 13, 1794. Robert d. Jan. 17, 1862, at Amhurst, Ohio. Chil. : 1. MARY. 2. GALILEO, 3. SAMUEL. 4. ELLEN, 5. SUSAN. Res. Grand Travers, Mich.
4. ELIZABETH ANN CARHART, b. Mar. 21, 1809, m. Sept. 1, 1831, John Clark, of London, Eng., b. June 30, 1807. Elizabeth d. Aug. 22. 1832, at Auburn, Mich.
5. HIRAM CARHART, b. Aug. 21, 1811, d. July 10, 1842. He was a soldier, and is buried on Governor's Island, N. Y. Bay.
6. JAMES CARHART, b. Jan. 28, 1813, m. Oct. 4, 1840, Sarah Buck, b. June 27, 1817. Res. Pontiac, Mich. Chil. :
7 G. 1. HARRIET L., b. July 27, 1841. 2. LAFAYETTE J., b. Dec. 24, 1843. 3. PHEBE M., b. Oct. 28, 1846, m. Oct. 2, 1870, John Hall, of Staley Bridge, Eng., b. Jan. 14, 1842. 4. ELIJAH B., b. Mar. 28, 1849, 5. GEORGE, b. May 27, 1852. 6. JUDSON, b. Oct. 14, 1855. 7. MARY E., b. Jan. 24, 1857. 8. ESTELLE, b. April 1, 1858.
6 G.—7. LUCRETIA CARHART, b. Mar. 12, 1815, m. Aug. 15, 1844, Robert Brown, b. Dec. 2, 1817. Res. Pontiac, Mich. Chil. :
7 G.—1. EDITH B. BROWN. 2. BERTHA BROWN. 3. LULA BROWN.
6 G.—8. ANNIE CARHART, b. May 21, 1817, d. Mar. 16, 1878.
9. GEORGE W. CARHART, M. D., b. May 20, 1820, m. April 30, 1851, Lefa Jane Wiley, m. 2nd wife, June 6, 1860, Sarah B. Carter, m. 3d wife, Dec. 14, 1870, Ellen G. Driscoll. G. W. C. d. at his residence, Jackson, Mich., April 21, 1872. Chil. :
7 G.—1. HAMILTON B. CARHART, res. Grand Rapids, Mich., 2. PAUL, 3. JOHN. 4. EMMA.
6 G.—10. LAFAYETTE CARHART, b. Oct. 14, 1824, d. Aug. 20, 1828.
5 G.—III. NATHAN CARHART—son of Thomas³—m. Phebe Armstrong, of Albany Co., N. Y., and had one son, James, who died in N. Y. city.

5 G.—IV. SUSAN CARHART, m. Joshua Pinckney (*Note* 8), of East Chester, N. Y. (son of Philip Pinckney and Elizabeth Townsend). Res. Rye, N. Y. Chil.:

6 G.—1. MARIA PINCKNEY, d. 1859. 2. CLARA PINCKNEY, m. Gilbert H. Smith. 3. LYDIA PINCKNEY, m. William Onderdonk, 4. JOHN TOWNSEND PINCKNEY, m. Miss Pell of East Chester, N. Y.

5. THOMAS CARHART PINCKNEY, b. 1803, m. Caroline Smith, (dau. of Rev. Mordecai Smith, of Rockville Centre, N. Y.) T. C. P. d. Feb. 2, 1878. He was a lawyer in N. Y. city for many years. Res. Brooklyn, N. Y. He gave very valuable assistance in tracing the family of Mary Lord, wife of Thomas Carhart. Chil.:

7 G.—1. MARY AUGUSTA PINCKNEY, m. Edward E. Roberts.

2. JULIA VICTORIA PINCKNEY, m. Dr. Lloyd Stevens, of Lloyd's Neck, son of Dr. Alexander H. Stevens, of New York.

3. LOUISE MATILDA ADELINE PINCKNEY, m. Wm. Youngblood, of New York.

4. J. H. HOBART PINCKNEY, b. 1828, d. July 28, 1877.

5. THOMAS COATSWORTH PINCKNEY, m. Cornelia M. Stevens, of Sing Sing.

5 G.—V. CLORINIA CARHART, m. John Durie.

VI. ANNIE CARHART, m.—Cregier, of Charleston, S. C. Nothing known of their descendants.

VII. JENNIE CARHART, d. unm.

VIII. PETER CARHART, of whom nothing is known.

IX. MARY CARHART, m. Isaac Jerolomon of Coeymans, N. Y. Chil.:

6 G.—1. WILLIAM JEROLOMON, m. Elizabeth Blodgett. 2. NATHAN JEROLOMON, m. Miss Lattin. 3. NICHOLAS JEROLOMON, m. Miss Rairack, 4. DAVID JEROLOMON, m. Phebe Ann Whitbeck, and married 2nd wife, Phebe Ann Wallace. Chil.:

7 G.—1. LANSING, 2. MARTIN, 3. EGBERT, 4. DAVID. By 2nd wife, 5. OLIN.

6 G.—5. NELLIE JEROLOMON, m. Bleecker Platt. 6. MARY JEROLOMON, m. John Van Zandt, 7. ANN ELIZA JEROLOMON, m. Jacob Hallenbeck.

FAMILY OF DANIEL,[2] of *Coeymans, Albany Co., N. Y., Son of* THOMAS,[2] *of Rye, Westchester Co., N. Y.*

4 G.—DANIEL[3] CARHART, b. 1746, at Rye, N. Y., m. 1773, Elizabeth Bloomer, b. 1757 (daughter of Capt. Robert Bloomer (*Note* 9), of Rye). Daniel removed to Coeymans, Albany Co., N. Y., in 1793, and died there, Aug. 24, 1829, aged 83 years. Chil.:

I. JAMES[3]. II. ANNIE. III. DANIEL[3]. IV. HACKALIAH[3]. V. SOLOMON[3]. VI. ROBERT[3]. VII. THOMAS D. VIII. ISAAC. IX. BARBARA.

5 G.—I. JAMES[3] CARHART, b. 1774, at Rye, m. Susan Jerolomon, of Coeymans, N. Y., in 1799. James d. April 13, 1840. Chil.:

6 G.—1. NICHOLAS, b. 1800, m. March 7, 1830, Eliza Litchfield, of

Coeymans. and m. second wife, Miss Sharbraum. Nicholas d. 1862. Res. Coeymans. Chil.:

7 *G.*—1. HENRY. b. 1831, d. 1854. 2. IRA. m. Martha White. 3. CHARLOTTE. m. Staats Vanderheyden, 4. HANNAH, m. Wm. Van Cleef, res. New York. 5. LEWIS, m. Elizabeth Wiltsie.

6 *G.*—2. ROBERT CARHART. m. Katie Sutton. Chil.:

7 *G.*—LOUISE M. CARHART, who m. Henry Caswell, (son of Charles Caswell, of Coeymans. N. Y.)

6 *G.*—3. NELLIE CARHART, b. 1810, m. Jacob Wyncoop, of Bethlehem. N. Y. Nellie died at Coeymans, 1867. Jacob resides at Troy, N. Y. Chil.:

7 *G.*—1. PETER WYNCOOP. m. Elizabeth Terrell. Res. Waterford, N. Y. 2. ANN ELIZA WYNCOOP, m. Alanson Beebe. Res. Chatham. N. Y. 3. JOHN WYNCOOP. m. Eliza Sherman. Res. Waterford, N. Y. 4. HENRIETTA WYNCOOP. m. Barent Van Eyck. Res. Coeymans, N. Y. 5. ELIZABETH WYNCOOP. m. Peter Hogle, of Troy.

6 *G.*—4. ELIZA CARHART. m. Charles Ball. Chil.:

7 *G.*—1. DAVID BALL. 2. CHARLES BALL.

6 *G.*—5. HANNAH CARHART. d. at the age of 16 years.

6 *G.*—6. JANE CARHART, m. Garret Waldron. Garret d. 1850. Jane is living at Waterford. N. Y. Chil.:

7 *G.*—1. MARGARET J. WALDRON. m. Sylvanus Haverly. Res. Troy, N. Y. 2. SUSAN WALDRON. m. Lewis Smith. Res. Troy, N. Y. 3. PETER WALDRON, m. Margaret Van Antwerp. Res. Waterford, N. Y. 4. JAMES WALDRON. 5. ASA WALDRON. m. Sarah Parter. 6. ELIZA WALDRON, m. Samuel Snyder. Res. Waterford. N. Y.

6 *G.*—7. ALANSON CARHART. m. Lucy Rairack. Chil.:

7 *G.*—1. EDWARD. 2. PETER. 3. LUCY. d. 1868.

6 *G.*—8. ESTHER CARHART. b. Oct. 14, 1820. m. 1836, Lewis Towne, of Coxsackie. N. Y. Lewis d. 1843. Chil. :

7 *G.*—1. EMMA E. TOWNE. 2. FRANCES L. TOWNE. m. Benjamin Wager. Res. Amity. N. Y. Mrs. Towne m. 2nd husband, John Ryan, of Waterford. N. Y. Chil.: 3. SARAH RYAN.

6 *G.*—9. HARRIET CARHART, m. George Evander. No children.

5 *G.*—II. ANNIE CARHART, dau. of Daniel¹, b. 1776. m. Elijah Utter, of Coeymans, N. Y., and removed to western part of N. Y. State. Chil.:

6 *G.*—1. DANIEL. 2. ISAAC. 3. PALMER. 4. ROBERT. 5. LAVINIA. 6. SARAH, 7. ELIZABETH, 8. BARBARA.

FAMILY OF DANIEL², *of Coeymans, N. Y., son of Daniel¹.*

5 *G.*—III. DANIEL² CARHART (son of Daniel¹,) b. Sept. 14. 1777, m., Oct. 5, 1799, at King Street, Conn., Rebecca Sutton (dau. of Sands and Mary Sutton (*Note* 10), of Harrison, Westchester Co., N. Y.) b. Mar. 16, 1775. Rebecca. d. at Coeymans, N. Y.. Mar. 19, 1842. Daniel d. April 10, 1861, aged 84. Res. Coeymans, Albany Co., N. Y. Chil.:

1. MARY. 2. ISAAC D.. 3. ELIZABETH. 4. HENRY. 5. ANNA. 6. DANIEL SUTTON. 7. DEBORAH. 8. BARBARA. 9. CALVIN.

6 G.—1. Mary Carhart, b. July 26, 1800, m. Feb. 25, 1821, Christopher Reynolds, b. Aug. 27, 1800. Chil.:
7 G.—1. Daniel Reynolds, b. April 19, 1823, m. Jane Leddings. Jane d. Aug., 1870. Chil.:
8 G.—1. Mary Ann Reynolds, m. John Burtell. Chil.:
9 G.—1. Edwin Burtell, 2. John Wesley Burtell, 3. Lucy Burtell, 4. Sanford Burtell, 5. Agnes Burtell.
7 G.—2. Peter Reynolds, b. May 25, 1825, m. Catharine Boyce. Chil.:
8 G.—1. George, 2. Christopher, 3. William, 4. Edward, 5. Alanson, 6. Sarah Ann, 7. Mary, 8. Katie, 9. Jacob.
7 G.—3. Ann Reynolds, b. Oct. 12, 1827, m. Peter Holbrook. Chil.:
8 G.—1. Isaac Holbrook. Res. Albany, N. Y. 2. Nancy Holbrook, 3. Peter Holbrook.
7 G.—4. John Reynolds, b. July 23, 1830, m. Margaret Hickman. Chil.:
1. Edward, 2. Richard, 3. Hiram, 4. David, 5. Stephen, 6. Sarah E., 7. Frank, 8. William, 9. Annie, 10. Georgianna.
7 G.—5. Levi Reynolds, b. Feb. 27, 1833, m. Nancy Brandt. Chil.: 1. Albert, 2. Eva.
7 G.—6. Isaac Reynolds, b. Dec. 12, 1836, m. Mrs. Catharine (Halfe) Carl. Chil.: Carrie Reynolds.

6 G.—2. Isaac D. Carhart—son of Daniel.²—b. July 31, 1802, at Coeymans, N. Y., m. Nancy Bangs (dau. of Rev. John Bangs and sister of Revs. Nathan and Heman Bangs, of the M. E. Church). Res. Trempealeau, Wis. Chil.:
7 G.—1. Mary Lavinia Carhart, b. 1831, m. N. T. Manly. Res. Parkersburg, Iowa. Has two children.
7 G.—2. Rev. Lewis Henry Carhart, b. 1833, m. Mary F. Tomlinson, of Conn. Married, in 1872, second wife, Clara H. Lully, of Davenport, Iowa. Chil.:
8 G.—1. Alfred Bangs, 2. Jessy Peck.
Rev. L. H. C. was pastor of the Tabernacle M. E. Church at Dallas, Texas, in 1877. In 1879, he was engaged, with his brother-in-law, Rev. Richard W. A. Allen, in organizing plans of emigration, and founding the town of Clarendon, Donley Co., Texas.

7 G.—3. Delia A. Bangs Carhart, b. 1836, m. L. G. Huntley. Res. Trempealeau, Wis. Has four children.
7 G.—4. John McKendree Carhart, b. 1838, died in the army of U. S., at Bull Run, July 21st, 1861. Res. Middleburgh, N. Y.
7 G.—5. Andrew Rickey Carhart, b. 1841, m. Josie Gillies.
7 G.—6. Isaac Whitfield Carhart, b. 1843, m. Julia Scott, of Arkansas, and is Postmaster at Hot Springs, Ark.
7 G.—7. Emma Frances Carhart, b. 1846, m. Rev. Richard W. A. Allen. Res. Waterloo, Iowa. Removed to Clarendon, Texas.
7 G.—8. Nathan H. Carhart, b. 1848. Res. Trempealeau, Wis.
7 G.—9. Charlotte Ophelia Carhart, b. 1850, m. Benjamin F. White. Res. Anamosa, Iowa.

THE CARHART FAMILY.   37

7 *G.*—10. CLARA JOSEPHINE CARHART, b. 1855, at Fox Lake, Wis. Res. Trempealeau, Wis. Unm.

6 *G.*—3. ELIZABETH CARHART, b. March 20, 1804, m. Francis Terry, whose 1st wife was her sister Barbara. No chil.
6 *G.*—4. HENRY CARHART, b. April 19, 1806, m. his cousin, Eliza Carhart, dau. of Robert. Res. Gilderland, N. Y. Chil. :
   7 *G.*—1. CATHARINE R., b. 1840, m. Nov., 1871, William Ward, of Gilderland, N. Y.
   2. ROBERT SEYMOUR, b. 1852, m. Maggie Hotaling, Dec., 1875.

6 *G.*—5. ANNIE CARHART, b. Oct. 10, 1808, m. Alanson M. Titus, of New Baltimore, Greene Co., N. Y., b. Feb. 23, 1813. Res. Wilton, Rock Co., Ill. Chil. :
   7 *G.*—1. ISAAC HENRY TITUS, b. June 7, 1836, m. Jan. 13, 1867, Carrie M. Osman, of England. Chil. :
      8 *G.*—1. WILLIAM HENRY TITUS. 2. DAVID ALLEN TITUS. 3. CHARLES JEFFERSON TITUS.
   7 *G.*—2. DAVID TITUS, b. June 27, 1838, m. Feb. 18, 1864, Elizabeth Gascoygne, of England. Res. Nebraska. Chil. :
      8 *G.*—1. ELIZABETH TITUS. 2. ANN TITUS.
   7 *G.*—3. MARY ELIZABETH TITUS, b. June 27, 1840, m. Feb. 20, 1864, William Frisbie. Chil. :
      8 *G.*—1. ALANSON FRISBIE. 2. ELLEN LOUISE FRISBIE.

6 *G.*—6. DANIEL SUTTON CARHART, b. Dec. 10, 1810, m. Dec. 8, 1830, Margaret Martin (dau. of John and Catharine Martin, of New Scotland, Albany Co., N. Y.), b. Feb. 9, 1809. Residence, Coeymans. Chil. :
   1. CATHARINE REBECCA. 2. MARGARET ANN. 3. JOHN WESLEY. 4. EDWIN M. 5. SARAH ELIZABETH. 6. HENRY SMITH. 7. BARBARA LAVINIA.

7 *G.*—1. CATHARINE REBECCA CARHART, b. Jan. 21, 1832, m. Dec. 11, 1850, Tunis G. Hotaling, b. Dec., 1828 (son of Garret and Catharine Hotaling, of Bethlehem, Albany Co., N. Y.) Res. Schodack, Rensselaer Co., N. Y. Chil. :
   8 *G.*—1. FRANK H. HOTALING, b. Nov. 27, 1851.
   2. EDWIN OLIN HOTALING, b. Sept. 27, 1857, m. June 4, 1879, Luella S. Moul, (dau. of William and Charity Moul, of Schodack, N. Y.)
   3. WILLIAM B. HOTALING, b. Sept. 7, 1859.
   4. HENRY L. HOTALING, b. Nov. 29, 1866.

7 *G.*—2. MARGARET A. CARHART, b. April 9, 1833, m. Dec. 22, 1855, at New Baltimore, Greene Co., N. Y., Rev. Jotham H. Hauxhurst, b. May 10, 1834 (son of Jotham and Elizabeth Hauxhurst, of Ellenville, Ulster Co., N. Y.) M. A. C. graduated at Warnersville Seminary, Scoharie Co. [This lady furnished the record of Daniel.⁶] Chil. :

38   *GENEALOGY OF*

8 *G.*—OSMAN BAKER HAUXHURST. b. Dec. 15, 1857, a student at N. W. University, Evanston, Ill.

7 *G.*—3. Rev. JOHN WESLEY CARHART, D. D. (*Note* 11). b. June 26, 1834. m. Oct. 6, 1857. Theresa A. Mumford. b. 1837 (only child of John H. and Mary Mumford, of Richmondville, N. Y.) Res. 1880, Oshkosh, Wis. Chil.:

8 *G.*—1. MARY THERESA CARHART, b. Aug. 30, 1858. M. T. C. is editress of " Early Dawn," Oshkosh, Wis. "A paper devoted to the promotion of pure Christianity, Temperance, and news from the Churches." An inquiry from this lady, as to " What I knew in relation to the Carhart ancestors ?" gave rise to investigations which resulted in the compiling of this record.
2. MATILDA E. CARHART, b. July 3, 1861.   3. EDWARD E. CARHART, b. Dec. 15, 1863, publisher of " Early Dawn."   4. NINA BEACH CARHART, b. Feb. 25, 1866.   5. CHARLES CARHART. b. Oct., 1869.   6. HALLIE CARHART. b. April, 1875.   7. SARAH ETHELINE.

7 *G.*—4. EDWIN M. CARHART, m. Oct. 16, 1856. Emily J. Gurney, b. Nov. 24, 1836 (only child of Jacob and Mary Gurney, of New Baltimore, Greene Co., N. Y. and niece of Gurney, photographer, of N. Y. city. Emily d. Dec. 23, 1865. Res. New Baltimore, N. Y. Chil.:
8 *G.*—1. JACOB GURNEY, b. Sept. 22, 1857. Res. New Baltimore. 2. JULIA S., b. Dec. 13, 1858. Res. New Baltimore.   3. BENJAMIN IRVING, b. Oct. 17, 1860. Res. New Baltimore.
E. M. C. m. 2d wife, Oct. 17, 1867. Caroline Amanda Vanderpool, of New Baltimore, N. Y., b. Dec. 16, 1838. Chil.: 4. EMILY J., b. March 21, 1870.   5. ADDIE SWEET, b. May 10, 1873.

7 *G.*—5. SARAH ELIZABETH CARHART, m. Sept. 4, 1872, Washington Carhart Terry, b. April 11, 1843 (son of Francis Terry and Barbara Carhart, dau. of Daniel²). Res. Stanton Hill, Coeymans, Albany Co., N. Y.

7 *G.*—6. Prof. HENRY SMITH CARHART (*Note* 12). b. Mar. 27, 1844. m. Aug. 30, 1876, at Sing Sing, N. Y., Ellen M. Soulé (*Note* 13). b. Sept. 10, 1846 (only dau. of Rev. Frank and Susan Sprague Soulé, and grandniece of Bishop Soulé, of the M. E. Church). Chil.:
8 *G.*—MARGARET SPRAGUE SOULÉ. b. June 28, 1877, at Evanston, Ill.

7 *G.*—7. BARBARA LAVINIA CARHART, b. Feb. 15, 1850. Res. Coeymans, N. Y. Unm. A graduate of Claverack Female College, Claverack, N. Y.

6 *G.*—7. DEBORAH CARHART (dau. of Daniel²), b. March 2, 1813. Unm. Res. Iowa.

6 *G.*—8. BARBARA CARHART, b. Sept. 5, 1815, m. Francis Terry, of Coeymans, Oct. 28, 1840. Barbara d. March 17, 1845. Chil.:
7 *G.*—WASHINGTON CARHART TERRY, b. April 11, 1843, m. Sept. 4, 1872, Sarah Elizabeth Carhart (dau. of Daniel Sutton Carhart).

Francis Terry m. 2nd wife, Jan. 12, 1848. Elizabeth Carhart, sister of Barbara, his 1st wife. Francis d. Nov. 19, 1869. Res. Stanton Hill, Coeymans, N. Y.

6 G.—9. CALVIN CARHART, b. July 12, 1818, m. Ann Garrett, of New Baltimore, N. Y., Nov., 1842. Calvin was killed by a fall from a horse, May 6, 1848. Res. New Baltimore, N. Y. Chil.:
  7 G.—1. EDWARD E. CARHART, b. Jan. 7, 1844, m. Feb. 27, 1867, Hannah Ray, b. April 11, 1843. Chil.:
    8 G.—1. CALVIN, b. April, 1868. 2. FRANCIS TERRY, b. Jan. 2, 1878.
  7 G.—2. CAROLINE E. CARHART, b. May 12, 1845, d. April 30, 1872, but a short time before she was to have been married.

5 G.—IV. HACKALIAH[2] CARHART (son of Daniel,[1] of Coeymans), b. 1780, m. Elizabeth Flansburg, of Bethlehem, Albany Co., N. Y. Chil.:
  6 G.—1. MARY, 2. ELIZABETH, 3. RACHEL.

FAMILY OF SOLOMON, *of Coeymans, Son of* DANIEL.[1]

5 G.—V. SOLOMON CARHART, b. Sept. 6, 1782, at Coeymans, m. Mar. 16, 1804, Catharine Fires, of Coeymans, b. April 4, 1784. Solomon d. at Coeymans, Aug. 30, 1861, aged 79 years. Catharine d. Dec., 1871. Chil.:
  1. ANNA. 2. CATHARINE. 3. SARAH MARIA. 4. HACKALIAH.[2] 5. PETER. 6. SOLOMON,[2] 7. JANE ELIZA. 8. LEVI. 9. JUDITH. 10. MARGARET. 11. LEONARD A. 12. FLETCHER.

6 G.—1. ANNA CARHART, b. April 24, 1805, d. unm., 1858.

6 G.—2. CATHARINE CARHART, b. Aug. 20, 1806, m. Oct. 30, 1830, William Tuttle, of Coeymans, N. Y. Catharine d. Feb., 1877. Chil.:
  7 G.—1. LEVI CARTER TUTTLE, b. June 2, 1834. 2. CHARLOTTE ANN TUTTLE, b. Mar. 26, 1838. 3. MARY TUTTLE, b. June 22, 1840. 4. HENRIETTA TUTTLE, b. Sept. 1, 1843. 5. CATHARINE TUTTLE, b. July 4, 1848, d. Oct. 6, 1871.

6 G.—3. SALLIE MARIA CARHART, b. Sept. 2, 1808, at Coeymans, Albany Co., N. Y., m. in 1828, Hiram Tompkins Litchfield, b. Feb. 13, 1810, at Waterloo, Albany Co., N. Y. Sallie d. Nov. 1, 1868, at Washington, D. C. Hiram d. Dec. 27, 1875, at Washington, D. C. Chil.:
  7 G.—1. HIRAM SANFORD LITCHFIELD, b. Feb. 27, 1830, at Coeymans, Albany Co., N. Y. 2. EDWARD HENRY LITCHFIELD, b. Oct. 2, 1832, at Coeymans. Res. Washington, D. C. 3. JANE ANN LITCHFIELD, b. July 27, 1834, at Coeymans. 4. HANNAH MARIA LITCHFIELD, b. Feb. 22, 1836, at Coeymans. 5. SOLOMON CARHART LITCHFIELD, b. Mar. 10, 1838, at Coeymans. 6. WILLIAM ELBERT LITCHFIELD, b. July 13, 1842, at Coeymans. 7. JAMES ALLEN LITCHFIELD, b. Oct. 9, 1844, at Cicero, Onondaga Co., N. Y. 8. JOHN VAN BEUREN LITCHFIELD, b. Oct. 4, 1846, at Cicero, N. Y.

6 G.—4. HACKALIAH² CARHART, b. July 6, 1810, m. Elizabeth Shultz, in 1834. Res. Penn Yan, N. Y. Chil.:
7 G.—1. CATHARINE, m. George Armstrong. 2. HARRIET, m. James Pipe. 3. HENRIETTA, m. George Clark. The last two are twins.

6 G.—5. PETER CARHART, b. April 19, 1812, m. Ellen Coonly, Feb., 1842. Res. Janesville, Wis. Chil.:
7 G.—1. ELMA, m. William Swaney. Elma d. in 1876, leaving four children. 2. HENRY, unm.

6 G.—6. SOLOMON² CARHART, b. Feb. 4, 1814, m. Hester Hotaling, in 1844. Chil.:
7 G.—1. JASPER. Res. Boston, Mass. 2. GARRET. Res. Washington, D. C. 3. EDWARD. 4. CATHARINE. 5. FRANCES.

6 G.—7. JANE ELIZA CARHART, b. April 21, 1816, m. James Terry, Oct., 1834. Res. Michigan. Chil.:
7 G.—1. MARY TERRY. 2. JAMES TERRY. 3. PETER LANSING TERRY. 4. EMMA E. TERRY. 5. FRANK TERRY. 6. IDA TERRY. 7. MALVINA TERRY. 8. SIDNEY TERRY.

6 G.—8. LEVI CARHART, b. April 20, 1819, m. Catharine Springstead, March, 1844. Res. Schodack, N. Y. Chil.:
7 G.—1. ALFRED, 2. CATHARINE, m. William Van Vosberg, 3. CLARA, m. Willard Van Vosberg.

6 G.—9. JUDITH CARHART, b. June 16, 1821, m. Jan. 1, 1851, George Martin, of New York city, b. Oct. 10, 1827. George d. in Minnesota, June 21, 1865. Res. Dodge Co., Minn. Chil.:
7 G.—1. MARIA LOUISE MARTIN, b. Feb. 3, 1853, m. Sept. 12, 1871, William A. Garver, of Dodge Co., Minn. 2. ADA C. MARTIN, b. Sept. 26, 1855, m. June 4, 1873, Frederick D. Palin, of Minn. 3. HELEN C. MARTIN, b. Aug. 1, 1857, m. Oct. 5, 1876, John Shepherdson, of Minn.
Mrs. Judith Martin m. 2nd husband, Aug. 12, 1867, George Durfey, of Claremont, Dodge Co., Minn., b. Jan. 20, 1817.

6 G.—10. MARGARET LOUISE CARHART, b. June 6, 1823, m. Oct. 17, 2842, John Van Beuren, of Schodack, Rensselaer Co., N. Y., b. Nov. 13, 1820. Margaret d. Sept. 8, 1874. Res. Ellington, Dodge Co., Minn. Chil.:
7 G.—1. HENRIETTA VAN BEUREN, b. Oct. 28, 1843, in New York, d. Dec. 20, 1870, at Ellington, Dodge Co., Minn.
7 G.—2. IDA LOUISE VAN BEUREN, b. July 17, 1847, in New York, m. Sept. 27, 1871, David Ward, of Ellington, b. Mar. 1, 1838. Chil.:
8 G.—1. FRANK ARTHUR WARD, b. Feb. 1, 1872. 2. ZETTIE WARD, b. Feb. 11, 1874, d. Mar. 30, 1875. 3. ALBERTO WARD, b. Sept. 18, 1875. 4. HATTIE JULIA WARD, b. Jan. 23, 1877.
7 G.—3. ESTELLE VAN BEUREN, b. Sept. 14, 1852, in New York, d. Mar. 6, 1854.
7 G.—4. ADELLE BERTHA VAN BEUREN, b. Feb. 24, 1856, in New York city, m. July 23, 1874, John B. Cottier, of Ellington, Minn., b. July 23, 1852. Res. Ellington, Minn. Chil.:
8 G.—1. CLAUDE VAN BEUREN COTTIER, b. Dec. 7, 1877.
7 G.—5. GRACE EVELYN VAN BEUREN, b. April 18, 1861, in New York.

THE CARHART FAMILY.

6 G.—11. LEONARD A. CARHART, b. May 22, 1825, m. Sept. 14, 1851, Elizabeth Smith. Res. Coeymans, Albany Co., N. Y. Chil. :
7 G.—1. LEONARD ROMAINE, b. June 7, 1852. 2. ANNA G., b. Nov. 8, 1856. 3. ELLA M., b. Mar. 2, 1859. A graduate of the State Normal School, Albany, 1879. 4. TRUMAN S., b. Mar. 15, 1864. 5. H. WILBUR, b. July 31, 1867.
6 G.—12. FLETCHER CARHART, b. Mar. 24, 1827, m. Jane Weeks, in 1853. Res. Brooklyn, N. Y. Chil. :
7 G.—1. FRANK. 2. CHARLES. 3. ANN AUGUSTA. 4. EDWIN. 5. GEORGE. 6. FREDERICK. 7. WILLIAM.

FAMILY OF ROBERT,[2] *of Gilderland, Albany Co., N. Y., son of* DANIEL,[1] *of Coeymans.*

5 G.—VI. ROBERT CARHART,[2] (*Note* 14), b. July 2, 1784, at Rye, N. Y., m. June 29th, 1807, Catharine Rowe, of Coeymans, b. Mar. 8, 1785. Catharine d. Feb. 7, 1850. Robert d. 1872, aged 88 years. Chil. :
1. PETER. 2. MARGARET. 3. ELIZA. 4. SANFORD. 5. GARRETSON LYON. 6. ELMA.

6 G.—1. PETER CARHART, b. June 2, 1808, m. in 1835, Catharine Vedder, of Coeymans. He was in the Albany post-office for many years, and afterwards U. S. mail agent, between New York and Albany. Res. Albany, N. Y. Chil. :
7 G.—1. RICHARD CARHART, b. 1836, m. Lucinda A. Smith, of Albany. Richard was proprietor of the Irving House, Chicago, at the time of the great fire, when it was burnt, and he suffered an entire loss of property. He died Feb. 14, 1874, at Chicago. Mrs. C. resides at Kenosha, Wis. Chil. :
8 G.—1. CORA B., b. at Chicago, Dec. 26, 1865. 2. EVEREST L., b. April 1, 1867. 3. LOUIS P., b. Aug. 15, 1868, d. Nov. 30, 1872. 4. CHARLES ALBERT, b. June 3, 1870. 5. GEORGE T., b. Oct. 17, 1871. 6. ARCHIBALD MCBEAN, b. Nov. 6, 1873, d. Sept., 1877.
7 G.—2. ANNIE MARIA CARHART, b. 1837. Res. Waukegan, Ill. Unm. Peter, m. second wife, Abigail Taylor. Chil. :
7 G.—3. WILLIAM TAYLOR CARHART, b. 1859.

6 G.—2. MARGARET CARHART, (dau. of Robert,[2]) m. Cornelius Van Derzee. Chil. :
7 G.—1. ELIZABETH VAN DERZEE, b. 1833, m. Dr. Barney Wood, of Albany. 2. CATHARINE ANN VAN DERZEE, d. 1855, unm.

6 G.—3. ELIZA CARHART, (dau. of Robert[2]) m. Henry Carhart, her cousin, (son of Daniel,[2]) in 1839. Res. Gilderland, Albany Co., N. Y. Henry is a farmer. Record found in the family of Daniel.[2]

6 G.—4. SANFORD CARHART, m. Sophia Mead, of Gilderland, in 1848. Res. Gilderland. Farmer. Chil. :

42   *GENEALOGY OF*

7 G.—1. ABRAHAM CARHART, a soldier in the war of the Rebellion, drowned while bathing in the Mississippi, during the siege of Vicksburg.
7 G.—2. ROBERT CARHART, m. Elizabeth Vine, of Gilderland. Chil.: 1. ADA NEWTON. 2. IRENE.
7 G.—3. CHARLES CARHART, m. Kate Vine, of Gilderland. Prof. of Penmanship at Poultney, Vt.
7 G.—4. PERRY MEAD CARHART. Res. Gilderland. Unm.

6 G.—5. GARRETSON LYON CARHART, M. D., (*Note* 15) (son of Robert,² of Gilderland,) b. Mar. 28, 1824, at Gilderland, m. Mar. 27, 1850, Martha Boyland Bancroft, (dau. of Benjamin Bancroft, M. D., of Weathersfield Springs, N. Y.) Martha d. 1868. Res. Marion, Linn Co., Iowa. Chil.:
7 G.—1. GEORGE BANCROFT, b. July 21, 1852, d. 1863. 2. MARTHA EUNICE, b. Mar. 22, 1856. 3. ROBERT BENJAMIN. b. June 30, 1866, d. 1868. Dr. G. L. C. m. 2nd wife, Feb. 22, 1871, Elizabeth Dickson Spearman, of Manchester, Iowa (dau. of William D. Spearman, of Brooklyn, N. Y.) Chil.:
7 G.—4 WILLIAM GARRETSON CARHART, b. Sept. 3, 1875.
6 G.—6. ELMA CARHART, (dau. of Robert²), m. Charles Weaver, of Gilderland, in 1852, and d. Feb. 2, 1872. Res. Gilderland. Chil.:
7 G.—1. CATHARINE WEAVER. 2. ANNIE WEAVER.

FAMILY OF THOMAS D., *of Albany, Son of* DANIEL.[1]

5 G.—VII. THOMAS D. CARHART, b. Mar. 15, 1786, at Rye, Westchester Co., N. Y., m. Mar. 4, 1810, Mary Totten, of Gilderland, N. Y., b. July 23, 1785. Mary d. at Bethlehem, N. Y., Nov. 2, 1837. Thomas d. at Albany, N. Y., Jan. 2, 1861. Chil.:
1. WILLIAM. 2. ELISHA. 3. SAMUEL. 4. ANGELINE B. 5. STEPHEN. 6. CATHARINE.
6 G.—1. WILLIAM CARHART, b. Dec. 18, 1810, at Coeymans, N. Y., m. Mar. 13, 1834, Rosanna Austin, of West Scotland, Albany Co., N. Y. William d. Jan. 18, 1848. Res. Albany, N. Y. Chil.:
7 G.—1. MARY E. CARHART, b. July 24, 1838, m. Jan. 5, 1857, Edward Herron. Res. Albany, N. Y. Chil.:
8 G.—1. FANNY HERRON. 2. GEORGE HERRON. 3. ADA HERRON. 4. WILLIAM HERRON. 5. JANE HERRON. 6. ESTHER HERRON. 7. CHARLES HERRON. 8. JAMES HERRON.
7 G.—2. FANNY L. CARHART, b. 1840, m. Thomas Meadon, in 1858. Res. Greenpoint, Long Island. Chil.:
8 G.—1. ADA MEADON. 2. HOWARD MEADON. 3. GEORGE MEADON. 4. MARY MEADON.
7 G.—3. JAMES W. CARHART, b. at Bethlehem, N. Y., 1835, d. Oct. 28, 1837.
4. EMMA CARHART, b. Dec. 12, 1843, d. Jan. 26, 1848.
5. MARGARETTA A. CARHART, b. 1846, d. 1848.

THE CARHART FAMILY.

6. GEORGE W. CARHART, b. 1845, m. Nancy Schermerhorn. Res. Albany, N. Y. Chil.:
8 G.—1. HOWARD, res. Albany, N. Y. 2. GEORGE. 3. MARY.

6 G.—2. ELISHA CARHART, b. Oct. 15, 1812, at Coeymans, N. Y., m. Jan. 14, 1841, Ellen S. Beebe, of Gilderland, N. Y., b. Dec. 22, 1816. Res. Albany, N. Y. Chil.:
7 G.—1. MARY ELLEN CARHART, b. Feb. 8, 1842, in Gilderland, m. Dec. 30, 1868, Levi Fredendall, Albany, N. Y. Res. Gilderland, N. Y. Chil.:
8 G.—1. GEORGE FREDENDALL. 2. EDWARD FREDENDALL.
7 G.—2. HULDAH A. CARHART, b. Jan. 8, 1844, m. Jan. 17, 1861, Albert C. Hallenbeck. Res. Gilderland, N. Y. Chil.:
8 G.—1. LUELLA MINERVA HALLENBECK. 2. ERNEST A. HALLENBECK. 3. MARY C. HALLENBECK.
7 G.—3. ELIZA J. CARHART, b. Feb. 26, 1846, d. April 10, 1867.
7 G.—4. ELMIRA CARHART, b. Oct. 20, 1848, at Gilderland, N. Y., m. Nov. 13, 1870, Henry E. Flagler. Res. Albany, N. Y. Chil.:
8 G.—1. HENRY C. FLAGLER. 2. HATTIE B. FLAGLER.
7 G.—5. CATHARINE A. CARHART, b. Nov. 13, 1852, at Gilderland, N. Y., m. May 9, 1875, Walter Brasher. Chil.:
8 G.—ELLEN C. BRASHER.
7 G.—6. JACOB EDWARD CARHART, b. Aug. 22, 1855, at Gilderland, N. Y. Res. Albany, N. Y.

6 G.—3. SAMUEL CARHART, b. Dec. 3, 1815, d. Sept. 10, 1830, unm.
6 G.—4. ANGELINE B. CARHART, b. April 7, 1818, at Coeymans, N. Y., m. at Troy, N. Y., March 12, 1863, George Murray. Res. Albany, N. Y.
6 G.—5. STEPHEN CARHART, b. Nov. 21, 1820, at Coeymans, m. Aug. 30, 1845, Gertrude M. Groat, of Watervliet, N. Y., b. Sept. 25, 1823. Gertrude d. Dec. 20, 1857. Res. Albany, N. Y. Chil.:
7 G.—1. JESSIE F. CARHART, b. Dec. 20, 1857.
S. C. married 2nd wife, Sept. 29, 1859, Frances R. Vandenberg, of Albany, N. Y., b. July 28, 1833. Frances d. Sept. 29, 1866. Chil.:
7 G.—2. SARAH ANNA CARHART, b. July 13, 1860.
S. C. married 3rd wife, Oct. 12, 1871, Margaret Jacobson.
6 G.—6. CATHARINE E. CARHART, b. Aug. 12, 1825, at Coeymans, N. Y., d. Sept. 18, 1854, at Albany, unm.

FAMILY OF ISAAC CARHART, *of Manlius, N. Y., Son of* DANIEL.

5 G.—VIII. ISAAC CARHART, b. Mar. 4, 1789, at Rye, N. Y., m. May, 1807, Hannah Rowe, b. Nov. 6, 1790, at Coeymans, N. Y. He removed from Coeymans to Manlius, Onondaga Co., N. Y., in 1827, and died there, Mar. 17, 1845. Hannah d. Oct. 23, 1867. Chil.:

1. ELIZABETH. 2. JOHN. 3. CATHARINE. 4. BARBARA ANN, 5. HANNAH MARIA. 6. ISAAC ROWE. 7. HESTER. 8. PETER SANFORD. 9. HENRY DUNSTAN.

6 G.—1. ELIZABETH CARHART. b. Aug. 20, 1809, at Coeymans, N. Y., m. April 28, 1836, Leonard Wilkins, b. July 9, 1802, at Hillsboro Centre, N. H. (son of Andrew and Elizabeth Wilkins). Elizabeth d. April 18, 1858, at Cicero, N. Y. Leonard d. May 12, 1879, at Farwell, Mich. Chil.:

7 G.—1. LUCY A. WILKINS, b. July 8, 1839, at Syracuse, N. Y. Graduated at Cazenovia Seminary, N. Y., June, 1866. Occupation, bee-keeping. Res. Farwell, Mich.

2. AUGUSTINE H. WILKINS, b. Aug. 8, 1842, at Syracuse, N. Y. Enlisted in April, 1861, in the 12th N. Y. Regiment of Volunteers. Was taken prisoner at the battle of Malvern Hill, and spent three months in Libby prison. Is General Agent in the Southwest, for the publishing house of A. S. Barnes & Co., N. Y. Residence since 1870, New Orleans. Is also a partner in the firm of Lathrop & Wilkins, booksellers, N. O.

3. LETTIE A. WILKINS, b. July 15, 1845, at Syracuse, N. Y. Graduated at Cazenovia Seminary, N. Y., June, 1866. Occupation, bee-keeping. Res. Farwell, Mich.

4. GEORGE H. WILKINS, b. July 25, 1850, at Collamer, N. Y. He is a farmer at Farwell, Mich.

6 G.—2. JOHN CARHART, b. May 17, 1811, at Coeymans, N. Y., m. Oct. 22, 1840, Angeline Chesbro, of Knox, N. Y., b. March 24, 1817. Angeline d. Oct. 12, 1871. J. C. married second wife, July 16, 1872, Amanda Brooks, of Florence, Ohio, b. April 27, 1842. Removed in 1855, from Gilderland, N. Y., to Circle Grove, Amity, Scott Co., Iowa. Removed 1875, to Grinnell, Poweshiek Co., Iowa. Chil.:

1. SUSAN. 2. EDWARD CHESBRO. 3. ALBERT ELIJAH. 4. MELISSA. 5. LESTER BROWN.

7 G.—1. SUSAN CARHART, b. at Gilderland, N. Y., May 31, 1842, m. March 2, 1862, at Circle Grove, Iowa, George W. Talman (*Note* 16), b. Oct. 12, 1837, at Forrestville, Chatauqua Co., N. Y. Res. Gilman, Iowa. Chil.:

8 G.—1. GRACE MELISSA TALMAN, b. at Circle Grove, Iowa, Jan. 13, 1863, d. at Baton Rouge, La., Mar. 23, 1864. 2. IDA M. TALMAN, b. at Morganza Bend, La., Jan. 18, 1865, in camp of U. S. Army. 3. ANGELINE TALMAN, b. at Wild Rose Farm, Scott Co., Iowa, Dec. 15, 1866. 4. CLARA MABEL TALMAN, b. at Wild Rose Farm, Oct. 3, 1868. 5. GEORGE ALBERT TALMAN, b. in Jasper Co., Iowa, May 13, 1871. 6. SUSAN TALMAN, b. Dec. 15, 1872. 7. LUCY MARIA TALMAN, b. Nov. 2, 1874.

7 G.—2. EDWARD CHESBRO CARHART, b. at Gilderland, N. Y., Apr. 25, 1844, d. May 27, 1859, at Amity, Scott Co., Iowa.

7 G.—3. ALBERT ELIJAH CARHART, b. at Cicero, Onondaga Co., N. Y., July 11, 1846, m. Aug. 6, 1873, Maggie Dosh, of Scott Co., Iowa. A. E. C. entered Cornell College, Mount Vernon, Iowa, in 1866, and graduated from the Classical Department, with degree of A. M., in 1873. Was Principal of a school in Tama City, Iowa. Present res. Maquaketa, Jackson Co., Iowa. Chil.:

8 G.—1. KATIE GERTRUDE CARHART, b. June 5, 1874, d. Dec. 13, 1874. 2. RAYMOND ALBERT CARHART, b. Dec. 16, 1875.

7 *G*.—4. MELISSA CARHART. b. at Bridgeport. N. Y.. Mar. 15, 1848, d. of hydrophobia, at Amity. Scott Co.. Iowa. Jan. 23, 1860 (*Note* 17).

7 *G*.—5. LESTER BROWN CARHART, b. at Cicero. N. Y.. Jan. 1, 1850, m. Aug. 20, 1872. Addie W. Wright, of Clarance, Iowa.

L. B. C. entered Cornell College, at Mount Vernon. Iowa, in 1866, and graduated from Classical Department, in June, 1872, with degree of A. M. Was Principal of Eldora graded school for two terms. Moved to Hampton. Franklin Co., Iowa, where he is at present (1877) engaged in book and music business.

6 *G*.—3. CATHARINE CARHART (dau. of Isaac, of Manlius). b. June 22, 1813, at Coeymans. N. Y.. m. April 13, 1835, at Collamer. N. Y., Michael Leyden, b. May 5, 1809, in Ireland. M. L. was a farmer at Collamer, until 1869, when he removed to Syracuse, N. Y. Chil.:
1. MAURICE. 2. HANNAH MARIA. 3. ISAAC H. 4. HART C. 5. HESTER A. 6. MARY ELIZABETH. 7. ELIZA J. 8. BARBARA M. 9. ELLA LOUISE. 10. CATHARINE. 11. EDWIN C. 12. LUCY F.

7 *G*.—1. MAURICE LEYDEN. b. Oct. 18, 1836, at Collamer, m. 1865, Margaret L. Garriguz. of Rochester. M. L. is of the firm of Davis & Leyden, Dental Depot, Rochester. He served a term of four years in the war of the Rebellion, with the rank of Lieutenant and Captain. Was taken prisoner during an engagement, in 1864, and suffered the horrors of Libby and Danville. He was honorably mustered out, at the close of the war, with the rank of Major. Chil.:

8 *G*.—BLANCHE ELOISE LEYDEN, b. 1874.

7 *G*.—2. HANNAH MARIA LEYDEN, b. May 26, 1838, at Collamer, m. July 28, 1860, Edwin R. Clark. Chil.:
1. ORVILLE L. CLARK, b. 1867. 2. WALTER E. CLARK, dead. 3. EDWIN R. CLARK, d. July 25, 1872.

7 *G*.—3. ISAAC H. LEYDEN, b. May 1, 1840, at Collamer. N. Y., m. Feb. 12, 1867, Nellie A. Hart. I. H. L. is a clothing merchant at Syracuse. Chil.: ELLEN LOUISE LEYDEN, b. 1872.

7 *G*.—4. HART C. LEYDEN. b. June 3, 1843, at Collamer. Is of the firm of J. H. Leyden & Bro., Dental Depot, Syracuse, N. Y.

7 *G*.—5. HESTER A. LEYDEN, b. March 9, 1845, at Collamer. Is engaged in teaching in Syracuse.

7 *G*.—6. MARY ELIZABETH LEYDEN, b. Sept. 4, 1846, at Collamer, d. Aug. 9, 1848.

7 *G*.—7. ELIZA J. LEYDEN, b. Feb. 16, 1848, at Collamer. Is Principal of a Grammar School, at Burlington, Vt.

7 *G*.—8. BARBARA M. LEYDEN, b. Sept. 9, 1850. Is teaching in Syracuse.

7 *G*.—9. ELLA LOUISE LEYDEN, b. April 9, 1853, at Collamer, N. Y., d. Nov. 17, 1862, at Syracuse.

7 *G*.—10. CATHARINE LEYDEN. b. June 13, 1855, at Collamer.

7 *G*.—11. EDWIN C. LEYDEN, b. Dec. 27, 1857, at Collamer, N. Y., m. Nov. 27, 1879, at Cleveland, N. Y., Minnie Long, dau. of Rev. Wm. Long, Rector of St. James' Church, of Cleveland, N. Y. Res. Rochester. N. Y.

7 *G*.—12. LUCY F. LEYDEN, b. Nov. 26, 1862, at Syracuse, N. Y.

6 *G*.—4. BARBARA ANN CARHART (dau. of Isaac, of Manlius). b. Nov. 15, 1815, at Bethlehem, Albany Co., N. Y., m. George W. Huntley, of

Kirkville, Onondaga Co., N. Y. Barbara d. Oct. 20, 1851. She had five children, none of whom survived her.

6 G.—5. HANNAH MARIA CARHART, b. Feb. 16, 1818, at Bethlehem.

6 G.—6. ISAAC ROWE CARHART, b. June 9, 1820, at Bethlehem, m. Catharine Ann Thompson, of North Manlius, N. Y., in July, 1846. Catharine died July 13, 1847. Chil. :

7 G.—KATE LOUISE CARHART, b. May 12, 1847, m. June 4, 1866, George R. Cook, of Syracuse, N. Y., an attorney at law, and present Surrogate of Onondaga Co. Chil. :

8 G.—1. CHARLES CARHART COOK, b. Jan. 17, 1868. 2. HENRY LANSING COOK, b. Oct. 6, 1871, d. Jan. 12, 1876. 3. FLORENCE LUCY COOK, b. Sept. 6, 1874, d. Jan. 20, 1876. 4. MABEL LOUISE COOK, b. Nov. 12, 1877.

Isaac R. Carhart m. second wife, Lucy A. Morris, of Syracuse, Sept. 9, 1858. He was a lumber merchant at Syracuse, and d. Sept. 3, 1863.

6 G.—7. HESTER CARHART, b. April 4, 1824, at Coeymans, N. Y., m. Sept. 1, 1848, Henry Furbeck. Hester d. at Dewitt, N. Y., Dec. 7, 1854. Chil. :

7 G.—1. DUANE L. FURBECK, res. Trenton, Mo. Occupation, grocer. 2. GEORGE FURBECK, late of Toledo, O. Killed, Oct., 1879, by falling from a car and being crushed.

6 G.—8. PETER SANFORD CARHART, b. July 22, 1826, at Coeymans, m. Lucia E. Hulbert, of North Manlius, Onondaga Co., b. Oct. 25, 1841. P. S. C. is a farmer, and inventor and manufacturer of Carhart's Cultivator, and a Reversible Harrow. Res. Collamer, Onondaga Co., N. Y. Chil. :

7 G.—1. HERBERT ADDISON, b. May 21, 1868. 2. ANGIE ELECTA, b. Dec. 16, 1871. 3. RAYMOND HENRY, b. July 14, 1874. 4. ELMER HOWARD, b. April 21, 1876. 5. ORLETTA LOUISE, b. June 28, 1878.

6 G.—9. HENRY DUNSTAN CARHART, b. July 31, 1830, at Manlius, N. Y. He was Captain in the 185th Regiment, N. Y. Volunteers, and d. Dec. 4, 1864, in camp, before Petersburg, Va.

5 G.—IX. BARBARA CARHART (dau. of Daniel¹), b. 1792, in Rye, N. Y., m. Stephen Rowe, brother of the wives of her brothers, Robert and Isaac. Stephen died, leaving no issue. Barbara Rowe m. second husband, Samuel Goodfellow, of Syracuse, who died, leaving one son. Barbara m., third husband, Mr. Pray, who died without issue, as is supposed. Her residence is Indiana.

FAMILY OF JAMES CARHART, *of Babylon, L. I., Son of* THOMAS,² *of Rye.*

4 G.—JAMES CARHART, b. about 1750, m. July 30, 1782, Elizabeth Vanderbilt. James was a Quaker ; occupation, farming. Chil. :

5 G.—HENRY CARHART, who adopted the profession of the law. His health failing, he went to one of the West India Islands, where he died. No descendants.

FAMILY OF HACKALIAH,[1] *of West Greenwich, Fairfield Co., Conn., Son of* THOMAS,[2] *of Rye, Westchester Co., N. Y.*

4 G.—HACKALIAH[1] CARHART (*Note* 18), b. Jan. 30, 1755, at Rye, N. Y., m. April 2, 1785, Margaret Anderson, b. Nov. 19, 1760, (dau. of Isaac Anderson (*Note* 19), and Hannah Purdy, of King Street (*Note* 20), West Greenwich, Conn.) Hackaliah d. June, 1837, aged 83 yrs. Margaret d. Feb. 4, 1845, aged 85 yrs. Chil.:
I. MARY. II. HACKALIAH.[2] III. GULIELMA. IV. ALFRED. V. HANNAH ANDERSON. VI. ISAAC ANDERSON. VII. JOSHUA. VIII. MARGARET. IX. ELIZABETH.

5 G.—I. MARY CARHART, b. June 9, 1786, d. 1796.

5 G.—II. HACKALIAH[2] CARHART, b. May 30, 1788, at King Street, m. Jan. 1, 1815, Susan Steadwell, (dau. of Benjamin and Sarah Steadwell, of King Street). Susan d. Sept. 4, 1837. He m. second wife, Mary Fluellen, Mar. 11, 1842. Mary d. Nov. 7, 1869, at Glenville. Hackaliah d. at Glenville, Conn., Aug. 10, 1876, aged 88 yrs., being the last of the name of Carhart in that vicinity, or in Rye. Buried in Anderson Cemetery (*Note* 21). Chil.:

6 G.—1. WILLIAM HENRY CARHART, b. Mar. 15, 1816, at King Street, m. Nancy Maria Dickinson, of Bedford, N. Y. Chil.:
7 G.—GEORGE HENRY CARHART, who m. Sarah Adams, of Bedford, and had:
8 G.—1. ANNA. 2. IDA. 3. JANE. 4. GEORGE HENRY.

6 G.—2. ANN ELIZA CARHART, b. May 7, 1818, at King Street, m. Oct. 10, 1837, John B. Willson, b. Oct. 25, 1812, (son of Major Jotham Willson and Sarah Green, of King Street.) J. B. W. was a farmer, and resided at Glenville, Conn., where he d. Sept. 23, 1874. Chil.:
7 G.—1. MORTIMER B. WILLSON, b. at Glenville, Jan. 22, 1839, m. July 29, 1863, Mary E. Dusenbury, (dau. of James Dusenbury and Sarah Morton Palmer, of New York). M. B. W. is a farmer, and resides at Glenville, Conn. Chil.:
8 G.—EDITH WILLSON, b. April 17, 1864, a student at Rye Seminary, N. Y.

7 G.—2. ADELINE E. WILLSON, b. at Glenville, Conn., Jan. 11, 1842, m. April 29, 1867, Francis Manton Holly, M. D., (son of William Wells Holly, of Stamford, Conn., and Annie, dau. of John J. Glover, of New York, b. in England, and Sarah Cornell, of Long Island). Res. Greenwich, Conn. Chil.:
8 G.—1. FRANCIS GLOVER HOLLY, b. Mar. 11, 1868. 2. ALICE MAUD HOLLY, b. April 17, 1871. 3. MARY CHARLOTTE HOLLY, b. Sept. 24, 1872. 4. CARRIE RENSHAW HOLLY, b. April 2, 1875.

7 G.—3. JOTHAM S. WILLSON, b. April 4, 1844, at Glenville, unm.

7 G.—4. MARY HAIGHT WILLSON, b. Sept. 1, 1856, graduated at Rye Seminary, in 1877, and m. April 30, 1879, at Glenville, William F. Duncan, M. D. of New York. Res. New York.

6 G.—3. MARIA AMELIA CARHART, b. at King Street, Sept. 2, 1820, m. Asbury Wooster. Maria d. May 21, 1861. Chil.:
   7 G.—1. ADELINE WOOSTER. 2. FRANK WOOSTER, d. Jan. 21, 1880.
6 G.—4. CATHARINE AMANDA CARHART, b. at King Street, Nov. 30, 1822. Res. Glenville. Unm.

5 G.—III. GULIELMA SPRINGAT PENN CARHART, b. Aug. 20, 1791, at King Street, m. Simeon Redfield, of Portchester, N. Y., Jan. 19, 1817 (*Note* 22). S. R. died in New York city, Oct. 28, 1823. No chil. Mrs. Redfield m. second husband, Nathaniel Dayton, in 1842, and d. May 17, 1845. Buried in Anderson Cemetery.

5 G.—IV. ALFRED[1] CARHART, b. at King Street, Mar. 9, 1793, m. Dec. 3, 1812, Phebe Totten, b. Mar. 7, 1785, (dau. of Samuel Totten, (*Note* 23) of King Street, and Esther Steadwell, of North Castle, Westchester Co., N. Y.) Phebe d. Dec. 18, 1817, and was buried in the Orthodox Quaker burying-ground, at Purchase, Westchester Co., N. Y.
   A. C. lived at Riversville, on the Byrum, or Armonck river, Fairfield Co., Conn., until 1826, when he moved to New York city, where he became engaged in mercantile and other business. He was elected to the N. Y. Legislature in 1839-40. Removed to Peekskill in 1869. Chil.:
   6 G.—1. MARY ELIZABETH CARHART (Author and Compiler of the Carhart Record), b. July 23, 1814, at King Street, m. Sept. 12, 1838, in New York city, Thomas Gilcrist Dusenbury, b. Mar. 19, 1810, (son of David and Hannah Anderson Dusenbury, and grandson of Wilsey Dusenbury, of White Plains, N. Y.) Res. New York city. Chil.:
   7 G.—MARY JOSEPHINE DUSENBURY, b. in New York city, Nov. 3, 1839, d. Dec. 3, 1849. Buried in Anderson Cemetery.

6 G.—2. MOSES TOTTEN CARHART, b. Aug. 11, 1817, at Riversville, Conn., d. Jan. 10, 1837. He was engaged in business in 1836, with Haviland, Harrell & Allen, druggists, of Charleston, S. C. By imprudence in bathing in the Ashley river, in the spring of 1836, he contracted a cold, which developed consumption; from which he died at St. Augustine, Fla., where he had gone for the winter in the hope of relief. He was buried at St. Augustine, in the ground of the Presbyterian Church, whose pastor in 1837, was Rev. Dr. Schoonmaker.

ALFRED[1] CARHART married second wife, June 5, 1818, Anna Peck, (*Note* 24) of Peeksland, Conn., b. Nov. 15, 1797. Anna d. Sept. 7, 1843. Buried in Anderson Cemetery. Chil.:
   6 G.—3. ELMA MARIA CARHART, b. June 12, 1819, at Riversville, m. in New York, Nov. 20, 1844, Henry Rutgers Cannon, M. D., (son of P. Cannon, Pres. of Rutgers College, New Brunswick, N. J.) Elma d. May 9, 1862. Buried in Anderson Cemetery. Chil.:
   1. ALFRED SPENCER CANNON. 2. HENRY LYMAN CANNON. Both died in infancy.
   6 G.—4. ROBERT NELSON CARHART, b. Aug. 7, 1821, at Riversville, Conn., d. Oct. 7, 1865, at Carmel, Putnam Co., N. Y., unmarried. Buried at the Baptist Church, Red Mills, Putnam Co.

6 G.—5. LAVINIA ANNA CARHART, b. Nov. 3. 1825, at Riversville, m. in New York, May 26, 1844, Stephen Thorne Munson, b. Nov. 23, 1815, (son of Ira Munson, who was son of Ebenezer, of Danbury, Conn.; and Mrs. Elizabeth Whitney—born Price—dau. of John Lloyd Price (*Note* 25), of Flintshire, Wales, and Euphemia Pell Hunt (*Note* 26), fourth in descent from John Pell, 2nd Lord of the Manor of Pelham (*Note* 27), Westchester Co., N. Y.)

S. T. M. was a book publisher in New York for several years. Was in Quartermaster's Department during the War of the Rebellion, and for many years in New York Custom House, and an efficient member of the Board of Education in Hoboken, N. J. Chil. :

7 G.—1. FRANK BEECHER MUNSON, b. Dec. 29, 1845, in New York city, d. Aug. 31, 1846, at White Plains. Buried in Disbrow Cemetery at Mamaroneck, Westchester Co., N. Y.

7 G.—2. GRACE MUNSON, b. Aug. 31, 1847, in New York, d. Jan. 6, 1859. Buried at Greenwood, L. I.

7 G.—3. MARY JOSEPHINE MUNSON, b. April 20, 1851, in New York, m. Nov. 25, 1873, at Hoboken. N. J., Carl Heinrich Bruckner, b. April 18, 1847 (son of Rudolph Bruckner and Elise Eglin, of Basel, Switzerland, and nephew of Christof Eglin, of Havre, an officer of the Legion of Honor of France). Chil. :

8 G.—RUDOLPH EGLIN BRUCKNER, b. Jan. 13, 1875, at Hoboken, N. J.

7 G.—4. LOUISE WEED MUNSON, b. May 20, 1853, in New York, d. Dec. 15, 1858. Buried in Greenwood.

6 G.—6. LYMAN BEECHER CARHART, b. Aug. 5. 1828, in New York, m. May 29, 1862, in Brooklyn, Ophelia Merle d'Aubigné, b. Sept. 28, 1835 (dau. of Guillaume Merle d'Aubigné (*Note* 28), of Brooklyn—brother of Rev. Dr. John Henri Merle d'Aubigné, of Geneva, Switzerland, author of the " History of the Reformation,"—and Ophelia Geer, dau. of Capt. Joshua Geer, of Groton, Conn.)

L. B. C. was engaged in dry goods business at Davenport, Iowa, for many years, in the firm of Kehoe & Carhart. He resided in Brooklyn, from 1856 to 1873, when he removed to Peekskill, N. Y., where he now resides. Chil. :

7 G.—1. WILLIAM MERLE CARHART, b. May 21, 1863, at Brooklyn, N. Y. 2. CHARLES LYMAN CARHART, b. Nov. 13, 1865, at Brooklyn, N. Y. Students at the Military Academy, Peekskill. 3. BESSIE MERLE CARHART, b. Oct. 29, 1869, at Brooklyn, N. Y. 4. ELOISE OPHELIA CARHART, b. Oct. 19, 1871, at Brooklyn, N. Y. 5. ANNA GEORGINE CARHART, b. Sept. 4, 1874, at Peekskill, N. Y.

6 G.—7. JAMES ALFRED CARHART, b. April 5, 1832, d. Aug., 1833, in New York.

6 G.—8. FRANCES HENRIETTA CARHART, b. Dec. 6, 1835, in New York, m. July 18, 1854, Daniel W. Terry, of Coeymans, N. Y., (brother of Revs. David and Milton S. Terry, of the M. E. Church). [The latter is Presiding Elder of the New York District, N. Y., 1880]. Frances d. Oct. 28, 1865. Buried in the Anderson Cemetery. Chil. :

7 G.—1. ALFRED CARHART TERRY, b. Sept. 9, 1855, in Jersey City, N. J., d. Feb. 27, 1856. 2. MARVIN BARTLETT TERRY, b. Jan. 14, 1857, at Coeymans, N. Y.

6 G.—9. MARIA LOUISE CARHART, b. Sept. 3. 1840, died in infancy.
ALFRED CARHART, married third wife, Nov. 21, 1871, Mary Horton, dau. of Gilbert Horton, of Carmel, Putnam Co., N. Y.

5 G.—V. HANNAH ANDERSON CARHART, b. Mar. 22, 1795. m. Feb. 8, 1817, F. Garretson Lyon, of North Castle, N. Y. (grandson of Roger Lyon, of Revolutionary memory, and Mary Willson, of King Street). Hannah d. Nov. 13, 1877, at Mamaroneck, N. Y., aged 82 years. Res. New York city and Mamaroneck, N. Y. Chil. :
6 G.—1. NATHAN EMORY LYON, b. Jan. 2, 1818, in New York, m. April 15, 1840, Catharine Coles. Res. New York city. Chil. :
7 G.—1. SARAH MARIA LYON, b. June 26, 1841. m. Dec. 18, 1861, Peter Sheldon Coles. Res. Tivoli, Dutchess Co., N. Y. Chil. :
8 G.—1. EMERY GARRETSON COLES, b. Oct. 13, 1864. 2. MARY E. COLES, b. Sept. 18, 1865. 3. FRANK COLES, b. Oct. 21, 1867. 4. GERTRUDE ADELIA COLES, b. June 16, 1869. 5. JENNIE ADELAIDE COLES, b. Aug. 6, 1871. 6. Twin sons, b. Jan. 13, 1875.
7 G.—2. EMERY GARRETSON LYON, b. Aug. 25, 1843, m. Dec. 30, 1867, Mary W. Lewis. Chil. :
8 G.—1. NATHAN EMERY, b. Sept. 9, 1868. 2. EMMA AUGUSTA, b. Sept. 18, 1869, died. 3. ELLA ELIZABETH, b. Mar. 17, 1872. 4. EMMA MARY. b. May, 1874.
7 G.—3. EMMA E. LYON, b. Jan. 10, 1846, m. April 17, 1866, Halsey W. Knapp. Chil. :
8 G.—1. KATIE ESTELLE KNAPP, b. Feb. 21, 1868. 2. BURRAS FRANK KNAPP, b. Jan. 27, 1871, died.
7 G.—4. MARY JANE LYON, b. April 10, 1848, died.
7 G.—5. ANDREW SIMPSON LYON, b. Jan. 15, 1851, m. Mary A. Morgan, April 10, 1870. Chil. :
8 G.—1. CHARLES EMERY, b. March, 1871, died in infancy. 2. ALICE MARY, b. June, 1872. 3. IDA LUELLA, b. Feb., 1874.
7 G.—6. CHARLES BENJAMIN LYON, b. May 14, 1854. 7. WILLIAM WARREN LYON, b. Oct. 25, 1856.

6 G.—2. GILBERT LYON, b. May 28, 1828, died.
6 G.—3. ALBERT LYON, b. Aug. 18, 1821, m. Harriet Newell Van Zyle, Nov. 18, 1845. A. L. is a Justice at Mamaroneck. Chil. :
7 G.—1. CALVIN AUGUSTUS, b. May 2, 1847. 2. WILLIAM EDWIN, b. May 22, 1849, d. Feb. 13, 1852. 3. ALBERT EDWARD, b. Nov. 21, 1851, d. May 26, 1866. 4. GEORGE NELSON, b. May 17, 1854. 5. LIZZIE SANFORD, b. Jan. 19, 1856, m. Dec. 25, 1876, Elsworth White. 6. EDWIN ANDERSON, b. Aug. 8, 1859. 7. HARRY GEDNEY, b. Oct. 30, 1862. 8. WILBER CARHART, b. July 11, 1865. 9. HATTIE FRANCES, b. Sept. 8, 1869.

6 G.—4. WILLIAM EDWIN LYON, b. in New York, Feb. 8, 1824, m. Jane Sloat, Aug. 8, 1859. Res. Mamaroneck. Chil. :
7 G.—1. ELLA FRANCES, b. July 20, 1860. 2. WILLIAM EDWIN, b. April 14, 1863. 3. MARGARET JANE, b. April 12, 1865. 4. CHARLES WARREN, b. June 26, 1866. 5. IRVING, b. May 4, 1868. 6. JAMES NEWMAN, b. April 18, 1870. 7. MINNIE ESTELLE, b. Nov. 19, 1872. 8. LILLIE LYON, b. Mar. 23, 1877.

6 G.—5. ADDISON LYON, b. Dec. 14, 1825, died in infancy.
6 G.—6. MARGARET LYON, b. June, 1827, died in infancy.

6 G.—7. WARREN LYON, b. in New York, Nov. 2, 1829, m. May 22, 1856, Mary A. Ferguson. Mary A. d. Mar. 29, 1864. Res. New York city. Chil. :
7 G.—1. OLIVIA AUGUSTA, b. May 2, 1857. 2. LEONORA, b. Feb. 28, 1859. 3. EMMA, b. Aug. 21, 1862, died. 4. MARY AUGUSTA, b. Jan. 22, 1864.
Warren Lyon m. second wife, Lucy Atkins, of England, Apr. 27, 1868.

6 G.—8. ELMIRA LYON, b. at King Street, Aug. 2, 1832, m. May 3, 1859, Matthew R. Rooke. Res. New York city and Mamaroneck. Chil. :
7 G.—1. THEODORE AUGUSTUS ROOKE, b. Mar. 18, 1860, d. June 8, 1862. 2. FRANK AYDELOTT ROOKE, b. Nov. 17, 1862. 3. IDA JEAN ROOKE, b. Jan. 13, 1866. 4 and 5. JESSIE and CARRIE, twins, b. Jan. 4, 1868. 6. WARREN AUGUSTUS ROOKE, b. Sept. 27, 1873.

5 G.—VI. ISAAC ANDERSON CARHART, b. at King Street, Dec. 3, 1796, m. Sept. 15, 1819, Eliza Matthews, b. July 10, 1800 (dau. of Daniel Matthews and Charity Smith, of North Castle, Westchester Co., N. Y., and aunt of Cornelius Matthews, author and poet, of New York). Eliza d. May 30, 1823. Isaac d. Mar. 6, 1847. Res., until 1839, New York city, then Binghamton, Broome Co., N. Y. Chil. :
6 G.—1. SAMANTHA B. 2. DANIEL M. 3. MARGARET A. 4. GEORGE W. 5. CHARLES B. 6. ADELINE. 7. ISAAC A., JR. 8. JOHN D. 9. JAMES I. 10. THOMAS N.

6 G.—1. SAMANTHA BRUSH CARHART, b. Jan. 14, 1821, at King Street, m. Sept. 26, 1844, at Binghamton, N. Y., Henry E. Hotaling, of that city. Samantha d. Nov. 6, 1854, at Cleveland, Ohio. Chil. :
7 G.—1. HERBERT EUGENE HOTALING. 2. EMILY HOTALING, m. Mr. Platt, of Jersey City, N. J. 3. HENRY HOTALING.

6 G.—2. DANIEL MATTHEWS CARHART, b. Dec. 8, 1822, m. July 2, 1844, Charlotte A. Hight, of Jersey City (dau. of Robert Hight, of New York, and grand dau. of John Hight, of England). D. M. C. d. July 4, 1861. Res. Cleveland, Ohio. Chil. :
7 G.—1. CHARLES HIGHT, b. Oct. 24, 1848. 2. CHARLOTTE, b. Dec. 6, 1849, d. June 15, 1864. 3. DANIEL MATTHEWS, JR., b. Nov. 16, 1852. 4. FREDERICK, b. Jan. 22, 1854, d. Aug. 26, 1860.

I. A. C. m. Feb. 29, 1824, second wife, Susan Woolley Burt, of Flushing, L. I., and New York city, b. Aug. 13, 1798 (dau. of Charles Burt). Chil. :
6 G.—3. MARGARET ANN CARHART, b. Nov. 13, 1825, in New York city, m. Sept. 22, 1844, Richard M. Squires, of Ohio. Res. Binghamton, N. Y. Chil. :
7 G.—1. RICHARD SQUIRES, b. Aug. 9, 1845, at Binghamton. 2. CHARLES SQUIRES, b. Oct. 26, 1847, d. Aug. 17, 1849. 3. MARGARET ADELINE SQUIRES, b. Dec. 25, 1850, m. Oct. 18, 1877, Albert H. Bixby, of Webster, Mass. 4. ISAAC CARHART SQUIRES, b. May 28, 1854. 5. WILLIAM THEODORE SQUIRES, b. Oct. 12, 1869.

6 G.—4. GEORGE WASHINGTON CARHART, b. Mar. 3, 1827, in New York city. Res. Binghamton. Is a farmer, and unmarried. G. W. C. enlisted at Binghamton, Oct. 8, 1861, in the 89th New York Regiment, Col. Fairchild—Burnside's Corps. He was at the battles of Roanoke Island, Camden, Newbern—marched through Dismal Swamp and North Carolina to Norfolk, then to Newport News, Washington, and Hagerstown. Was also in the battles of South Mountain, Antietam, and Fredericksburg, and was discharged, ill, at the latter place.

6 G.—5. CHARLES BURT CARHART, b. Aug. 30, 1828, in New York city, m. Aug. 31, 1850, his cousin, Louise Hawkshurst (dau. of Stephen Hawkshurst and Penelope Burt). C. B. C. d. Aug. 26, 1878. Res. Chicago, Ill. Chil.:
7 G.—1. LIZZIE ADELINE, b. Aug. 23, 1851. 2. CHARLES, b. Oct. 24, 1853. 3. FREDERICK MARK, b. Jan. 28, 1859. 4. SUSAN MAY, b. May 23, 1867.

6 G.—6. ADELINE CARHART, b. Nov. 6, 1830, in New York city, m. George Allen, of Binghamton, N. Y. Adeline d. Nov. 3, 1852. Res. Binghamton, N. Y.

6 G.—7. ISAAC A. CARHART, JR., b. July 25, 1832, d. Aug. 3, 1832.

6 G.—8. JOHN DERBIN CARHART, b. June 27, 1835, d. July 18, 1835.

6 G.—9. JAMES ISAAC CARHART, b. Jan. 9, 1837, at King Street, Conn., m. Sept. 24, 1860, Sarah Ennis, of New York city. Chil.:
7 G.—1. JAMES HENRY, b. Jan. 5, 1862, d. June 5, 1863. 2. MARY ADELINE, b. Dec. 15, 1863. 3. CELIA M., b. Mar. 11, 1866.

6 G.—10. THOMAS NEWMAN CARHART, b. Oct. 25, 1840, in New York, m. Oct. 20, 1860, Nellie Gose, of Scranton, Pa. Chil.:
7 G.—SUSAN BURT CARHART, b. Jan. 2, 1862, at Scranton, Pa., d. April 5, 1862. T. N. C. is an engineer in Missouri. Res. Leavenworth, Kansas.

5 G.—VII. JOSHUA^2 CARHART, b. Sept. 28, 1798, at King Street, West Greenwich, Conn., m. May 20, 1818, Mary Anderson, (dau. of Stephen Anderson, of New Rochelle, Westchester Co., N. Y.), b. Mar. 9, 1798. Mary d. Feb. 18, 1833. Joshua d. Nov. 29, 1876. Buried in Anderson Cemetery. Res. New York city and Brooklyn, N. Y. Chil.:

6 G.—1. MARY ELIZABETH CARHART, b. Feb. 26, 1819, unm.

6 G.—2. HENRY AUGUSTUS CARHART, b. July 20, 1820, in New York, m. Caroline Langdon, of New Rochelle, N. Y. Caroline d. 1849. Henry d. at Greytown, Nicaraugua, in 1851. Chil.:
7 G.—1. GEDNEY, who d. in 1849. 2. JAMES, d. Feb., 1868, at Yokohama, Japan.

6 G.—3. JOHN CARHART, b. at New Rochelle, Sept. 4, 1821, m. Eliza Furman, of Newtown, L. I. Res. Newtown. Chil.:
7 G.—1. LEONARD, b. 1845. 2. HANNAH MARIA, b. 1847, m. Harvey Smith, of Brooklyn, N. Y. Res. California. 3. ALBERT, b. Jan., 1856. 4. SUSAN, b. April, 1859.

THE CARHART FAMILY.

6 G.—4. WILLIAM EDGAR CARHART, b. Aug. 31, 1823, in New York, m. Feb. 20, 1851, Virginia Lilly Billops (dau. of Richard Lilly and Mary Respass Billops, of Portsmouth, Va.) Res. Baltimore, Md. Produce commission merchant at Newbern and Elizabeth City, N. C., and Baltimore, Md. Chil. :

7 G.—1. MARY ELLA CARHART, b. Nov. 24, 1851, m. June 8, 1871, Calder Smith Sherwood, (son of Oscar Biddle and Carrie Williams Sherwood, of Portsmouth, Va.) C. S. S. is a watchmaker and jeweller, at Portsmouth, Va. Chil. :

8 G.—1. MABEL RANDOLPH SHERWOOD, b. May 12, 1872. 2. MARY VIRGINIA SHERWOOD, b. Oct. 20, 1877.

7 G.—2. WILLIAM EDGAR CARHART, JR., b. Mar. 13, 1853, machinist and engineer. Res. Baltimore, Md.

7 G.—3. ADELIA CORA CARHART, b. July 31, 1854. d. Aug. 5, 1855.

7 G.—4. CHARLES WATKINSON CARHART, b. Mar. 23, 1857. Carpenter. Res. Baltimore, Md.

7 G.—5. ERNEST MCALPINE CARHART, b. Jan. 8, 1859. Jeweller. Res. Portsmouth, Va.

7 G.—6. CLAUDE MORTIMER CARHART, b. Nov. 23, 1860. Salesman in dry goods, at Baltimore, Md.

7 G.—7. MATTIE RANDOLPH CARHART, b. May 14, 1863.

7 G.—8. CLARA VIRGINIA CARHART, b. Jan. 30, 1865.

7 G.—9. FRANK BILLOPS CARHART, b. Oct. 23, 1867.

7 G.—10. LILLY RUTH CARHART, b. Jan. 15, 1870. d. May 28, 1871.

7 G.—11. CARROLL KEARNS CARHART, b. June 12, 1873.

6 G.—5. CHARLES CARHART, b. in New York city, Feb. 7, 1826, died in childhood.

6 G.—6. GEORGE CARHART, b. July 1, 1831, d. June 26, 1849.

JOSHUA married, Aug. 20, 1833, second wife, Esther Ann Vredenberg, of White Plains, N. Y., b. Oct. 27, 1806. Esther d. Feb. 18, 1838. Chil. :

6 G.—7. URANIA ESTHER CARHART, b. Dec. 25, 1835, m. Oct. 16, 1858, William Cuthbert Wren, of London, England, b. Oct. 9, 1835, res. Brooklyn, N. Y. Chil. :

7 G.—1. DOLLIE LOUISE WREN, b. at Boonville, Mo., Oct. 12, 1859. 2. JESSIE WREN, b. in Brooklyn, N. Y., Jan. 7, 1861. 3. CHARLES WREN, born in Brooklyn, N. Y., Feb. 25, 1863. 4. WILLIE CUTHBERT WREN. b. in Brooklyn, N. Y., Mar. 22, 1871. 5. AMY WREN, b. in Brooklyn, N. Y., Dec. 8, 1872. 6. EMMA JOSEPHINE WREN, b. in Brooklyn, N. Y., May 9, 1878.

6 G.—8. SUSAN CARHART, b. Jan. 5, 1837, d. July 3, 1837.

JOSHUA married, April 30, 1839, third wife, Jannette Fisher, of White Plains, N. Y., b. Mar. 11, 1812. Jannette d. April 15, 1842. Chil. :

6 G.—9. JANNETTE MARIA THERESE CARHART, b. April 15, 1840, m. May 24, 1859, George Fisher, of New York city. Chil. :

7 G.—1. SARAH AUGUSTA FISHER, b. Feb. 23, 1860. 2. LUCY FISHER, b. June 14, 1862. 3. CLARA FISHER, b. Feb. 25, 1870.

5 G.—VIII. MARGARET CARHART, b. Dec. 11, 1800, m. Mar. 3, 1828, Rev. Thomas Newman (*Note* 29), of the M. E. Church, b. Nov. 1, 1800, at Stamford, Conn. Rev. T. N. died at Fulton, Oswego Co., N. Y., May 1, 1875. Chil. :

6 G.—1. SARAH ELMA NEWMAN, b. at Saratoga, Aug. 15, 1831, m. Dec. 14, 1853, Rev. W. Smith Titus, of Victory, Cayuga Co., N. Y. (son of Jared Titus, of Hyde Park, and Rebecca Green, of Wayne Co., N. Y.) Rev. W. S. T. is of the M. E. Church. Chil. :

7 G.—1. ELMA MARGARET TITUS, b. Dec. 14, 1854, at Ogdensburgh, St. Lawrence Co., N. Y. 2. FRANK WILLIS TITUS, b. Nov., 1856, at Canton, St. Lawrence Co. 3. EDMUND JANES TITUS, b. July 1, 1859, at Camden, Oneida Co., d. Mar. 22, 1861. 4. WILLIAM SMITH TITUS, b. Jan. 8, 1864, at Mexico, Orange Co., N. Y., d. June 27, 1864. 5. ELENOR EDITH TITUS, b. Sept. 7, 1868, at Walcott, Wayne Co., N. Y.

6 G.—2. ENOCH GEORGE NEWMAN, b. July 7, 1833, at Stillwater, Saratoga, N. Y., m. Feb. 25, 1862, Laura A. Winchell, (dau. of Asa Winchell, and Mary Morgan, of North Hammel, N. Y., b. at Rutland, Vt.) Res. near Fulton, Oswego Co., N. Y. Chil.

7 G.—1. EVA MYRA NEWMAN, b. Jan. 15, 1863. 2. GEORGE NATHAN NEWMAN, b. Sept. 14, 1869. 3. MARY EMMA NEWMAN, b. Jan. 7, 1873.

6 G.—3. MARY FLETCHER NEWMAN (*Note* 30), b. April 9, 1838, at New Windsor, Orange Co., N. Y., m. Jan. 8, 1862, Rev. Henry Abbott, of the M. E. Church (son of Henry and Mary Abbott, of Schoharie Co., N. Y.) Mrs. A. d. Feb 2, 1874. Chil. :

7 G.—1. GRACE MARY ABBOTT, b. Dec. 11, 1862, at Florence, Oneida Co., N. Y., d. Feb. 26, 1874. 2. GEORGE IRVING ABBOTT, b. Mar. 12, 1864, at Sandy Creek, Oswego Co., N. Y. 3. ANNA LAURA ABBOTT, b. Jan. 4, 1868, at Butler, Wayne Co., N. Y. 4. GRACE MARY ABBOTT, b. Nov. 30, 1873, at Hamilton, St. Lawrence Co., N. Y.

This child was adopted at her mother's death, by her father's sister, Mrs. Maria Mayer.

6 G.—4. HENRIETTA BANCROFT NEWMAN, b. Feb. 7, 1842, at Monroe, Orange Co., N. Y., m. Aug. 7, 1872, Norman G. H. Haviland, M. D., of Granby Centre, (son of Garretson Haviland and Aurelia Chapman, of Hoosack, N. Y.) Res. Fulton, Oswego Co., N. Y. Chil. :

7 G.—CLARENCE FLOYD HAVILAND, b. Aug. 5, 1875.

6 G.—5. GRACE BEVERAGE NEWMAN, b. Oct. 27, 1844, at Montgomery, Orange Co., N. Y., m. 1877, Eber Granville Hubbard, (son of Halsey Hubbard and Rachel Hugunin, pioneers in the settlement of Oswego Co., N. Y.)

5 G.—IX. ELIZABETH CARHART, b. at King Street, Feb. 7, 1803, m. June 12, 1831, Barnabas Seureman Adams, b. at New Rochelle, Westchester Co., N. Y., Sept. 15, 1804, (son of Jesse Adams and Mary Secor—dau. of Johnathan Secor and Sarah Flandreau (*Note* 31), of Huguenot descent). Elizabeth d. May 22. 1860. B. S. A. d. May 15, 1867. Res. New York city. Buried in Anderson Cemetery. Chil.:

6 G.—1. WASHINGTON IRVING ADAMS, b. Mar. 25. 1832. in New York city. m. Oct. 30, 1860, Marion Lydia. (dau. of Hon. GEORGE BRIGGS.) (*Note* 32). W. I. A. is manager of Scoville Manufacturing Co., New York city. Res. Montclair, N. J. Chil.:
7 G.—1. BRIGGS BOOTH ADAMS, b. Sept. 5, 1861, in New York city, d. Dec. 24, 1878, at Montclair, N. J.

B. B. A. was a promising young man, amiable in disposition, and beloved by all who knew him. He was well advanced in his Academic Course, and it was his intention to enter College during the next year.

His death was sudden, and has left a void in the hearts of his parents and friends that cannot be filled.

7 G.—2. CHARLOTTE E. ADAMS, b. Nov. 24. 1862. in New York city, d. Feb. 24, 1864. in New York. 3. W. IRVING LINCOLN ADAMS, b. Feb. 22. 1865. in New York. 4. MARY WILSON ADAMS, b. July 8, 1869, at Montclair. N. J.

6 G.—2. ELIZABETH ARMENIA ADAMS, b. June 19, 1836, in New York city, m. Nov. 24. 1870. Edwin C. Fuller. of Stockbridge, Mass., and Montclair, N. J. Res. Montclair. No children.

6 G.—3. MARGARET EMILY ADAMS, b. May 20, 1840. in New York, m. May 20, 1862. Henry M. Price. (son of Edward Price. M. D., of New York). Res. Montclair, N. J. Chil.:
7 G.—1. HARRY IRVING PRICE, b. Sept. 11, 1864. in New York. 2. OSCAR BENSON PRICE, b. Feb. 2. 1868. at Carmansville. N. Y. 3. GEORGE BRIGGS PRICE. b. Dec. 11. 1871. at Watsessing. N. J.

6 G.—4. MARY LOUISE ADAMS. b. April 30, 1842. in New York, m. Sept. 5, 1865, Ferdinand Ungar, of New York. Res. Montclair, N. J. Chil.:
7 G.—1. MARY ERNESTINE UNGAR, b. June 4, 1866. in New York.
7 G.—2. FERDINAND ADAMS UNGAR, b. Aug. 8, 1870, in New York.
6 G.—5. ELMA MARIA ADAMS, b. Dec. 3, 1843, m. Aug. 25, 1863, Oscar S. Follet, of ——, Vt. Res. Montclair, N. J. Chil. :
7 G.—WILLIE IRVING FOLLET, b. Mar. 27, 1867.

FAMILY OF JOSHUA,[1] *of Washington, Dutchess Co., N. Y., Son of* THOMAS,[2] *of Rye, Westchester Co., N. Y.*

4 G.—JOSHUA[1] CARHART, b. Dec. 27. 1757, m. Mar. 27, 1782, Phebe Baker. He lived for some years at White Plains, Westchester Co., N. Y., and then removed to Washington, Dutchess Co., N. Y. Was a farmer and a Quaker.
5 G.—I. WILLIAM. II. and III. RICHARD and JORDAN (twins).

IV. SARAH. V. RACHEL. VI. ELIZABETH. VII. JOHN. VIII. PHEBE. IX. ANNIE. X. MARY.

5 G.—I. WILLIAM CARHART, b. June 15, 1783, m. Armenia Greene, of Dutchess Co., b. 1786, aunt to Fitz Greene Halleck, and Mrs. Judge Martin, of Green Bay, Wis., a well known magazine writer and author. Mrs. Armenia Carhart d. in 1878, at Duck Creek, near Green Bay, Brown Co., Wis., aged 92 years. Chil. :

6 G.—WILLIAM CARHART, b. May 20, 1807. Res. Green Bay, Wis.

5 G.—II. RICHARD CARHART. b. May 31, 1786, m. Nov. 30, 1833, Catharine Andrews, b. April 25, 1797. Richard d. Sept. 23, 1868. Catharine d. Aug. 31, 1876. Chil.:
1. DANIEL H. 2. PHEBE. 3. JAMES. 4. JOHN. 5. SARAH.

6 G.—1. DANIEL H. CARHART. b. Dec. 16, 1834, m. Oct. 5, 1854, C. C. Briggs, b. Aug. 7, 1829. D. H. C. resides at Pleasant Plains, and is the last of the name in Dutchess Co., N. Y., in 1880. Chil.:

7 G.—EDWARD W. and GEORGE R. (twins). EDWARD W. CARHART graduated at Albany Medical College, and is practising medicine in Albany, N. Y. GEORGE R. graduated at De Graw Institute, Rhinebeck, N. Y.

6 G.—2. PHEBE J. CARHART, b. June 6, 1836.

6 G.—3 and 4. JAMES and JOHN CARHART (twins), b. Aug. 7, 1838. John died in infancy.

6 G.—5. SARAH CARHART, b. Mar. 14, 1841, d. Jan. 13, 1843.

5 G.—III. JORDAN CARHART, b. May 31, 1786, twin brother to RICHARD, had ANNIE, who m. Mr. Losee.

5 G.—IV. SARAH CARHART, dau. of Joshua,[1] b. July 19, 1788, m. Aug. 3, 1809, at Friends' Meeting, Matinecock, L. I., John Robbins (son of Jeremiah and Hannah Robbins, of Roslyn, L. I.) Sarah d. Nov. 19, 1826. John d. April 24, 1834. Chil.:

6 G.—1. WILLIAM B. ROBBINS, b. July 5, 1811, m. Mary E. Hewlett. William d. April 18, 1869, leaving three sons.

6 G.—2. SARAH C. ROBBINS, b. July 5, 1813, m. Richard C. Hubbs, April 10, 1836. They had six children.

6 G.—3. EDWARD ROBBINS, b. Sept. 3, 1816, m. 1841, Martha Whitson. Martha d. July 17, 1847. Edward d. 1856. Had one daughter.

6 G.—4. WALTER W. ROBBINS, b. Oct. 26, 1818, m. Jan., 1857, Cornelia Strong. Walter d. Dec. 27, 1863. Two sons living.

6 G.—5. PHEBE ANN ROBBINS, b. Sept. 23, 1821, m. Mar. 5, 1839, Thomas J. Seaman. Thomas d. Jan. 18, 1856. Two sons living.

6 G.—6. JOHN ROBBINS, b. April 15, 1824, m. June 22, 1858, Selinda E. Smith. Has one son and two daughters. Res. Babylon, L. I.

5 G.—V. RACHEL CARHART, b. April 9, 1790, m. James Prior, of Jericho, L. I. Chil.:

6 G.—WILLIAM H. PRIOR, of Jericho, L. I.

5 G.—VI. ELIZABETH CARHART, b. Aug. 10, 1792, d. in 1812.

5 G.—VII. JOHN CARHART, b. June 27, 1794, m. Jan. 30, 1817, Helen Layton, b. Sept. 28, 1792, (dau. of Garret and Jane Layton, of

Maple Hill, Roslyn, L. I.) Helen d. April 14, 1830. John d. March, 1831. Res. New York city. Chil.:

6 G.—1. WILLIAM H. CARHART, b. June 8. 1818, m. Sept. 3. 1840, Maribah Marshall. W. H. C. has been a merchant in New York city for many years. Res. New York city. Chil. :
7 G.—1. WILLIAM, who died in infancy. 2. HELEN. 3. LOUISE, d. at the age of 20 years. 4. WILLIAM, 2nd, d. aged 16 years. 5. MARIBAH. 6. SARAH ADELE, d. aged 3 years. 7. LEILA. 8. CARRIE.

6 G.—2. JANE CARHART, b. Nov. 16, 1819, d. July 31, 1821.
6 G.—3. ANNIE ELIZABETH CARHART, b. Oct. 21, 1821, d. Oct. 22, 1826.

6 G.—4. SARAH HELEN CARHART, b. April 15, 1824, m. June 5, 1844, James M. Ludlum, (son of Joseph Ludlum, of Oyster Bay, L. I.) Res. Oyster Bay, L. I. Chil.:
7 G.—1. HELEN LUDLUM, b. June 1, 1846, d. Apr. 5, 1852. 2. JAMES HENRY LUDLUM, b. Jan. 7. 1848, m. Oct. 22, 1873, Mary A. Sammis, of Oyster Bay, L. I. 3. LILLIE LUDLUM, b. April 6, 1853. 4. FREDERICK LUDLUM, b. May 5, 1857. 5. LOUISE CARHART LUDLUM, b. Sept. 29, 1862.

5 G.—VIII. PHŒBE CARHART, b. Jan. 13, 1798, m. Joshua Divine. Chil. : PHEBE A. DIVINE, m. Mr. Clement.
5 G.—IX. ANNIE CARHART, b. Aug. 19, 1799, d. in 1817.
5 G.—X. MARY CARHART, b. Jan. 22, 1805, m. Grant Haviland, of Glenn's Falls, N. Y., and m. second husband, Joseph Haviland, of Dutchess Co., N. Y., May 29, 1878. Res. Glenn's Falls, N. Y. No children.

GENEALOGY

OF THE

Carhart Family.

NEW JERSEY BRANCHES.

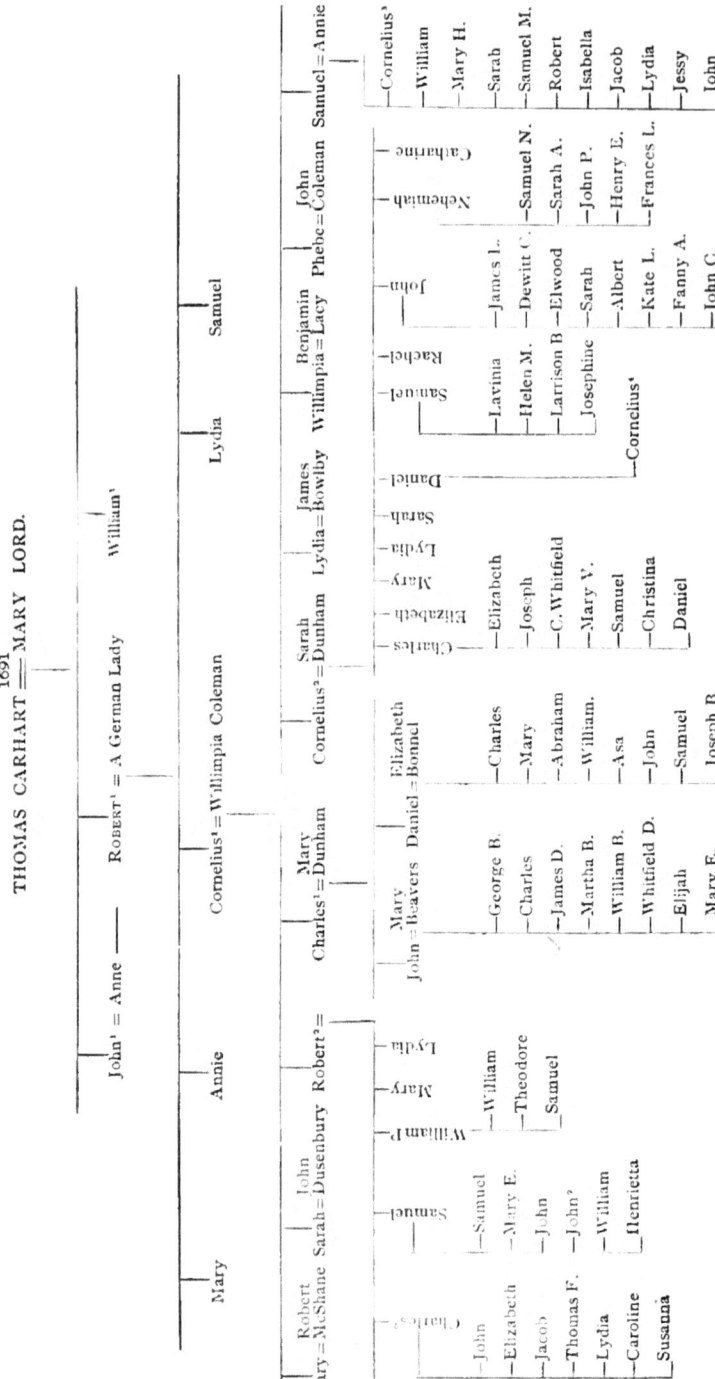

2.—CHART OF ROBERT[1].

THE NEW JERSEY BRANCHES.

The descendants of ROBERT[1] and WILLIAM[1] CARHART—known as the New Jersey branches—seem not to have possessed. in a great degree, the migratory spirit of their cousins of Rye, Westchester Co., N. Y., but rather to have followed the custom of their ancestors of Cornwall, where, as related by Clarendon: "Landed property did not, as elsewhere, constantly change hands. The same families have lived there for centuries, surrounded by the same families of farmers and laborers."

Of the Rye family, not one is to be found at present in the locality selected by their ancestor, while on the contrary, many of those of New Jersey are still owning and occupying lands which were at first selected by their progenitors. As an example, see *Note* 41.

Not all the New Jersey families, however, have manifested that strong local attachment as seen in the Perryville family ; or they have been moved by ambition, or the love of change, to find new fields to conquer, and new avenues to competence. Such have left the roof-tree of the fathers and founded homes and established themselves in prosperous business occupations elsewhere. Should the facts of history contained in this record, tend to strengthen the family bond between the three great branches, by bringing them into nearer acquaintance, the author will be partially compensated for her labors.

FAMILY OF ROBERT,[1] *of Matawan, Monmouth Co., N. J., Son of* THOMAS.[1]

Records furnished by Messrs. CHARLES and ELWOOD CARHART.

ROBERT[1] CARHART, the second son of THOMAS,[1] seems not to have been a landholder, after selling what he inherited from his father's estate to his brothers, John and William, as no records of purchase can be found in his name. From all information that can be gathered, he lived a man of leisure, until his death, in 1752. He is supposed to have lived at, or near, Matawan, Monmouth Co., N. J. Descendants have only been found from his son Cornelius.[1]

2 G.—ROBERT[1] was born on Staten Island, in 1693. He married in 1725—tradition says, "a German lady." He died Feb. 12, 1745. Chil. :

3 G.—I. MARY CARHART, b. July 24, 1726. II. ANNIE CARHART, who d. Aug. 10, 1837. III. CORNELIUS[1] CARHART, b. Sept. 6, 1729. IV. LYDIA CARHART, b. Aug. 30, 1732. V. SAMUEL[1] CARHART, b. June 22, 1737. There are no records of Mary and Annie.

3 G.—CORNELIUS[1] CARHART (*Note* 33), b. Sept. 6, 1729. m. in 1754, Willimpia Coleman.

After his father's death—wishing to start in the battle of life, and tiring of the lowlands of Monmouth Co.—he went, about 1753, with his cousins, the Warnes, and cousins Jacob and Richard, sons of his uncle William Carhart, to the more fertile lands of the northern part of Hunterdon Co., later known as Sussex Co. At the present day, the part on which he settled is known as Warren Co. Here he first rented, and subsequently bought a tract of land. Eighty acres of this land is still in the possession of his descendants. A part of the town of Washington, Warren Co., is built upon the original tract. He is said to have been "honest and upright in all his doings." He was a Captain in the 3rd Regiment of Hunterdon Co., in 1778, and third Major, in 1781, in the Continental Army. He died June 3, 1810, and is buried in the Mansfield Cemetery, near Washington, N. J. Chil.:
I. MARY. II. SARAH. III. ROBERT.[2] IV. CHARLES.[1] V. CORNELIUS.[2] VI. LYDIA. VII. WILLIMPIA. VIII. PHEBE. IX. SAMUEL.[2] X. JOHN.[1]

4 G.—I. MARY CARHART, b. Jan., 1756, m. Robert McShane. Lived at Perryville, Hunterdon Co., N. J., on the farm now owned by Charles[4] Carhart.

4 G.—II. SARAH CARHART, b. Feb., 1758, m. John Dusenbury, of Sussex Co., N. J. Her descendants are living in Northern New Jersey.

4 G.—III. ROBERT[2] CARHART, b. at Mansfield, Sussex Co., N. J., Aug. 17, 1760. He was a private in the 2nd Regiment, Hunterdon Co., in 1778. After the war he settled at Hampton, Hunterdon Co. He died May 1, 1834. Buried in Mansfield Cemetery. Robert was a farmer. Chil.:
1. CHARLES.[2] 2. SAMUEL.[3] 3. WILLIAM P. 4. MARY. 5. LYDIA.

5 G.—1. CHARLES[2] CARHART, b. Oct. 15, 1791, at Hampton, N. J., m. May 17, 1817, Rebecca Allshouse, b. Feb. 9, 1800, at Harmony, N. J. Charles was a farmer, and lived at Harmony, N. J. He died July 11, 1868. Chil.:
1. JOHN.[2] 2. ELIZABETH. 3. JACOB. 4. THOMAS F. 5. LYDIA. 6. CAROLINE. 7. SUSANNAH.

6 G.—1. JOHN[2] CARHART, b. Dec. 11, 1818, m. June 20, 1840, Elizabeth Metz, b. May 20, 1820, at Harmony, N. J. John d. April 12, 1870. He was a carpenter. Chil.:

7 G.—1 WILLIAM[2] CARHART, b. Aug. 19, 1844. m. Aug. 3, 1864, Lizzie Lomson, b. May 21, 1848. Res. Harmony, N. J. Chil.:

8 G.—1. JENNIE, b. Mar. 8, 1866. 2. JESSIE, b. Dec. 2, 1870. 3. CHARLES, b. Feb. 8, 1874.

6 G.—2. ELIZABETH CARHART, b. Oct. 4, 1820, m. Anthony Oberly.

6 G.—3. JACOB CARHART, b. Mar. 23, 1823, unm. Res. Harmony, N. J.

6 G.—4. THOMAS F. CARHART, b. Sept. 27, 1828, m. Dec., 1859, Louise Castera. Business, New York city. Res. White Plains, N. Y.

THE CARHART FAMILY.

He left the paternal roof when a young man, and commenced business in New Orleans. He finally changed to New York, and is now one of the prominent business men of the city. He gave efficient service in research for the record. Chil.:

7 G.—1. MARIA L., b. Jan., 1872. 2. THOMAS F., Jr., b. July, 1873. 3. JOHN WARREN, b. Oct., 1874. 4. RALPH, b. Jan., 1876.

6 G.—5. LYDIA CARHART, b. April 11, 1831, m. Dec. 20, 1857, Levi Raub.

6 G.—6. CAROLINE CARHART, b. Nov. 28, 1833, d. Sept. 10, 1836.

6 G.—7. SUSANNA CARHART, b. May 23, 1837, m. Jan. 7, 1858, Jacob Cline, of Harmony, N. J., a farmer.

5 G.—2. SAMUEL³ CARHART (son of Robert²), b. March 31, 1802, m. Jan. 24, 1827, Mary Mond, of Sussex Co., N. J., b. Oct. 5, 1804. Samuel died in Philadelphia, in 1869. Chil.:

6 G.—1. SAMUEL⁴ CARHART, b. April 6, 1828, in New York city, d. July 2, 1856, at Philadelphia. Buried in Odd Fellows' Cemetery, Phil.

6 G.—2. MARY ELIZABETH CARHART, b. Aug. 31, 1830, m. William C. Marlow. Res. Camden, N. J.

6 G.—3. JOHN CARHART, b. Dec. 6, 1833, d. May 19, 1835.

6 G.—4. JOHN² CARHART, b. Mar. 20, 1836, d. Jan. 12, 1842.

6 G.—5. WILLIAM CARHART, b. Mar. 13, 1840, d. Dec. 3, 1840.

6 G.—6. HENRIETTA M. CARHART, b. Mar. 21, 1843, m. her cousin, Theodore Carhart. Res. Scranton, Pa.

5 G.—3. WILLIAM P. CARHART, b. at New Hampton, 1799, d. July 12, 1863. Chil.:

1. WILLIAM. 2. THEODORE. 3. SAMUEL.⁵

6 G.—1. WILLIAM CARHART, b. 1816. Res. Phillipsburg, Warren Co., N. J. Chil.:

7 G.—1. ROBERT CARHART, b. 1844. Chil.:

8 G.—1. EDWINA, b. 1868. 2. HENRY, b. 1871. 3. BERTRAND, b. 1874.

7 G.—2. MARY CARHART. 3. THEODORE CARHART, m. Henrietta, dau. of Samuel³ Carhart, of Philadelphia. 4. EMMA. 5. ANNIE. 6. WILLIAM. 7. JOSEPH CARHART.

6 G.—2. THEODORE CARHART, b. Jan. 31, 1819, m. Jan. 29, 1839, Rachel Allbright. T. C. is a merchant at Belvidere, N. J., a sterling business man. Chil.:

7 G.—1. MARY S. CARHART, b. Dec. 29, 1839, d. Dec. 16, 1840.

7 G.—2. PHINEAS M. CARHART, b. Sept. 21, 1841, m. May, 1873, Elizabeth Helm. P. M. C. is Cashier of Bank at Wilkesbarre, Pa.

7 G.—3. EMMA L. CARHART, b. Oct. 29, 1843, m. March, 1862, William Hageman, of Trenton, N. J., travelling salesman.

7 G.—4. ELLEN E. CARHART, b. Dec. 10, 1846, m. Sept. 22, 1871, James Dillon, of Philadelphia, salesman.

7 G.—5. MATILDA D. CARHART, b. April 10, 1848, m. April 4, 1871, E. G. Wire, civil engineer, Belvidere, N. J.

7 G.—6. HENRY S. CARHART, b. July 10, 1850, d. Feb. 25, 1855.

7 G.—7. EDMUND H. CARHART, b. Jan. 7, 1853, m. Oct. 22, 1879,

Mary Kellogg (dau. of Henry Redfield, Esq., of Plainfield, N. J.) E. H. C. is of the firm of Carhart & Co., clothiers, Broadway, New York.
7 *G*.—8. RODERICK CARHART, b. Mar. 3, 1855. Res. Belvidere, N. J.

6 G.—3. SAMUEL⁵ CARHART, b. Oct. 23, 1832, m. Feb. 2, 1853, Sarah Voorhes. Res. Phillipsburgh, N. J. Chil.:
7 *G*.—1. SAMUEL,⁶ b. April, 1854. Res. Phillipsburgh, N. J. 2. EDMUND, b. Dec. 8, 1856, d. Jan. 2, 1869. 3. MARY S., b. April 2, 1860, d. Dec. 18, 1876. 4. ELMER ELSWORTH, b. July 14, 1861. Res. Phillipsburgh, N. J. 5. CORNELIUS V., b. Nov. 17, 1862. Res. Phillipsburgh, N. J. 6. WILLIAM S., b. Oct. 17, 1864. Res. Phillipsburgh, N. J.

5 G.—4. MARY CARHART (dau. of Robert²), m. Mr. Sigman, of Warren Co., N. J.
5 G.—5. LYDIA CARHART, m. Mr. Phillips, of Port Murray, N. J.

4 G.—IV. CHARLES¹ CARHART (son of Cornelius¹), b. Jan. 3, 1763, at Mansfield, N. J., m. 1784, Mary E. Dunham, (dau. of Jacob Dunham, of Clinton, N. J.) Charles went with his sister, Mrs. Lydia Bowlby, to Virginia, Monongalia Co., and settled on land owned by his father. Two of his wife's brothers (Dunham) accompanied them. Charles lived but a short time, and after his death, his widow, with two sons—JOHN and DANIEL—returned to New Jersey. She subsequently married her cousin, James Dunham, the owner of a large estate, which he managed and worked with slaves. Chil.: 1. JOHN². 2. DANIEL¹.

5 G.—JOHN² CARHART, b. Oct. 15, 1786, in Jefferson Co., Va., m. Aug. 21, 1810, Mary Beavers, b. May 22, 1789 (grand-dau. of Col. Joseph Beavers (*Note* 34), who resided near Greenwich, N. J.) Mary d. Nov. 20, 1871. John d. March 21, 1872. "He was a man of much influence, and highly respected in his neighborhood." Chil.:
1. GEORGE BEAVERS. 2. CHARLES¹. 3. JAMES DUNHAM. 4. MARTHA BEAVERS. 5. WILLIAM BEAVERS. 6. WHITFIELD DUNHAM. 7. ELIJAH H. 8. MARY E.

6 G.—1. GEORGE BEAVERS CARHART, (*Note* 35) b. Jan. 12, 1812, m. Feb. 17, 1850, Mary E. Rose (dau. of Simri Rose, (*Note* 36) of Branford, Conn., and Macon, Ga.—and Lavinia Helen Elizabeth Blount, of Clinton, Ga., dau. of James Blount, (*Note* 37) and Elizabeth Gregoire de Roulhac, of the Hermitage, Beaufort, N. C.) Res. Brooklyn, N. Y. Chil.:
7 *G*.—AMORY SIBLEY CARHART, b. Dec. 28, 1851, in New York city. Res. Brooklyn, N. Y.

6 G.—2. CHARLES¹ CARHART, (*Note* 38) b. April 22, 1813, m. May 4, 1843, Matilda Stiger, b. Oct. 8, 1814, d. July 22, 1864, (dau. of Adam Stiger). C. C. m. 2nd wife, Nov. 22, 1866, Emily Mattison, (grand dau. of Col. Corson, of the war of 1812, who owned a fine estate at Freedom, Sussex Co., N. J.) C. C. resides at Perryville, N. J. Chil.:
7 *G*.—1. MARY E. CARHART, b. Jan. 23, 1844, m. Dec. 2, 1863, Randolph Kenyon, (*Note* 39) b. Oct. 30, 1836. Res. Raritan, N. J. Chil.:

8 G.—1. MINNIE MATILDA KENYON, b. Mar. 24, 1865. 2. ANGELINE DALES KENYON, b. Nov. 16, 1867. 3. CHARLES CARHART KENYON, b. Aug. 9, 1871.
7 G.—2. GEORGE B. CARHART, b. Feb. 9, 1848, d. Oct. 17, 1852.
7 G.—3. SARAH VIRGINIA CARHART, b. Aug. 25, 1849, d. Feb. 22, 1854.
7 G.—4. JAMES DUNHAM CARHART, b. Dec. 24, 1853, d. Aug. 26, 1854.

6 G.—3. JAMES DUNHAM CARHART, b. May 2, 1815, m. June 8, 1845, Sarah V. Curd, of Macon, Ga. J. D. C. d. March 23, 1878, (*Note* 40). Business, wholesale grocer in New York city. Res. Brooklyn. Chil.:
7 G.—1. JAMES DUNHAM CARHART, Jr., b. Nov. 1, 1846, at Macon, Ga., m. Nov. 16, 1870, Fanny Rockwell (adopted dau. of James Rockwell, of Brooklyn, N. Y.) J. D. C., Jr., d. Aug. 5, 1878. Res. Brooklyn. Chil.:
8 G.—1. KATIE ROCKWELL CARHART, b. March 5, 1875, d. Dec. 27, 1878. 2. JAMES SIDNEY ROCKWELL CARHART, b. June 14, 1877.
Mrs. Fanny Rockwell Carhart, m. Feb. 5, 1880, Fred. S. Dennis, M.D., of Brooklyn, N. Y.
7 G.—2. WILLIAM EDWARD CARHART, b. Sept. 3, 1850, in New York city, m. June 6, 1872, Augusta Richards (granddau. of Admiral Stringham, U. S. Navy). Chil.:
8 G.—1. WILLIAM E. CARHART, b. July 20, 1874. 2. CHARLES RICHARDS CARHART, b. June 1, 1876.
7 G.—3. MARY LOUISE CARHART, b. June 26, 1853, was educated at Paris, France, and m. Dec. 15, 1875, at Brooklyn, N. Y., Julius Walker Lewis. Res. Knoxville, Tenn. Chil.:
8 G.—JOHN WALKER LEWIS, b. Mar. 11, 1878, at Knoxville, Tennessee.
7 G.—4. HENRY BRIGHAM CARHART, b. July 6, 1855. Res, Knoxville, Tenn. Unm.

6 G.—4. MARTHA BEAVERS CARHART, b. July 5, 1818, m. Dec. 31, 1839, James Scott Kels, Esq., b. Oct. 8, 1816, d. Dec. 15, 1872. Res. Perryville, Hunterdon Co., N. J. Chil.:
7 G.—1. MARY CATHARINE KELS, b. July 24, 1841, m. Feb. 11, 1864, Joseph Bird, M. D. Res. Ashville, N. C. Chil.:
8 G.—LEWIS E. BIRD, b. April 6, 1866.
7 G.—2. GEORGIANNA BILLS KELS, b. Mar. 24, 1846, m. Nov. 23, 1865, Joseph B. Bird, Esq. Res. Clinton, N. J. Chil.:
8 G.—1. WALTER BIRD, b. Jan. 18, 1869. 2. JAMES K. BIRD, b. May 5, 1872.
7 G.—3. WILLIAM WHITFIELD KELS, b. Nov. 2, 1847, m. Oct. 22, 1873, Frances Arabella Allen. Res. Perryville, N. J. Chil.:
8 G.—HENRY C. KELS, b. April 3, 1876.

6 G.—5. WILLIAM BEAVERS CARHART, b. Oct. 22, 1820. Res. Brooklyn, N. Y. Unm. Senior partner in the New York business, "Carhart Brothers," wholesale grocers.

6 G.—6. WHITFIELD DUNHAM CARHART, b. June 23, 1825, m. June 10, 1860, Mary E. Rockafeller. W. D. C. d. August 29, 1873. He was a farmer at Clinton, N. J. Chil.:

7 G.—1. JOHN B. LAMAR, b. Mar. 18, 1864, d. July 29, 1864. 2. WILLIAM B., b. April 2, 1865. 3. JAMES D., b. Jan. 11, 1867. 4. GEORGE B., b. July 10, 1868. 5. WHITFIELD D. CARHART, b. Sept. 28, 1871.

6 G.—7. ELIJAH H. CARHART, b. Aug. 11, 1827. Res. Macon, Ga. Unm. He is a prominent hardware merchant and extensive cotton planter at Macon, Ga.

6 G.—8. MARY E. CARHART, b. July 17, 1829, m. March 24, 1853, Sylvester Van Syckel. M. D. Res. Clinton, N. J. Chil.:

7 G.—1. JOHN H. VAN SYCKEL, b. Jan. 30, 1854. Res. Macon, Ga. 2. GEORGE C. VAN SYCKEL, b. June 28, 1855, d. Mar. 26, 1860. 3. CHESTER VAN SYCKEL, b. Feb. 18, 1858, d. May 7, 1861. 4. WILLIAM C. VAN SYCKEL, b. April 4, 1863. 5. LAMAR VAN SYCKEL, b. Jan. 26, 1866. 6. MARY E. VAN SYCKEL, b. Aug. 6, 1868, d. Dec. 11, 1872.

5 G.—2. DANIEL[1] CARHART (son of Charles[1]), b. June 11, 1788, near Clarksburgh, Va., m. Feb. 16, 1812, Elizabeth Bonnell (dau. of Clement Bonnell, of Clinton, N. J.) Daniel d. Dec. 3, 1879, aged 91 years. He resided at Perryville until his marriage, then bought a farm near Clinton. Later in life, having a large family of sons, and needing more land, he removed to Cecil Co., Md.; and also bought a large tract in Eastern Virginia. He being a Union man, the Rebellion of 1861 drove him out of Virginia, and he lost all of that estate. He finally removed to Elwood, Atlantic Co., N. J. All his children reside at Clinton, N. J., except JOSEPH B., who lives at Elwood, Atlantic Co. Chil.:

1. CHARLES.[5] 2. MARY. 3. ABRAHAM. 4. WILLIAM. 5. ASA. 6. JOHN.[5] 7. SAMUEL. 8. JOSEPH B.

6 G.—1. CHARLES[5] CARHART, b. 1814, at Clinton, N. J. Is a farmer at Annandale, Hunterdon Co., N. J. Chil.:

7 G.—1. MARY ELIZABETH CARHART, b. Jan. 15, 1849, at Clinton, N. J., d. Sept. 8, 1865, at Oak Grove, Westminster Co., Va.

7 G.—2. CLARENCE CARHART, b. April 7, 1855, in Virginia, d. Mar. 17, 1868, at Clinton.

7 G.—3. SARAH CARHART, b. July 21, 1865, at Clinton, N. J. Res. Annandale, N. J.

6 G.—2. MARY CARHART, b. Jan. 25, 1816, at Clinton. Res. Elwood, N. J. Unm.

6 G.—3. ABRAHAM CARHART, b. June 11, 1818, at Clinton, d. Aug. 29, 1867, in Virginia, unm.

6 G.—4. WILLIAM CARHART, b. Jan. 11, 1821, at Clinton. Farmer. Unm.

6 G.—5. ASA CARHART, b. May 23, 1822, at Clinton, m. 1st wife, Belinda Lutz; 2d wife, Elmira Woodruff. Res. Clarksville, N. J. Chil.:

7 G.—1. EDWINA CARHART, b. Aug. 8, 1853, in New York city, m. June 21, 1875, Henry D. Watts, of Brooklyn, N. Y.

6 G.—6. JOHN⁶ CARHART, b. March 2, 1825, at Clinton, m. Oct. 31, 1849, Amanda Larison. J. C. is a farmer at Clinton, N. J. Chil.:
7 G.—1. MARY F., b. Oct. 29, 1850. 2. GEORGE, b. Dec. 16, 1859. 3. BEDFORD, b. Jan. 25, 1861. Res. Clinton. N. J.
6 G.—7. SAMUEL CARHART, b. Sept. 20, 1827, at Clinton, N. J. Served in Union Army during the Rebellion. Res. Elwood, N. J. Unm.
6 G.—8. JOSEPH B. CARHART, b. June 5, 1830, at Clinton, m. Feb. 19, 1857, in Cecil Co., Md., Susan Bever, of Lancaster Co., Pa. J. B. C. is a dentist at Elwood, Atlantic Co., N. J. Chil.:
7 G.—1. LAVINIA, b. Dec. 3, 1857. 2. ELMER E., b. Nov. 20, 1860. 3. CARRIE L., b. Oct. 26, 1865. Res. Cecil Co., Md. 4. GEORGE CARHART, b. Dec. 8, 1867, at Philadelphia, d. Dec. 23, 1867.

4 G.—V. CORNELIUS² CARHART (*Note* 41), (son of Cornelius¹), b. Oct. 5, 1765, at Mansfield, Sussex Co., N. J., m. 1785, Sarah Dunham, sister of the wife of his brother Charles. Settled at Perryville, N. J. Built the brick hotel at that place. Cornelius d. Dec. 6, 1818. Sarah d. Dec. 24, 1843, at Philadelphia. Buried at Bethlehem, Hunterdon Co., N. J. Chil.: 1. CHARLES.³ 2. ELIZABETH. 3. MARY. 4. LYDIA. 5, SARAH. 6. DANIEL.² 7. SAMUEL. 8. RACHEL. 9. JOHN.⁵ 10. NEHEMIAH. 11. CATHARINE.

5 G.—1. CHARLES³ CARHART, b. Nov. 16, 1786, at Clinton, N. J., m. Oct. 19, 1823, Christina Bird Carhart, widow of his brother Daniel².
He bought 345 acres of land, opposite the old homestead, and brought it up to a high state of cultivation. He was an earnest Christian, in communion with the Presbyterian Church; and died June 4, 1863, at a good old age, "honored and remembered with respect by all who knew him." Res. Perryville, N. J. Chil.:
6 G.—1. ELIZABETH CARHART, b. March 24, 1826, m. Sept. 25, 1844, William F. Hoffman. Elizabeth d. 1866. Chil.:
7 G.—1. CHRISTINA HOFFMAN. 2. SARAH HOFFMAN, m. James Dunham. Res. Salisbury, N. C.
6 G.—2. JOSEPH B. CARHART, b. Nov. 10, 1829, m. Feb. 16, 1856, Christina G. Emory. Res. Maple Grove farm, Perryville, N. J. No issue.
6 G.—3. C. WHITFIELD CARHART, b. Oct. 25, 1832, m. Jan. 21, 1858, Mercy G. Emory, sister of brother Joseph's wife. Res. Maple Grove farm. Chil.:
7 G.—1. EMMA O., b. at Maple Grove farm, June 1, 1859. 2. CLARENCE M., b. Sept. 17, 1864.
6 G.—4. MARY V. CARHART, b. Dec. 26, 1833, m. Feb. 3, 1859, William Humphrey. Res. Philadelphia.
6 G.—5. SAMUEL CARHART (*Note* 42), b. Nov. 3, 1835, m. Mar. 8, 1854, Louise J. Hoffman. Res. Ocean Beach, N. J. Civil engineer and surveyor. S. C. d. May 13, 1879. Chil.:
SAMUEL LOUIS CARHART, b. July 31, 1876, at Ocean Beach.
6 G.—6. CHRISTINA CARHART, b. April 5, 1837, m. Jan. 28, 1864, Whitfield Dunham, b. Jan. 12, 1829. Farmer near Clinton, N. J. Chil.:
7 G.—1. MARY ELIZABETH DUNHAM, b. Sept. 5, 1865. 2. CHARLES C. DUNHAM, b. July 1, 1868. 3. CATHARINE H. DUNHAM, b. Feb. 26, 1871. 4. HELEN MAR DUNHAM, b. Jan. 4, 1877.

68   GENEALOGY OF

6 G.—7. DANIEL³ CARHART, b. Jan. 28. 1839, m. April 16, 1867, Josephine Story. Daniel was Professor of Mathematics and Civil Engineering in Polytechnic Institute, Philadelphia. In 1878, removed to Danville, Southern Virginia. Chil.:
  7 G.—1. CHARLES F., b. Sept. 23, 1868, in Philadelphia. 2. ELMORE C., b. Feb. 21, 1870, in Philadelphia. 3. HELEN JOSEPHINE, b. Sept. 12, 1877, in Philadelphia.

5 G.—2. ELIZABETH CARHART (dau. of Cornelius²), b. March 3, 1789, m. Oct. 13, 1810, John Eckel, of Mount Pleasant, N. J., farmer. Elizabeth d. Jan. 25, 1847. Chil.:
  6 G.—1. SAMUEL CARHART ECKEL, b. Feb. 10, 1812, m. Mary Duckworth, July 4, 1837. S. C. E. was a merchant at Mount Pleasant, Hunterdon Co., N. J. A prominent man in his neighborhood, and Elder in the Presbyterian Church. He died Jan. 27, 1859. Chil.:
    7 G.—1. STANFORD J. ECKEL. He was a promising young lawyer at Phillipsburgh, N. J., and was drowned while bathing at Milford, N. J. 2. C. VIRGINIA ECKEL. 3. MARTHA J. ECKEL. 4. ALBERT S. ECKEL, res. near Milford, N. J. 5. HANNAH E. ECKEL.
  6 G.—2. SARAH DUNHAM ECKEL, b. May 29, 1813, m. Furman Van Syckel. Sarah d. Feb. 10, 1875. Res. Clinton, N. J. Chil.:
    7 G.—1. MARY ISABELLA VAN SYCKEL. m. Isaac Aller. 2. FANNY VAN SYCKEL. m. Holcomb Opdyke; m. 2nd husband, Elijah Hewitt. 3. JOHN E. VAN SYCKEL.
  6 G.—3. HANNAH BAKER ECKEL, b. Feb. 4, 1816, m. William B. Alpaugh, June 3, 1851. Hannah d. April 20, 1869. Res. Frenchtown, N. J. No children.
  6 G.—4. SELINA ECKEL, b. Mar. 12, 1818, m. Mahlon Mattison, a merchant of New York city. Res. Jersey City, N. J. Selina d. Jan. 11, 1852. Chil.:
    7 G.—SAMUEL MATTISON, of New York city.
  6 G.—5. AMANDA ECKEL, b. Nov. 1, 1820, m. Mar. 11, 1840, James B. Cooley, a farmer in Hunterdon Co., N. J. Amanda d. Sept. 25, 1868. Res. Palmyra, N. Y. Chil.:
    7 G.—1. JAMES COOLEY. 2. ELIZABETH COOLEY. 3. SAMUEL COOLEY. 4. MAHLON COOLEY.
  6 G.—6. JOHN JORDAN ECKEL, b. Oct. 29, 1822, d. Dec. 4, 1869, unm. Res. New York city.
  6 G.—7. JOSEPH HENRY ECKEL, b. May 16, 1829, d. Dec. 18, 1829.
  6 G.—8. ELIZABETH ECKEL, b. Jan. 26, 1832, m. Isaac Mettler, a prominent merchant of New York city. Res. Jersey City, N. J. Chil.:
    7 G.—1. MARY V. METTLER. 2. CARRIE C. METTLER.

5 G.—3. MARY CARHART (dau. of Cornelius²), b. April 30, 1791, m. Aug. 24, 1811, Daniel Van Syckel, of Milford, N. J. Mary d. Oct., 1856. Res. Milford, N. J. Chil.:
  6 G.—1. HOLLOWAY W. VAN SYCKEL. m. Jane Wilcox, of Illinois. Res. Illinois. Chil.:
    7 G.—1. DANIEL VAN SYCKEL. 2. GEORGE VAN SYCKEL. 3. HOLLOWAY VAN SYCKEL. 4. EOLINE VAN SYCKEL.
  6 G.—2. ISABELLA VAN SYCKEL, m. James E. Negus, a farmer, at Bound Brook, N. J. Chil.:

THE CARHART FAMILY.

7 G.—1. ROBERT P. NEGUS. 2. SUSAN E. NEGUS. 3. JAMES E. NEGUS. 4. WILLIAM S. NEGUS.
6 G.—3. SELINDA VAN SYCKEL, m. Samuel Parry, of Clinton. N. J., a prominent public man. Chil. :
7 G.—1. EDWARD PARRY, a merchant miller, of Clinton. N. J. 2. Rev. SAMUEL PARRY.
6 G.—4. ELBRIDGE VAN SYCKEL. m. Bethany Dunham. E. Van S. was a commission merchant in New York city. Now (1879) a farmer at Bound Brook. N. J. Chil. :
7 G.—1. ELBRIDGE VAN SYCKEL. JR. 2. CATHARINE VAN SYCKEL. 3. MARY VAN SYCKEL. 4. ISABELLE VAN SYCKEL. 5. NEHEMIAH VAN SYCKEL.
6 G.—5. SANFORD VAN SYCKEL. m. Sarah Eddum. of Illinois.
6 G.—6. HORATIO D. VAN SYCKEL, m. Emeline Voorhes, of New York city. Res. New York city.
6 G.—7. ALBERT VAN SYCKEL, m. Maria Fisher, of Illinois, and resides in St. Louis. Mo.
6 G.—8. GUSTAVUS A. VAN SYCKEL, m. Elizabeth Gardyne, and resides in San Francisco, Cal.
6 G.—9. VIRGINIA VAN SYCKEL, m. Edward Thomas, and resides at Milford. N. J. Chil. :
7 G.—1. ISABELLE THOMAS. 2. FANNY THOMAS. 3. HOWARD THOMAS.

5 G.—4. LYDIA CARHART (dau. of Cornelius²), b. Jan. 18, 1793, m. 1813. John Van Buskirk, of Warren Co.. N. J. Chil.:
6 G.—1. CORNELIUS VAN BUSKIRK, m. Elizabeth Mayberry, of Warren Co., N. J. Chil.:
7 G.—1. JOHN M. VAN BUSKIRK, of Hunterdon Co., N. J. 2. WILLIAM D. VAN BUSKIRK., of Belvidere. N. J.
6 G.—2. SARAH ANN VAN BUSKIRK, m. William M. Apgar, of Milford. Hunterdon Co. Res. Milford, N. J. Chil.:
7 G.—1. M. VIRGINIA APGAR. 2. JANE E. APGAR. 3. CORNELIUS V. APGAR. 4. EMILY C. APGAR. 5. WILLIAM HENRY APGAR, d. in youth. 6. EDWIN APGAR.
LYDIA m. second husband, Jacob Bunn, of Hunterdon Co.
6 G.—3. MARY E. BUNN, m. Levi Case, of Hunterdon Co. Res. Milford, N. J. Chil.:
7 G.—1. DEWITT CASE. 2. ELIZABETH CASE. 3. LUCY B. CASE.
6 G.—4. CAROLINE BUNN, m. Samuel V. Eckel, of Little York, Hunterdon Co. Res. Little York. Chil. :
7 G.—1. PAUL H. ECKEL. 2. STEWART ECKEL. 3. M. BELLE ECKEL.
6 G.—5. ISABELLA D. BUNN, m. George H. Van Syckel, of Hunterdon Co. Res. Milford. Chil. :
7 G.—1. JACOB B. VAN SYCKEL. Res. Rio Vista, Cal. 2. LYDIA E. VAN SYCKEL. 3. J. AUGUSTA VAN SYCKEL. 4. GEORGE H. VAN SYCKEL.
6 G.—6. PAUL H. PROVOST BUNN. d. 1838.
6 G.—7. MELINDA BUNN, m. William C. Alpaugh, of Little York, Hunterdon Co., N. J. Res. Milford. N. J. Chil. :
7 G.—1. JAMES ALPAUGH. 2. CAROLINE E. ALPAUGH. 3. WIL-

LIAM ALPAUGH. 4. LAMBERT ALPAUGH. 5. EDWARD ALPAUGH.
6. MARY E. ALPAUGH.
Jacob Bunn d. 1851. Lydia Bunn d. 1852.

5 G.—5. SARAH CARHART (dau. of Cornelius²), b. Dec. 18, 1794, m. Aug. 24, 1815, Philip Runckel, who d. March, 1833. She m. 2nd husband, Daniel Van Syckel. Chil.:
6 G.—1. GEORGE RUNCKEL, m. Jane Laqueer, of Kingwood, N. J. George d. July 22, 1870.
6 G.—2. SARAH RUNCKEL, m. Jacob Besson, wholesale tea and coffee merchant, New York city. Res. Hoboken, N. J. Chil.:
7 G.—1. ELBRIDGE V. S. BESSON, Mayor of Hoboken, N. J., in 1879. 2. JOSEPHINE BESSON, m. Charles Rudolphy, of Hoboken, N. J. 3. LOUISE BESSON. 4. JAMES BESSON, a farmer in Dorchester Co., Md. 5. CHARLES BESSON.
6 G.—3. NELSON RUNCKEL, m. Sarah Voorhes. Res. Williamsport, Pa. Wholesale grocer. Chil.:
7 G.—1. CHARLES V. RUNCKEL. 2. VIRGINIA RUNCKEL.
6 G.—4. ALMIRA W. RUNCKEL, m. Dr. Dewitt Hough, of Rahway, N. J. Chil.:
7 G.—1. JANE HOUGH. 2. H. PAGE HOUGH.
6 G.—5. JOHN C. RUNCKEL, m. Helen Chichester. J. C. R. is a tea merchant, New York city. Chil.:
7 G.—1. HELEN RUNCKEL. 2. PHILIP H. RUNCKEL.

5 G.—6. DANIEL² CARHART (son of Cornelius²), b. Mar. 6, 1797, m. Sept. 25, 1818, Christina Bird. Resided adjoining Maple Grove farm. Daniel d. Sept. 29, 1819. Buried at Bethlehem, N. J. Chil.:
6 G.—CORNELIUS³ CARHART, b. July 7, 1819, m. Jan. 12, 1843, Elizabeth Bird, sister of Hon. John S. Bird, ex-Congressman from Hunterdon Co., N. J. Elizabeth d. 1861. Cornelius m. second wife, Matilda Pierce, Nov. 28, 1865. C. C. gave valuable information of early New Jersey ancestors. Res. Washington, N. J. Chil.:
7 G.—1. DIANA V. CARHART, b. June 13, 1844. Res. Somerset Co., N. J.
7 G.—2. MARY A. CARHART, b. Sept. 14, 1845, d. Jan. 30, 1867.
7 G.—3. CHRISTINA CARHART, b. Dec., 1846, m. Mar. 22, 1872, Dwight Davis. Res. Bradford, Mercer Co., Pa. Chil.:
8 G.—ROSE E. DAVIS, b. Oct. 3, 1872, in Nebraska.
7 G.—4. SANFORD M. CARHART, b. May 10, 1851. Res. Ogden city, Utah. Engineer on Central Pacific R. R.
7 G.—5. EMILY A. CARHART, b. Nov. 19, 1854, m. Mar. 22, 1876, Allen Crowe, farmer, Burt Co., Nebraska. Chil.:
8 G.—MILTON CROWE, b. Oct. 28, 1876.
7 G.—6. JOSEPHINE CARHART, b. Dec. 16, 1853. Res. Washington, N. J. Unm.
7 G.—7. JAMES B. CARHART, b. Jan. 16, 1856. U. S. mail carrier, Nebraska.
7 G.—8. DANIEL D. CARHART, b. Nov. 4, 1859, d. Nov. 3, 1866.
Cornelius³ had by second wife, Matilda Pierce:
7 G.—9. LYNDON A. CARHART, b. Dec. 7, 1866. 10. MARY EMMA CARHART, b. Nov. 8, 1868. 11. ELLA CARHART, b. Nov. 6, 1870.

THE CARHART FAMILY.

5 G.—7. SAMUEL CARHART (son of Cornelius²), b. May 10, 1779, m. Jan. 14, 1826, Lavinia Larison (*Note* 44), who d. Jan. 22, 1827. He m. second wife, April, 1829, Fanny Britton, who d. Sept., 1851. Samuel belonged to the firm of Britton & Co., of Milford, in 1827. Was proprietor of the hotel at Lambertsville in 1843. Bought 300 acres of land in Cecil Co., Md., in 1849, and removed there. He d. July 5, 1851. Fanny d. Sept., 1851. Both buried at Zion, Cecil Co., Md. Chil.:

6 G.—1. LAVINIA CARHART, b. Dec., 1826, m. Jan. 14, 1846, Gershom Moore. Res. near Trenton, N. J. Chil.:

7 G.—1. MARY L. MOORE. 2. GEORGE L. MOORE.

6 G.—2. HELEN MAR CARHART, b. Feb. 10, 1831, at Milford, N. J., m. Oct. 7, 1851, Samuel L. Bonnell, b. Nov. 18, 1822. Farmer at Clinton, N. J. Chil.:

7 G.—1. AMY H. BONNELL, b. Sept. 25, 1852. 2. ALEXANDER BONNELL, b. Nov. 15, 1854, d. Jan. 18, 1866. 3. LILLIE BONNELL, b. Feb. 6, 1857. 4. CHARLES BONNELL, b. April 3, 1859. 5. ELMER E. BONNELL, b. Aug. 18, 1861. 6. JOSEPHINE C. BONNELL, b. April 10, 1865. 7. ALEXANDER CARHART BONNELL, b. July 14, 1867.

6 G.—3. LARISON B. CARHART, b. Aug. 18, 1832, at Milford, m. Oct. 22, 1851, Damana C. Hamilton, who d. Feb. 18, 1866. He m. second wife, Mary A. Trace, Jan. 19, 1869. L. B. C enlisted in 6th Maryland Regiment, Sept., 1862. Appointed Brigade Commissary of Wagons in 3rd Division, Sixth Army Corps, under Gen. Wright. Discharged June 24, 1865. Farmer at Norton, Hunterdon Co., N. J. Chil.:

7 G.—1. SAMUEL J. CARHART, b. Dec. 5, 1852, at Zion, Cecil Co., Md., m. Oct. 14, 1875, Lucinda Gano. Samuel is a travelling salesman. Res. Newton, Bucks Co., Pa. Chil.:

8 G.—1. JOHN BRITTON CARHART, b. Aug. 22, 1876. 2. MARY DAMARIS CARHART, b. Sept. 28, 1877. 3 and 4. OLIVER ALLEN and ARTHUR IVENS CARHART, twins, b. June 12, 1879.

7 G.—2. EDWARD D. CARHART, b. July 14, 1855, in Cecil Co., Md., m. Oct., 1878, Louise Cathers. Res. near Oxford, Chester Co., Pa.

7 G.—3. MARY F. CARHART, b. July 28, 1858, in Maryland. Res. Hamilton, Cecil Co., Md. Unm.

6 G.—4. JOSEPHINE CARHART, b. Mar. 14, 1840, at Lambertsville, N. J. Res. Clinton, N. J.

5 G.—8. RACHEL CARHART (dau. of Cornelius²), b. Oct. 15, 1801, at Perryville, Hunterdon Co., N. J., m. June 30, 1821, Moses Craig. Res. Peapack, Somerset Co., N. J. Chil.:

6 G.—1. Rev. AUSTIN CRAIG, b. at Peapack, Somerset Co., N. J., Pres. of Antioch College, Ohio. He m. Adelaide Churchill. Chil.:

7 G.—1. LUCRETIA CRAIG. 2. ADELAIDE CRAIG. 3. MOSES CRAIG.

6 G.—2. EMILY CRAIG, m. Dr. Edward Parry. Res. Peapack, N. J. Chil.:

7 G.—RACHEL PARRY.

5 G.—9. JOHN⁵ CARHART (*Note* 43), (son of Cornelius²), b. March 6, 1804, near Clinton, N. J., m. Sept. 25, 1829, Kesiah Larison (*Note* 44). He resided near Clinton until April, 1822. Commenced business life as a clerk at Evartstown, N. J. In 1824, he engaged in business for himself at Frenchtown, N. J. In 1827, he removed to Milford, N. J., and remained there till 1830. Until 1834, he was a member of the firm of Carhart & Curtis, at Lambertsville, N. J. From 1834 to 1849, he was engaged in various departments of business. In 1849, he bought 300 acres of land at Zion, Cecil Co., Md., where he is living in 1880. Chil.:

6 G.—1. JAMES LARISON CARHART, b. July 5, 1830, at Lambertsville, N. J., m. Dec. 15, 1852, Kate Smith, of Cecil Co., Md. Was a merchant at Zion, Cecil Co., from 1849 to 1869; then removed to Philadelphia, and engaged in flour and grain commission business. Res. Philadelphia, 1878. Chil.:

7 G.—1. MARY S. CARHART, b. Sept. 16, 1853, at Zion, Md., m. Oct. 7, 1875, Theodore Evans, wholesale grocer, Philadelphia. Res. Philadelphia. Chil.: 1. ELSIE EVANS, b. Aug., 1876. 2. J. LACY HOUGH EVANS.

7 G.—3. ELLA N. CARHART, b. Jan. 15, 1857. Res. Philadelphia. Unm.

7 G.—3. CHARLES CARHART, b. at Zion, Md. Res. Philadelphia.

6 G.—2. DEWITT CLINTON CARHART, b. July 19, 1834, at Lambertsville, N. J., m. Jan. 25, 1858, Elizabeth Smith, of Zion, Md. Dewitt was a farmer until 1866; since, of firm of Carhart Brothers, Oxford, Chester Co., Pa. Chil.:

7 G.—1. VIRGINIA CARHART, b. Jan. 18, 1860, at Zion, Md. 2. KATE CARHART, b. Jan. 6, 1866, at Zion, Md.

6 G.—3. ELWOOD CARHART (*Note* 45), b. Dec. 20, 1836, at Bound Brook, N. J., m. Dec. 20, 1865, Minnie E. Lambert, of Philadelphia. Elwood was a farmer until 1866; since, of firm of Carhart Brothers, Oxford, Chester Co., Pa. Chil.:

7 G.—EMMA S. CARHART, b. Sept. 24, 1866, at Philadelphia.

5 G.—4. SARAH E. CARHART, b. Feb. 9, 1839, at Bound Brook, N. J., m. 1861, E. Parshall. Sarah d. at Oxford, Pa., May 15, 1863. Buried at Zion, Md.

6 G.—5. ALBERT CARHART, b. Sept. 10, 1841, at Bound Brook, N. J., m. June 14, 1865, Margery A. Smith, of Cecil Co., Md. Albert was a farmer until 1866; since, of firm of Carhart Brothers, Oxford, Pa. Is an officer in the State troops and a representative in the town councils. Chil.:

7 G.—1. KESIAH CARHART, b. Nov. 6, 1866, at Zion, Md. 2. HELEN CARHART, b. Aug., 1875, at Oxford, Pa., d. Aug., 1875.

6 G.—6. KATE L. CARHART, b. Nov. 18, 1843, at Bound Brook, N. J., m. Nov., 1873, William Rutherford, of Oxford, Pa. Kate d. Feb. 15, 1875. Buried at Oxford Cemetery. William d. March, 1879. Chil.:

7 G.—KATE RUTHERFORD, b. Feb. 9, 1875, at Oxford, Pa. Res. Zion, Md.

6 G.—7. FANNY A. CARHART, b. April 9, 1845, at Evertstown, N. J. Res. Zion, Md. Unm.

6 G.—8. JOHN CLAYTON CARHART, b. Feb. 23, 1849, at Bound Brook, m. Sept. 15, 1875, Ruth Gifford, of Cecil Co., Md. John C. is of the firm of Carhart & Co., at Zion, Md. Chil.:
 7 *G.*—LAWRENCE G. CARHART, b. June 20, 1876, at Zion, Md.

6 G.—9. AUSTIN CRAIG CARHART, b. April 3, 1853, at Zion, Md., of firm of Carhart & Co., Zion, Md. Unm.

5 G.—10. NEHEMIAH CARHART (son of Cornelius^3), b. Aug. 24, 1806, at Clinton, N. J., m. April 5, 1832, Sarah Patty, of Auburn, N. Y. He was in business at Frenchtown, N. J., until 1832, when he removed to Auburn, N. Y., and became a manufacturer of carpets and paper. He was a man of honest dealings, and secured many friends. Was an Elder of the Presbyterian Church, and a delegate to the General Assembly at Philadelphia, at the time of the reunion of the Old and New Schools of that Church. He died in 1873. Buried at Auburn. Chil.:
 6 G.—1. SAMUEL N. CARHART, b. May 6, 1835, at Auburn, m. Aug. 18, 1857, Cornelia Leonard. Res. Rochester, N. Y. Wholesale stationer. Chil.:
 7 *G.*—1. JOHN BRACKEN, b. Oct. 18, 1858, at Auburn, N. Y. 2. SYLVESTER LEONARD, b. May 5, 1862, at Auburn. 3. FRANK MATTHEW, b. Aug. 20, 1868, at Auburn. Res. Rochester.

6 G.—2. SARAH A. CARHART, b. Jan. 27, 1837, at Auburn. Res. Auburn. Unm.
 6 G.—3. JOHN P. CARHART, b. Sept. 6, 1845, at Buffalo, N. Y. Commercial traveller. Res. Auburn.
 6 G.—4. HENRY E. CARHART, b. Oct. 17, 1851, m. Feb. 7, 1876, Cornelia Dale, of Dryden, N. Y. Henry is a moulder in iron. Res. Auburn, N. Y.
 6 G.—5. FRANCES L. CARHART, b. Oct. 7, 1854, at Auburn, N. Y. Unm.

5 G.—11. CATHARINE A. CARHART (dau. of Cornelius^3), b. April 15, 1809.

4 G.—VI. LYDIA CARHART (dau. of Cornelius^1), b. Oct. 28, 1769, m. James Bowlby, and removed to Monongalia Co., Va. Nothing further can be obtained of the Bowlby family until we find:
 6 G.—A granddaughter of Mr. and Mrs. Bowlby, named WILLIMPIA CARHART BOWLBY, b. Feb. 12, 1793, m. Nov. 28, 1811, Stephen Smith, b. Oct. 7, 1789. Stephen d. Aug. 19, 1840. Willimpia C. Smith d. Aug. 15, 1847. Chil.:
 7 *G.*—1. LYDIA SMITH, b. Oct. 2, 1813, d. Feb. 11, 1871. 2. JAMES B. SMITH, b. Nov. 18, 1815. 3. REBECCA SMITH, b. March 14, 1818. 4. LUCINDA SMITH, b. July 25, 1821. 5. MARY A. SMITH, b. Jan. 29, 1824. 6. MATILDA SMITH, b. April 18, 1826, died same day. 7. *HENRY CLAY SMITH, b. Aug. 16, 1827. 8. ALVIN B. SMITH, b. Oct. 19, 1830. 9. ELMORE Y. SMITH, b. Oct. 29, 1833, is P. M. at Galion, Ohio.

74   GENEALOGY OF

* HENRY CLAY SMITH, born at Vermillion Springs. Richland Co., Ohio, studied law with the Hon. Jacob Brinkerhoff, Chief Justice of the Superior Court of Ohio, and Judge George W. Geddis, of Common Pleas. On account of the great number of Smiths, and because Carhart was a family name, he applied to the Court of Common Pleas of Richland Co.—on being admitted to the Bar in 1852—to have the name of Smith changed to that of Carhart. He has practiced in his profession at Galion, Ohio, since that time. He married Oct. 2, 1856, Elizabeth J. White, b. Dec. 29, 1833. Chil.:

8 G.—1. MARY ALICE CARHART, b. Feb. 28, 1858, d. Sept. 2, 1858. 2. JOSEPHINE CARHART, b. March 8, 1860, d. July 28, 1861. 3. CORA CARHART, b. Feb. 11, 1865. 4. ROBERT CARHART, b. Feb. 5, 1871.

4 G.—VII. WILLIMPIA CARHART (dau. of Cornelius¹), b. April 15, 1771, at Mansfield, Sussex Co., N. J., m. Benjamin Lacy, of Mansfield, N. J.

4 G.—VIII. PHEBE CARHART (dau. of Cornelius¹), b. Feb., 1774, at Mansfield, N. J., m. John Coleman, of Sussex Co., N. J.

4 G.—IX. SAMUEL² CARHART (son of Cornelius¹), b. Jan. 8, 1777, at Mansfield, N. J. His first wife was Annie, who d. Sept. 8, 1831. His second wife is living at Philadelphia, aged 84 years. Samuel d. April 24, 1852. He was a public spirited man of the time. Buried at Mansfield Cemetery. Chil.:
1. CORNELIUS.¹ 2. WILLIAM. 3. MARY H. 4. SARAH. 5. SAMUEL M. 6. ROBERT. 7. ISABELLA. 8. JACOB. 9. LYDIA. 10. JESSY. 11. JOHN.

5 G.—1. CORNELIUS¹ CARHART, b. Sept. 23, 1804, m. Margaret Lomson. C. C. d. 1865. A fine marble monument has been erected to his memory by his children, at Washington, N. J. Chil.:

6 G.—1. ELIZABETH CARHART, b. March 3, 1829, m. Nov. 23, 1848, Simon Youmans. Res. Washington, N. J. Chil.:

7 G.—1. HUGH YOUMANS, b. June 23, 1850, m. Nov. 25, 1874, Ellen Fritz. 2. TAMSON C. YOUMANS, b. May 8, 1858.

6 G.—2. MARY CARHART, b. May 5, 1831, m. Dec. 25, 1849, Simon Cummins. Res. Vienna, Warren Co., N. J. Chil.:

7 G.—1. CARHART L. CUMMINS. 2. JACOB P. CUMMINS. 3. THEODORE CUMMINS. 4. GEORGE CUMMINS.

6 G.—3. TAMSON CARHART, b. Dec. 27, 1841, m. Dec. 1, 1859, George P. Wycoff. Res. near Washingson, N. J. Chil.:

7 G.—1. JACOB K. WYCOFF. 2. MARY C. WYCOFF. 3. EDITH WYCOFF.

5 G.—2. WILLIAM CARHART, b. Oct. 4, 1806, m. Feb. 5, 1831, Julia A. Lomson. William d. April 26, 1852. Buried at Mansfield Cemetery. Chil.:

6 G.—1. CATHARINE CARHART, b. Jan. 11, 1832, m. Dec. 16, 1852, John H. Wycoff. Res. Washington, N. J. Chil.:

7 G.—1. JULIA A. WYCOFF. 2. SARAH C. WYCOFF. 3. DANIEL M. WYCOFF.

6 G.—2. ELIZABETH CARHART, b. Jan. 7, 1833, m. Oct. 15, 1853, Mr. Vannatta. Elizabeth d. Feb. 13, 1874.

THE CARHART FAMILY.

6 G.—3. SAMUEL CARHART, b. April 7, 1835. Res. Philadelphia. Chil.:
1. GEORGE B. CARHART, b. 1863. 2. ELMER CARHART, b. 1866. Res. Phillipsburg. N. J.
6 G.—4. WILLIAM CARHART, b. April 11, 1839. d. Dec. 11, 1850.
6 G.—5. SARAH L. CARHART, b. June 8, 1842, m. Mr. Case. Res. Washington, N. J.
6 G.—6. LOMSON CARHART, b. Oct. 31, 1845, m. Oct. 1, 1868. Margaret Hulsizer. Farmer, near Whitehouse, Somerset Co. N. J. Chil.:
7 G.—1. LILLIE CARHART, b. 1869. 2. SUSAN CARHART, b. 1871.

5 G.—3. MARY H. CARHART, b. Dec. 4, 1809, m. Dec. 6, 1831, Joseph Weller, of Warren Co., N. J.
5 G.—4. SARAH CARHART, b. July 29, 1812, m. first husband, Rev. Jessy Fritz ; second husband, Mr. Pitnord, of Illinois.
5 G.—5. SAMUEL M. CARHART, b. Oct. 5, 1814. Date of death not found.
5 G.—6. ROBERT CARHART, b. May 17, 1817, d. Oct. 19, 1818.
5 G.—7. ISABELLA CARHART, b. May 11, 1818, m. Mr. Rassenberg, of Martin's Creek, Northampton Co., Pa.
5 G.—8. JACOB CARHART, b. Aug. 10, 1823, at Mansfield, N. J., m. June 11, 1845, Mary Youmans. Res. Ackermansville, Northampton Co., Pa. Chil.:
6 G.—1. ISABELLA R. CARHART, b. May 2, 1846, m. Nov. 1, 1865, Joseph D. Shine. Res. Ackermansville, Pa. 2. MARY W. CARHART, b. Dec. 2, 1858, d. April 2, 1861.

5 G.—9. LYDIA CARHART, b. Nov. 1, 1825, m. Sept. 6, 1845. John W. Fitts. Res. near Washington, N. J. Chil.:
6 G.—1. SAMUEL. 2. JULIA. 3. JOHN. 4. ENOCH. 5. JOSEPH. 6. MARY. 7. SARAH. 8. ADA. 9. HENRY. 10. THYRZA. 11. MARGARET. 12. ROSA. 13. JESSIE FITTS.

5 G.—10. JESSY CARHART, b. April 6, 1838. Res. Phillipsburgh, N. J. Chil.: 1. FANNY, b. 1858. 2. SALLIE, b. 1860. 3. LEWIS R., b. 1871.

5 G.—11. JOHN CARHART, b. Dec. 17, 1836, d. 1871. Res. Washington, N. J. Chil. :
6 G.—1. IDA, b. 1859. 2. ANNIE, b. 1862. 3. EMMA, b. 1864. 4. ELLA, b. 1866. 5. ELIZABETH, b. 1869.

4 G.—X. JOHN CARHART, youngest child of Cornelius,[1] b. July, 1779, at Mansfield, N. J. John married, and inherited the Carhart homestead. He became intemperate, and died a poor man. No date of death. Buried at Mansfield Cemetery.

3 G.—IV. LYDIA CARHART (dau. of Robert[1]), of Matawan, N. J., and sister of Cornelius,[1] b. Aug. 30, 1732.
3 G.—V. SAMUEL[1] CARHART (second son of Robert[1]), and brother of

Cornelius,[1] resided in Monmouth Co., N. J. There is no record of his marriage. In the war of the Revolution he was first Ensign in Captain Burrow's Company, 1st Regiment of Monmouth Co., June 1st, 1776. Was promoted to Captain of 1st Regiment ; then Captain of State troops. Was taken prisoner, and paroled. Had sons:

4 G.—1. RICHARD CARHART.   2. ROBERT[2] CARHART.

4 G.—1. RICHARD CARHART, was a private in Monmouth Co. Regiment, in 1778, and was killed at the battle of Monmouth. No descendants.

4 G.—2. ROBERT[2] CARHART, was also a private in the same regiment. He lived at Matawan until 1820, then removed to New Brunswick, N. J., and was captain of a sailing vessel to New York city, carrying freight and specie for Government. He died about 1840, aged 78 years. He had children:

5 G.—1. SAMUEL CARHART, who left no descendants.

5 G.—2. CORNELIUS CARHART, who lived at Matawan. No date of marriage or death.

5 G.—3. MARY CARHART, d. in 1855. No record of birth or marriage.

5 G.—4. DEBORAH CARHART, m. Peter Van Pelt, and had a dau., who m. George Hyer, of Matawan, N. J. Deborah m. second husband, Mr. Wood, of Brooklyn, N. Y.

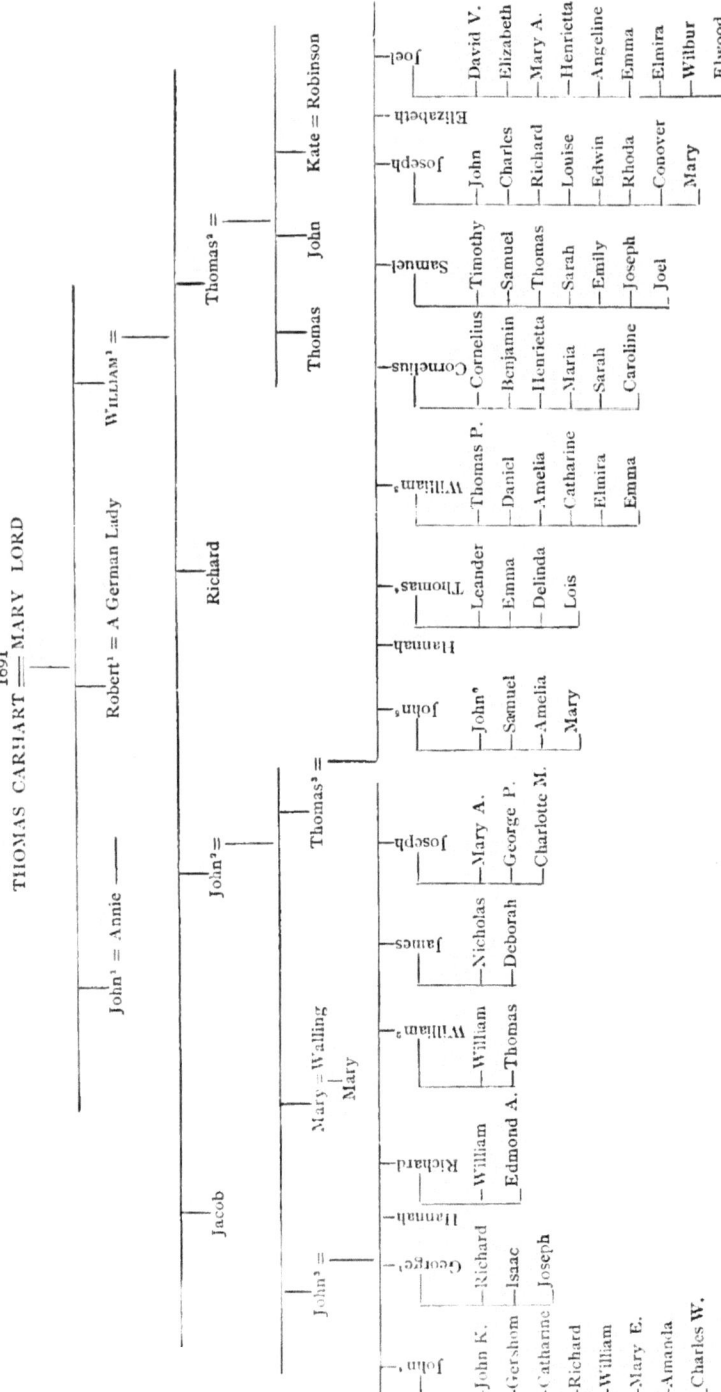

3.—CHART OF WILLIAM[1].

FAMILY OF WILLIAM,[1]

of Perth Amboy, N. J., third Son of THOMAS.

2 G.—WILLIAM[1] CARHART, b. about 1695, on Staten Island, resided after 1698, with his stepfather, Thomas Warne, in Monmouth Co., N. J. In 1723, he bought ninety acres of land of Thomas Ellison, at Perth Amboy, N. J. (*Book* 18, *or C. 2, p.* 570, *E. Jersey Records, Trenton, N. J.*) He had sons:

3 G.—1. JACOB CARHART, was Captain in 2nd Regiment of Hunterdon Co., N. J., 1777. Killed in battle. No descendants.

3 G.—2. JOHN[2] CARHART.

3 G.—3. RICHARD CARHART, was a private in Hunterdon Co. Regiment. Killed in battle. No descendants.

3 G.—4. THOMAS[2] CARHART, was a private in 3rd Battalion, and Corporal in 3rd Regiment, in 1778. After the war, he settled at Flemington, N. J. Occupation, blacksmith. Chil.:

4 G.—1. THOMAS CARHART, who left home, and was never heard from.

4 G.—2. JOHN CARHART, who went to Ohio, and died, leaving no descendants.

4 G.—3. KATE CARHART, who married M. Robinson, of Philadelphia.

FAMILY OF JOHN,[2] *Son of* WILLIAM,[1] *of Monmouth Co., N. J.*

3 G.—JOHN[2] CARHART, purchased land, March 2, 1758, near to what is now Keyport. (*Recorded in East Jersey Records at Trenton.*) No other dates can be found. Chil.:
I. JOHN.[3] II. MARY. III. THOMAS.[3]

4 G.—I. JOHN[3] CARHART, b. July 1, 1756, near Keyport, N. J., d. 1815. Buried at Matawan. He was enrolled as a private, in 1778, in Monmouth Co. Regiment (Militia). After the war, he settled near Keyport. Chil.:
1. JOHN.[4] 2. GEORGE.[4] 3. HANNAH. 4. RICHARD. 5. WILLIAM. 6. JAMES. 7. JOSEPH.

5 G.—1. JOHN[4] CARHART, b. Sept. 3, 1782. m. Feb. 15, 1811. d. Dec. 26, 1876, aged 94 years. Farmer at Port Monmouth, N. J. Chil.:
1. JOHN K. 2. GERSHOM. 3. CATHARINE. 4. RICHARD. 5. WILLIAM.[5] 6. MARY E. 7. AMANDA. 8. CHARLES W.

6 G.—1. JOHN K. CARHART, b. March 1, 1812, m. Nov. 6, 1834. Married second wife, Dec. 9, 1846. Freight agent between Keyport and New York city. Chil.:

7 G.—1. JOHN S. CARHART, b. Jan. 28, 1837, m. July 12, 1874, had
8 G.—CAROLINE, b. 1875.
7 G.—2. THOMAS J. CARHART, b. Sept. 29, 1841, m. 1868.
7 G.—3. CHARLES E. CARHART, b. March 12, 1843, m. 1869. Res. Tuckerstown, N. J. Chil.:
8 G.—1. WILLIAM. 2. ADA.
7 G.—4. Capt. PHILANDER CARHART, b. Aug. 24, 1848, m. Jan. 20, 1876. Captain of vessel at Keyport. 5. MARY F., b. Aug. 21, 1851. Res. Keyport. 6. CATHARINE, b. April 5, 1854. Res. Keyport. 7. LYDIA, b. Dec. 18, 1856. Res. Keyport. 8. ASENETH, b. Nov. 21, 1859. Res. Keyport. 9. VIRGINIA, b. July 28, 1862. Res. Keyport. 10. BISHOP, b. Dec. 24, 1869. Res. Keyport. 11. MARTHA, b. March 19, 1872. Res. Keyport. 12. RALPH, b. July 6, 1877. Res. Keyport.

6 G.—2. GERSHOM CARHART (son of John[1]), b. Aug. 8, 1814, m. Jan. 1, 1835 ; m. second wife, Nov. 14, 1842. Farmer near Bridgeboro, Monmouth Co., N. J. Chil.:
7 G.—1. STEPHEN E. CARHART, b. April 10, 1838, m. July 14, 1862. Res. Greenpoint, L. I. Chil.:
8 G.—1. SYLVANUS. 2. CLARA. 3. ELLA.
7 G.—2. PHEBE CARHART, b. Dec. 26, 1843, m. July 30, 1866.
7 G.—3. NELSON CARHART, b. Dec. 6, 1844, m. Dec. 23, 1869. Captain of a vessel at Port Monmouth, N. J. Chil.:
8 G.—1. MINNIE, b. Jan. 12, 1873. 2. CARRIE, b. Feb. 9, 1875. 3. THEODORE, b. Dec. 2, 1876.
7 G.—4. REUBEN CARHART, b. Dec. 5, 1845, m. Aug. 17, 1870. Farmer at Bridgeboro, N. J.
7 G.—5. HENRY CARHART, b. Sept. 20, 1847, m. July 30, 1870. Farmer at Bridgeboro, N. J. Chil.:
8 G.—1. WILLIAM, b. Oct. 4, 1871. 2. REBECCA, b. Aug. 31, 1874.
7 G.—6. JOSEPHINE CARHART, b. Feb. 15, 1849, m. Nov. 30, 1876.
7 G.—7. Rev. WILLIAM CARHART, b. Dec. 15, 1850. Methodist minister at Baltimore, Md.
7 G.—8. EDSON CARHART, b. Aug. 15, 1852, m. Nov. 30, 1873. Farmer at Bridgeboro, N. J. Chil.:
8 G.—LILLIE, b. Sept. 25, 1875.
7 G.—9. MARGARET CARHART, b. Jan. 8, 1857. 10. BURNETT CARHART, b. Sept. 22, 1858. 11. ARTHUR CARHART, b. Dec. 14, 1860. 12. GEORGE CARHART, b. Oct. 5, 1862. 13. ELMER CARHART, b. June 9, 1864. 14. EVELYN CARHART, b. Oct. 15, 1866.

6 G.—3. CATHARINE CARHART (dau. of John[1]), b. 1816, m. Mr. Grissom, of Buffalo, N. Y.
6 G.—4. RICHARD CARHART (son of John[1]), b. 1818, m. second wife, Feb. 24, 1856. Engineer. Res. Elizabeth, N. J. Chil.:
7 G.—1. CATHARINE A. CARHART, b. Feb. 27, 1849, m. John Holmes, a pilot. 2. LEROY, b. April 19, 1849. Res. Jersey City. 3. MARY E., b. May 16, 1851. 4. OSCAR, b. July 7, 1857. 5. AMBROSE, b. May 14, 1859. 6. AUGUSTA, b. Aug. 22, 1868.

6 G.—5. WILLIAM[3] CARHART (son of John[1]), b. March 15, 1827, m. Lydia Compton. He is a farmer at Port Monmouth, N. J. Chil.:

7 G.—1. DAVID B. CARHART, b. Nov. 12, 1850, m. Dec. 24, 1872, Mary E. Morris. Chil.:
8 G.—1. WILLIAM D. 2. JOSIE IDELL.
7 G.—2. LYDIA, b. Feb. 12, 1853, d. Feb. 12, 1855.

6 G.—6. MARY E. CARHART, b. Oct. 25, 1825, m. May 12, 1851, George F. Henry, of Port Monmouth, N. J.
6 G.—7. AMANDA CARHART, b. Aug. 27, 1832, m. July 2, 1851, Capt. Hiram Seely, of Port Monmouth, N. J.
6 G.—8. CHARLES W. CARHART, b. Nov. 24, 1834, m. Dec. 22, 1861, Sarah Irwin, of Keyport, N. J. Chil.:
7 G.—1. ESTELLA, b. April 28, 1864. 2. IRWIN, b. Jan. 10, 1870, d. July 25, 1870.

5 G.—2. GEORGE^4 CARHART (son of John^3), b. about 1784, at Port Monmouth. Chil.:
6 G.—1. RICHARD CARHART. Chil.:
7 G.—1. RICHARD.^{2} 2. GEORGE.^{2} 3. THOMAS. 4. CHARLES. 5. HENRIETTA. 6. EMMA.
6 G.—2. ISAAC CARHART. 3. JOSEPH CARHART. Chil.:
7 G.—LYDIA A. CARHART, b. Jan. 18, 1856, at Port Monmouth, N. J.

5 G.—3. HANNAH CARHART (dau. of John^3), b. Jan. 14, 1790, m. Dec. 6, 1810, d. July 6, 1851.
5 G.—4. RICHARD CARHART (son of John^3), b. Nov. 19, 1791, m. in 1817, Catharine Anmack, d. Dec. 26, 1875. He was a farmer, near Holmdell, Monmouth Co., N. J., and gave much information of the early history of the family. Chil.:
6 G.—1. WILLIAM CARHART, b. Sept. 8, 1822, m. Dec. 7, 1854, Sophia Greenwood. Res. Matawan, N. J. Chil.:
7 G.—1. CARRIE, b. Sept. 7, 1855. 2. ALFRED, b. Jan. 29, 1867.
6 G.—2. EDMOND A. CARHART, b. Nov. 4, 1824, m. July 1, 1856, Catharine H. Hoff. Chil.:
7 G.—1. TAYLOR CARHART, b. June 1, 1859. 2. LEILA, b. Feb. 15, 1861.

5 G.—5. WILLIAM^2 CARHART (son of John^3), b. Sept. 13, 1793, d. Aug. 17, 1824. He was a farmer. Chil.:
6 G.—1. WILLIAM^3 CARHART. Chil.:
7 G.—WILLIAM V., of Port Monmouth, N. J.
6 G.—2. THOMAS.

5 G.—6. JAMES CARHART (son of John^3), b. 1796, m. July 8, 1815, d. Feb. 15, 1844. He was a farmer at Marlboro, N. J. Chil.:
6 G.—1. NICHOLAS, who has one son. 2. DEBORAH.

5 G.—7. JOSEPH CARHART (son of John^3), b. Feb. 4, 1798, m. Aug. 17, 1820, Margaret Nowland. Res. Monmouth Co., N. J. and Brooklyn, N. Y. He is a mechanic. Chil.:
6 G.—1. MARY ANN, b. Nov. 8, 1821, d. in infancy.

6 G.—2. GEORGE P., b. May 22, 1823, m. Nov. 2, 1844, Mary Coyle. He died in the Federal army before Petersburgh, Va., in 1865. Chil.:
7 G.—1. CHARLES HENRY, b. Nov. 18, 1847. Res. Monmouth Co., N. J. 2. JOHN JOSEPH, b. March 21, 1849. J. J. C. is Professor of Elocution, at Green Castle, Indiana.
6 G.—3. CHARLOTTE M., b. Nov. 30, 1827, m. Aug. 8, 1847, Joseph La Fumée. Res. Brooklyn, N. Y. Chil.:
7 G.—1. EDWIN FOREST LA FUMÉE, b. Dec. 13, 1848, d. Dec. 28, 1879. 2. FRANCES ANGELINE LA FUMÉE, b. May 31, 1851, m. George Woodruff, of Brooklyn, N. Y. 3. CHARLOTTE LOUISE LA FUMÉE, b. Nov. 5, 1853, d. in infancy. 4. JOSEPHINE CLEMENTS LA FUMÉE, b. April 8, 1860, m. April 17, 1879, William L. Jones, of Jersey City, N. J.

4 G.—II. MARY CARHART (dau. of John²), b. 1758, m. John Walling. One dau., Mary Walling, still living, unmarried, at Keyport, aged 90 years. This lady furnished to Elwood Carhart the history, as far as obtained, of descendants of William,¹ son of Thomas.¹

4 G.—III. THOMAS³ CARHART (son of John²), b. Jan., 1761, d. near Keyport, in 1813. He was a farmer. Chil.:
1. JOHN.⁵ 2. HANNAH. 3. THOMAS.⁴ 4. WILLIAM. 5. CORNELIUS. 6. SAMUEL. 7. JOSEPH. 8. ELIZABETH. 9. JOEL.

5 G.—1. JOHN⁵ CARHART, b. about 1781. No date of marriage or death. Lived near Keyport, N. J. Chil.:
6 G.—1. JOHN⁶ CARHART, b. about 1803. No date of m. Res. Brooklyn, N. Y. Is a coal dealer. Chil.:
7 G.—1. JAMES, who is a farmer on Long Island.
7 G.—2. WILLIAM, who also resides on Long Island. Chil.:
8 G.—1. ANNIE. 2. MATILDA. 3. IDA. 4. CONOVER. 5. ALFRED. 6. THEODORE.
6 G.—2. SAMUEL CARHART (son of John⁵), lived and died at Burlington, N. J. Chil.:
7 G.—1. ELMIRA. 2. ADELAIDE. 3. SAMUEL. Living at Trenton, N. J. 4. JACOB.
6 G.—3. AMELIA CARHART (dau. of John⁵). 4. MARY CARHART.

5 G.—2. HANNAH CARHART (dau. of Thomas³), d. 1783.
5 G.—3. THOMAS⁴ CARHART. Chil.:
6 G.—1. LEANDER. 2. EMMA. 3. DELINDA. 4. LOIS.

5 G.—4. WILLIAM CARHART, b. 1789. Chil.:
6 G.—1. THOMAS P. CARHART. Chil.:
7 G.—1. EUGENE. 2. OSCAR. 3. CHARLES.
6 G.—2. DANIEL. 3. AMELIA. 4. CATHARINE. 5. ELMIRA. 6. EMMA.

5 G.—5. CORNELIUS CARHART (son of Thomas³), b. 1791. He was engaged in merchandise at Keyport, N. J., and retired from business in 1879. Chil.:
6 G.—1. CORNELIUS CARHART, who resides at Keyport. Chil.:

THE CARHART FAMILY.

7 G.—1. Minerva. 2. Newell. 3. Laura.
6 G.—2. Benjamin Carhart. Chil.: Melissa.
6 G.—3. Henrietta. 4. Maria. 5. Sarah. 6. Caroline.

5 G.—6. Samuel Carhart (son of Thomas³), b. 1793 ; lived at Keyport, N. J. Chil.:
  6 G.—1. Timothy. 2. Samuel, who has Crawford and Holmes, both living in Virginia. 3. Thomas. 4. Sarah. 5. Emily. 6. Joseph. 7. Joel.

5 G.—7. Joseph Carhart (son of Thomas³), b. 1796. He was a farmer, and is still living at Keyport. This gentleman gave much information for record. Chil.:
  6 G.—1. John Henry Carhart. Chil.: Virginia.
  6 G.—2. Charles. 3. Richard A., who has Chil.:
  7 G.—1. Lydia. 2. Malcomb. 3. Elenor. 4. Isabel. 5. Lina.
  6 G.—4. Louise. 5. Edwin. 6. Rhoda. 7. Conover. 8. Mary.

5 G.—8. Elizabeth Carhart (dau. of Thomas³), b. about 1800.

5 G.—9. Joel Carhart, b. Feb. 12, 1803, near Keyport, m. July 29, 1827, Mary A. Van Pelt. Joel is still living, near Brunswick, N. J., and engaged in farming. He is an active member of the Methodist Episcopal Church. Chil.:
  1. David Van Pelt. 2. Elizabeth. 3. Mary A. 4. Henrietta. 5. Angeline. 6. Emma V. 7. Elmira. 8. Wilbur. 9. Elwood.

6 G.—1. David Van Pelt Carhart, b. May 21, 1828, m. Nov. 16, 1849, Lydia Chambers. David is a farmer at Hightstown, Mercer Co., N. J. Chil.:
  7 G.—1. Jane L., b. Aug. 25, 1850. 2. Sarah J., b. April 30, 1852. 3. James N., b. Oct. 17, 1853. He is a merchant at Bordentown, N. J. 4. Zachariah, b. Dec. 19, 1856. 5. Lydia M., b. Oct. 12, 1862. 6. David E., b. June 6, 1865.
6 G.—2. Elizabeth Carhart (dau. of Joel), b. July 5, 1830, m. Ezekiel Gravatt. Elizabeth d. June 5, 1876.
6 G.—3. Mary A. Carhart, b. June 2, 1833, m. Girard Jones.
6 G.—4. Henrietta Carhart, b. July 10, 1835, m. H. Williams.
6 G.—5. Angeline Carhart, b. July 16, 1839, m. John R. Case.
6 G.—6. Emma V. Carhart, b. Nov. 11, 1843, m. Richard Biddle.
6 G.—7. Elmira Carhart, b. Feb. 10, 1846, m. Wellington W. Wright. Elmira d. March 29, 1876.
6 G.—8. Wilbur F. Carhart, b. June 7, 1848, m. Oct. 14, 1874, Annie M. Mull. Wilbur is a clerk in the Pennsylvania R. R. office at Philadelphia. Chil.:
  7 G.—1. Wilbur A. Carhart, b. Jan., 1876, at Camden, N. J.
6 G.—9. Elwood Carhart (son of Joel), b. July 27, 1851, m. March 9, 1870, Mary E. Lowe. Elwood is a farmer near Milltown, N. J. Chil.:
  7 G.—1. John L., b. May 31, 1871. 2. Alice R., b. June 28, 1873.

APPENDIX.

INDEX OF NOTES

SHOWING PAGE ON WHICH EACH REFERENCE OCCURS.

Note.	Page	Note.	Page
I	25	XXIV	48
II	25	XXV	49
III	26	XXVI	49
IV	26	XXVII	49
V	26	XXVIII	49
VI	28	XXIX	54
VII	31	XXX	54
VIII	34	XXXI	54
IX	34	XXXII	55
X	35	XXXIII	62
XI	38	XXXIV	64
XII	38	XXXV	64
XIII	38	XXXVI	64
XIV	41	XXXVII	64
XV	42	XXXVIII	64
XVI	44	XXXIX	64
XVII	45	XL	65
XVIII	47	XLI	61 & 67
XIX	47	XLII	67
XX	47	XLIII	71
XXI	47	XLIV	71
XXII	48	XLV	72
XXIII	48		

APPENDIX.

NOTE I.

"THOMAS LORD came to America in the ship Elizabeth and Ann, April 29, 1635, with Dorethy his wife, and six children."—*Chalmer's New England Families.*

"Thomas, aged 16 years, Ann, aged 14 years, William, aged 12 years, John, aged 10 years, ROBERT, aged 9 years, Annie, aged 6 years."

Savage says, "THOMAS LORD, may have been the one, by Porter, called the 'Sea Captain.'"

"ROBERT LORD married REBECCA PHILLIPS, dau. of Major William Phillips, of Saco, Maine. Chil. :

"1. Robert Lord, b. April 6, 1661, 2. Thomas Lord, b. May 18, 1663, died young. 3. A dau. b. at Cambridge, Mass., July 13, 1668."—*Savage's Genealogical Dictionary.*

[As subsequently appears, this daughter was MARY LORD, who married THOMAS CARHART. It is also found that a *second* daughter was born to them, named Sarah, who married English Smith. This appellation of "English" was probably not the proper name of Mr. Smith, though in two instances he is thus recorded. "In the early days," history informs us, it was the practice to thus designate persons by their nationality.]

[It may be inferred from a proviso in the will of Thomas Carhart commencing: "If it shall happen that my said wife shall be inclined to go for Auld England, with her children," etc., etc., that Robert and Rebecca Lord had removed there, probably soon after the birth of their daughter Mary, and before that of Sarah, of whose birth no record is found in Savage or elsewhere.]

NOTE II.

"WILLIAM PHILLIPS resided in Cambridge, Mass. until 1646, when he removed to Boston, and became a vintner. In 1660, he removed to Saco, Maine, where he became a large land proprietor, and extensively engaged—in connection with his son-in-law, Capt. John Alden—in lumbering operations. He was legally chosen to exercise the office of Commander of the Yorkshire forces; and his oath was given him at the Court holden at Wells, Sept 29, 1663. He was also appointed one of the King's Commissioners, and Justice, for settling the affairs of New England, and was afterwards appointed—in 1665—Major Commandant of the military forces of the Province of Maine.

"It was his good sense and his merits more than his wealth that gave him rank and influence. Amid all the political changes of his time he was highly esteemed by all parties, and much in office.

"He espoused the rights of Sir Ferdinand Gorges, from an honest conviction. This gave umbrage to Massachusetts, and when she resumed the Government of Maine, in 1668, she treated him with entire neglect; and appointed in his stead, Bryan Pendleton, to the command of the Regiment. Nicholas Shapleigh, an early settler in Kittery, was Major Commandant of the York Regiment, and was displaced for Wm. Phillips.

"MAJOR WM. PHILLIPS, A. D. 1661-4, took from Fluellen, Hobinowell, and Capt. Sundy—Indian Chiefs of the Saco River, and Newichowannock—several quit-claim deeds, of a territory extending from the river Saco, to Berwick and Lebanon, and from the rear line of Wells (exclusive of Lyman) so far back as to embrace about four townships of the usual size—about 10 miles sq.

"These were, Phillipstown—now Sanford—and Alfred, Massabesec—now Waterborough—a section of Little Falls plantation, or northern part of Phillipsburgh—now Hollis—and a part of Lymington.

"The above purchase, with revised bounds, was, in 1670, confirmed by Sir Ferdinand Gorges to the Grantee, or his son Nathaniel Phillips of Saco.

"Mr. Phillips removed to Boston on the breaking out of the Indian troubles, in 1675, in which year his house and mills were burnt, and died there, in 1683. His house stood on the north end of Salem St., where he owned 18 acres of land.

"Children of MAJOR WM. PHILLIPS, and his first wife, Mary.

1. Mary Phillips, who married Robert Field.
2. Martha Phillips, who married Richard Thurston.
3. REBECCA Phillips, who married ROBERT LORD.
4. Nathaniel Phillips, a merchant of Boston.
5. Phebe Phillips, who married Zackary Gillum.
6. Sarah Phillips, who married Ephraim Turner.
7. Elizabeth Phillips m. 1st husband, Abiel Averell.

"Her second husband, was Capt. John Alden, b. in Plymouth, in 1622, son of John Alden, 'the fair haired, taciturn stripling of the Mayflower,' and Priscilla Mullens, 'the loveliest maiden of Plymouth,' celebrated in Longfellow's poem of "Courtship of Miles Standish."

"Elizabeth Phillips and John Alden were married by Gov. John Endicott.

"From these persons are descended many of the families by the name of Alden, in America. Capt. John Alden resided in Alden Lane, near Alden St., Boston. He was imprisoned 15 weeks, on a charge of witchcraft : but made his escape."—*See Alden Genealogy.*

"MRS. MARY PHILLIPS died May 1, 1646, at Cambridge. The second wife of MAJOR PHILLIPS, was Susanna Stanley; who came to America with her husband Christopher Stanley, in the same ship with Robert Lord, in 1635 ; Susanna aged 31, and Christopher 32 years. No children. Christopher died in 1646.

"SUSANNA married MAJOR PHILLIPS, Sept. 10, 1650, and died Aug. 2, 1655." No children mentioned.

"In 1657, Major Phillips married his third wife, BRIDGET SANFORD; second wife, and widow of Gov. or Pres. John Sanford of R. I., who moved to Boston in 1637. She was the daughter of Wm. and Ann Hutchinson—'the prophetess of doleful heresies,' who was murdered by the Indians in 1643, at Pelham, Westchester Co., N. Y., near Hutchinson's river, to which place her family had removed on her banishment from Boston. Mrs. Bridget Phillips, being a quakeress, suffered severely from the persecutions inflicted upon that sect.'

"The children of this marriage, were 8. Samuel Phillips, b. Mar. 16, 1658, 9. William Phillips, b. Jan. 28, 1660."

[Savage thinks there was " John, b. Sept. 18, 1656, who died in infancy." But this must be an error, as that date comes after the death of his second wife and before his marriage with the third.]

"SAMUEL PHILLIPS was a bookseller in Boston. He married Hannah, daughter of Capt. Benjamin Gillum."

Dunton says, in his History of Printing, " Samuel Phillips, bookseller of Boston, at the Brick Shop west end of the Town house. If I may trust my eyes, he has a pretty and obliging wife, and he is young and witty, and the most beautiful man in the Town of Boston." [Samuel d. Oct., 1720.]

" JOHN PHILLIPS, 'Stationer's Arms,' Cornhill, was the son of Samuel, and succeeded him in business. He was a magistrate, Col. of the Boston Militia, a member of the General Court, and a deacon in the church in Brattle St. He died April 19, 1763, and was buried with military honours."

"WILLIAM PHILLIPS was the son of John, and succeeded him in business." [He died Jan. 6, 1772].

"The descendants of Samuel Phillips continued the bookselling business in Cornhill, until after the Revolution."

" By the will of Major Phillips, dated Sept. 29, 1683, he appoints his wife Bridget his executrix, and says : 'Having already given portions to each of my four daughters, and whereas, my beloved wife Bridget Phillips brought to me a considerable estate, and by her I have two sons, to whom I have not give portions ; I do give and bequeath my estate as follows." Then follows the boundaries, of about four miles square. " Also four hundred acres lying at Cape Porpus ; also four hundred acres of upland ; also an Island, called Cow Island, lying in Saco river ; also one-half of an Island, called ' Boniton's Island,' which one-half I bought of John Boniton, Sen., and which lyeth also on Saco river ; also my land in Winter Harbor township ; and I do give and bequeath all to my beloved wife Bridget Phillips, my second son, Samuel Phillips, and my youngest son, Wm. Phillips, to be equally divided between them.

"Mrs. Bridget Phillips, devised by will, Sept. 29, 1696, to Peleg Sanford, (a son of her former husband, and who was Gov. of Rhode Island from 1680–82,) what the Major had given to her, and what was included in the town now incorporated Sanford.

" The introduction of the names of Phillipstown and Sanford, arose from the foregoing facts.

" The estates of Wm. Sanford, son of Gov. Peleg, were divided in 1736. The deed of partition among his daughters (Mrs. Gov. Oliver and Mrs. Elisha Hutchinson, mother of Gov. Thomas Hutchinson of Mass.) is recorded in Taunton, Mass.

" The freeholders of Phillipstown, and Sanford, Maine, trace the title to their estates through this Deed."

"One half of the 'Fluellen tract,' comprising Alfred, Sanford, and Waterboro, called the ' 19,000 Acres,' was divided by Major Phillips, in 1676, among the following persons ; *viz.*, Nathaniel, his oldest son, (by first wife, Mary) and William, his youngest, (by third wife, Bridget) Mary Field, oldest daughter, Martha Thurston, second daughter, REBECCA LORD, third daughter, Elizabeth Alden, seventh daughter, Sarah Turner, Zackary Gillum, and ROBERT LORD, of London, mariner, (his sons-in-law); Peleg, John, and Elisha Sanford, (step-sons) Eliphel Stratton (wife of Bartholomew Stratton of Boston, and dau. of Gov. John Sanford), John Juliffe, John Woodman, Elisha Hutchinson, Theodore Atkinson, and Wm. Hadam, all of Boston, each 1,000 acres.

"The '19,000 acres,' was intended by Maj. Phillips, to be settled as a township by his children; incorporated under the name of Phillipstown—in 1768, changed to the present name of Sanford.

"Mr. Phillips provided for his son Nathaniel, merchant, of Boston, by giving him a deed for a tract of land on Saco river.

"The division of the Phillips estate, took place in 1718. Those who appeared, were Wm. Phillips, Deborah, the wife of Wm. Skinner, Sarah and Ann Phillips, single women, and Bridget, the wife of John Merrifield—all of Boston, grandchildren of Major Phillips.

"On the part of the other proprietors, John Briggs, of Boston, alone appeared.

"His son William was detained four years in captivity among the Spaniards. His children inherited his share of the property at a subsequent period."

[The 2,000 acres of land in York Co., Me., which ROBERT and REBECCA LORD, inherited from Major Wm. Phillips, appears to have descended to their daughter MARY. Her brother Thomas, according to Savage, "died young" and of Robert there is no record, as heir at law. Sarah, as per affidavit, died without issue: thus Mary Lord Carhart was the only heir to her estate. These estates, by right of primogeniture, descended to her son, John of Rye.]

[In 1807, the children of THOMAS[2] CARHART, son of John of Rye, brought a joint suit against Thomas Perkins, jr., of Arundell, Me., for the recovery of 20,000 acres of land, in said town of Arundell, which was once owned by John Carhart, late of Rye, their grandfather.

The proceedings in this suit are recorded in the office of the S. J. Court, Alfred, Me., as "having been discontinued in 1808, with costs to defendant," as I am informed by Thos. L. Allen, clerk of said court, (1877). The Hon. John Holmes, lawyer, and Member of Congress, in 1817, conducted this suit, and was afterwards appointed Agent for the sale of lands; but no returns were made to the heirs.

At the time of this suit, the old family Bible of John[1] Carhart, of Rye, was taken to Alfred, as evidence of descent and heirship, and was not returned. Hence the absence of dates, in some instances, connected with the families of John[1], and Thomas.[2]]

Part of an Indian Deed to Major Phillips.

"I, Mogg Megone, of Saco river, etc., etc., do confirm unto the said Major Phillips, a tract of land on Saco and Kenebeck rivers, in breadth, from one river to the other; and in length, beginning at the sea side, and running up the east river to Salmon Falls, on Saco river; and up the Kenebeck to opposite Salmon Falls."

In the 3d verse of Whittier's Poem of Mogg Megone; may be found a reference to Major Phillips, with a note attached, thus:

"MAJOR PHILLIPS, one of the principal men of the Colony. His garrison sustained a long and terrible siege by the savages. As a magistrate and a gentleman, he exacted of his plebeian neighbors a remarkable degree of deference. The Court Records of the settlement inform us, that an individual was fined for the heinous offence of saying that 'Major Phillips' mare was as lean as an Indian's dog.'"

[I have been unable to find historical data by which the family of Major Phillips can be traced in England. A lady of the Gorges family in England married a Mr. John Phillips. She inherited the family seat of Ashton, which was from that time called "Ashton Phillips." William Phillips may have been a descendant of this John Phillips, of Ashton, Somersetshire, as he was a firm adherent and supporter of the cause of Sir Ferdinand Gorges.]

The authorities consulted in compiling the sketch of Major Wm. Phillips, are; Wm. D. Williamson's "History of Maine," Falsom's "History of Saco and Biddiford," Drake's "History of Boston," "Savage's Genealogical Dictionary," "The History of Somersetshire, Eng.," "Dunton's History of Printing," "The Alden Genealogy," with some verbal communications from Thomas Carhart Pinckney, of New York.

NOTE III.

"The family of BROWN, of Rye, was descended from the BROWNS of BEACHWORTH, in the Co. of Kent, Eng., founded by SIR ANTHONY BROWN, who was created a KNIGHT of the BATH, at the coronation of Richard II.

"He left issue, two sons: SIR RICHARD, his heir, and SIR STEPHEN, LORD MAYOR of London, in 1439.

"SIR ROBERT BROWN, living in the time of HENRY V., was father of SIR THOMAS BROWN, treasurer of the Household of HENRY II. and SHERIFF of Kent in 1444 and 1460.

"THOMAS BROWN ESQ., of Rye, Co. of Sussex, Eng., emigrated to Concord, Mass., about 1632, from whence he removed to Cambridge, where he lived for some time.

"His sons were THOMAS and HACKALIAH[1], of Rye, Westchester Co., N. Y. Thomas d. in 1694, and Hackaliah in 1720.

"The latter left I. Deliverance, II. Peter, who d. in 1731 or 2, III. Thomas, who died in 1762, IV. Hackaliah[2], who died in 1784, V. Benjamin, VI. ANNIE, who married DANIEL[2] PURDY, VII. Mary.

[Daniel and Annie (Brown) Purdy had Hackaliah, Joshua, Daniel, ELIZABETH, who married THOMAS[2] CARHART of Rye.]

"The name of *Rye*, Westchester Co., N. Y., was given in honor of the Brown family, of Rye, Sussex Co., Eng.

"MAJOR HACKALIAH[2] BROWN, Justice in 1755, commanded the W. C. Co. levies, under Gen. Lord Amherst. He married Ann Kniffin and died in 1784."—*Bolton's History of Westchester Co.*

Arms—Three lions passant in bend, between two double cottesses, ar.
Crest—An eagle displayed. *Another Crest*—A stag, ppr. altered and ducally gorged and lined. or.

NOTE IV.

"FRANCIS PURDY, of Fairfield, Conn., who died in 1658, is believed to have been the common ancestor of the numerous race bearing this name, scattered widely throughout our country. Three sons of Francis (John, JOSEPH, Francis), came early to Rye ; John in 1670, Joseph in 1677, Francis in 1679.

"JOSEPH[1] PURDY, is first mentioned in 1677. He was a 'leading member of the community, being supervisor of the town in 1707-8, Justice of the Peace in 1712, and after, representative of the Co., for several years in the Assembly, and one of the chief promoters of the church,' writes the Rev. Mr. Wetmore, (many years later).

"With Col. Heathcote, and others in 1701, he purchased lands in North Castle, W. C. Co., N.Y., where some of his descendants settled. His will is dated Oct 5, 1709. He had seven sons : Joseph, DANIEL[2], Samuel, David, Johnathan, John, (called still John) and Francis.

"DANIEL[2] PURDY (son of JOSEPH[1]), who m. Annie Brown, was one of the patentees of Budd's Neck, W. C. Co., N. Y., in 1720. He was alive in 1750.

"His house stood on the site of Mr. Sylvanus Purdy's present tenement house ; and his farm lay below this point, on both sides of the road. He also owned one thousand acres in Courtland's Manor or North Salem, W. C. Co., N. Y., which he left to two of his grandsons. He had five children, 1. Hackaliah[3], 2. Joshua, and 3. Daniel[3], 4. ELIZABETH, m. THOMAS[2] CARHART of Rye, 5. Mary.

"Hackaliah[3], (eldest son of Daniel[2],) lived on the homestead, at Budd's Neck, and married Sarah, dau. of Elisha Budd.

"Joshua Purdy, (second son of Daniel[2],) was known as 'Captain.' Tradition speaks of him as a man of remarkable excellence. He lived until near the close of the last century. He was highly esteemed by his fellow townsmen. Like many of them, he adhered to the government side, in the great struggle which soon followed, and in 1776 was a prisoner at White Plains. The chairman of the Committee of Safety, wrote Aug. 20, recommending his release, as 'a man of influence,' towards whom lenity would be advisable, though he had never been friendly to the American cause.

"At his funeral, the brief eulogy was pronounced over him, 'a kind husband, a faithful master, a father to the poor, and a pillar to the church.' See *American Archives*, 4 series, *vol.* 1., *p.* 1524."—*Baird's History of Rye.*

Arms—Or. a chev, az. between three mullets, sa. pierced of the field.

NOTE V.

"THOMAS MERRITT came to Rye in 1673, John, in 1678. It is supposed they were brothers.

"Thomas Merritt, called 'senior,' in 1698, had married—perhaps his second wife—Mary, youngest daughter of Robert Francis of Weathersfield, Conn. 'She was born,' says Savage, 'in 1656.' He had proprietary rights with Robert Bloomer. Thomas Merritt was one of the principal men of Rye. He was sent with Deliverance Brown, in Jan. 1697, to Hartford, to petition the General Court of Conn. to take the town back into its Jurisdiction."—*Conn. Rec.*, vol. 4. p. 192.

"He was forward in building a 'meeting house' and parsonage and procuring a minister, while under Connecticut. He was living in 1713. His children were Thomas, Ephraim, and Samuel."—*Baird's History of Rye.*

[SYLVANUS MERRITT—father of HANNAH, wife of JOHN[3] CARHART, was his grandson. MARY MERRITT, wife of THOMAS[3] CARHART, was probably a sister, or cousin.]

NOTE VI.

"JEREMIAH CARHART possessed the stable qualities of English and German stocks. While yet a boy, he was obliged to rely upon his own exertions for support. He learned the trade of cabinet making at Binghamton, N. Y., and continued to labor at it for a few years. In 1836, he went to Buffalo, N. Y., where he married and remained ten years. During these years he made many experiments on the accordion with a view of its improvement. He discovered that the tone of the instrument was much better, when the wind was drawn through the reeds, than when it was expelled through them. This suggested the endeavor to produce a method by which a uniform quality of tone should be obtained. The idea of a 'suction bellows' was entirely novel, and deemed impracticable by other mechanicians and musical men; but he concentrated his energies on the invention of an apparatus which would cause the wind to rush *into* a bellows, with the same velocity by which it was expelled. He worked upon the idea for two years, and finally grasped the principle by which the suction bellows became a fact, and the melodeon, no longer a dream. He found also that the old style of reeds was ill adapted to his purpose, so he perforce invented a new kind of reed, much superior to the old, and new machinery for its manufacture. He may be considered as literally the inventor of the melodeon.

"Several other principles have been developed by him in the course of his long experience in the manufacture of musical instruments, so that some styles of his melodeons approximate to the grandeur of the pipe organ.

"At a fair of the American Institute, he exhibited a superb organ which was one of the chief features of the musical department, and was unanimously awarded the gold medal by the Judges of Musical Instruments.

"The most prominent organists and musicians have given flattering testimonials of their approval of the quality of these instruments."—*Fowler's Phrenological Journal.*

NOTE VII.

"JOHN GEDNEY, of Norwich, Suffolk Co., England,—a descendant of the Gedney family of Holbeach. Lincolnshire,—b. 1603, came to Salem, Mass., in May 1637, with his wife Mary, aged twenty-five. He had four sons, John, Bartholomew, Eleazar, and Eli. Eleazar the third, b. May 15, 1642, was the father of Eleazar, who in all probability was the ancestor of the family in Rye. The latter was born in 1666. The inscription on the tombstone in the Gedney cemetery, near Mamaroneck, reads, 1722, 'Here lies Eleazar Gedney, deceased Oct. 27. Born in Boston government.' 'Next lies Annie Gedney, his wife.'"

"John Gedney of Scarsdale, b. 1695, bought, in 1740, of Wm. Marsh, 116 acres of land in White Plains for 400 pounds. John died Oct. 3, 1766."—*Baird's History of Rye.*

[He was the father of JOSHUA GEDNEY who married ANNIE CARHART, dau. of Thomas[2] of Rye.]

[Capt. Thomas Robert Gedney, of the British Navy,—the discoverer of Gedney channel—brought from England just before his death, an old engraving of "Gedney church, near Holbeach, Lincolnshire." He also brought the coat of arms of the family.]

Arms. Shield, az. two lucies in saltier, ar. Crest, the same.

Communicated by Mrs. Rutherford, of Sing Sing.

NOTE VIII.

"THE PINCKNEYS of East Chester descend from PHILIP PINCKNEY, one of the first ten proprietors and patentees of that town, who originally emigrated from Fairfield, Conn, 1663–4.

"PHILIP PINCKNEY was a lineal representative of the Pinckneys of England, whose ancestor, GILO DE PINCKENIE, came into that country with William the Conqueror."—*Bolton's History of Westchester Co., N. Y.*

Arms, or, four fusils on fesse, gu. Crest, out of a ducal coronet, or, a griffin's head, p. p. r.

NOTE IX.

"ROBERT[1] BLOOMER bought land in Rye, in 1672. He had as on, Robert, Jr. who was a very active man in all public affairs. He owned Bloomer's Island and was proprietor of Bloomer's Mills. Was living in 1738.

"His grandson, Robert,[3] was Capt. Robert Bloomer, who, in 1775, commanded a company of the southern battalion W. C. Co. Militia.— *Bolton's History of Westchester Co., N. Y.*

[His daughter ELIZABETH married DANIEL[1] CARHART, of Coeymans, Albany Co., N. Y.]

NOTE X.

"The Sutton Family derive their origin from Joseph Sutton, whose father emigrated from the Co. of Lincolnshire, England to Mass.

"Joseph removed to Long Island, and died between 1760-70, aged about 80 years.

"He married Mary Sands, daughter of James² Sands, of Sands Point, Westchester Co., N. Y., and Sarah Cornell of Cow Neck, L. I."—*Bolton's Westchester Co., N. Y.*

[Joseph Sutton and Mary Sands, were the parents of Sands Sutton, whose daughter Rebecca married Daniel² Carhart of Coeymans, N. Y.]

Arms, ar. on a chevron, between three annulets gu. as many crescents, or.
Crest, a greyhound, head couped, erm. collared, gu. garnished and ringed, or. on collar, three annulets.

"The Sands Family were originally seated at St. Bees, in Cumberland Co., England and are descended from Richard del Sandys, who was returned Knight of the Shire, in 1377.

"James² Sands, of Sands Point, Long Island Sound, was born in 1673, and died in 1731. He was the son of Capt. James Sandys, of Reading, Berkshire, England who emigrated to Plymouth, Mass., in 1658. In 1660, he, with fifteen others, purchased Block Island.

"He was born in 1632, m. Annie Walker, of R. I., and died March 13, 1695."—*Baird's History of Rye.*

Arms, or. a fesse, dancettée between three crosses bottonée fitchée. gu. Crest, a griffin segreant per fesse. or. and gu.

NOTE XI.

"Rev. John Wesley Carhart, D. D., was a graduate of the Charlotteville Seminary, in 1854, and was appointed Prof. of Greek and Latin, in the Warnersville Union Seminary, in 1855. He united with the M. E. Church, in the summer of 1847, and was admitted into the Troy Conference, and licensed to preach in 1855. He was ordained a deacon in 1857, and an elder in 1859. He received the degree of D. D. from the University of Kentucky, in 1862.

"He published his volume of poems, 'Sunny Hours,' in 1859, and 'Poets and Poetry of the Hebrews,' in 1865.

"Since his 18th year he has been an almost constant contributor to various papers and magazines, and many of his Poems, Essays, and Sermons have found their way into the book literature of the times.

"In 1871, he was transferred to the Wisconsin Annual Conference of the M. E. Church. In 1876 he was appointed Presiding Elder of Appleton District, Wis."—*Communicated.*

NOTE XII.

"Prof. Henry Smith Carhart, entered Hudson River Institute, Claverack, N. Y., April 1862. Became Associate Principal of Oswego Village Institute, Dutchess Co. N. Y. (now Moon's Mills), remaining through 1863-4.

"He was admitted at Yale College in July 1865, but entered Wesleyan University, Middletown, Conn., in Sept. 1865, and was graduated in July 1869.

"From 1869 to 1871, was Instructor in Latin at Claverack Hudson River Institute, and College. Was at Yale Theological Seminary, in 1872-1873.

"Is at present Prof. of Civil Engineering, Physics, and Chemistry in the Northwestern University, at Evanston, Ill., having filled that chair since 1873.

"Was elected Vice Pres. of the Evanston Philosophical Association and Member of the American Electrical Society, in 1878."—*Communicated.*

NOTE XIII.

"Ellen M. Soulé was born at Kennebunkport, Maine. Was graduated at Hudson River Institute and Claverack Female College, in 1865, was Preceptress of Greenwich Academy, N. Y., in 1867-8, and Principal of Claverack College, in 1869-1870. From 1871-3, she was Principal of Van Norman's Institute, N. Y. city. From 1874 until the time of her marriage, she was Dean of the Women's College, and Prof. of French Language and Literature, in the Northwestern University, at Evanston, Ill."
—*Communicated.*

NOTE XIV.

"Robert Carhart became one of the first members of the antique, far-famed Stone M. E. Church in the town of Coeymans, N. Y. when in his thirteenth year.

"At this time he was the only member of his father's family that professed religion; so he covenanted with three neighbor boys to hold a weekly prayer-meeting on a rock, situated in a wood not far from his home.

"Young Robert's efforts were soon blessed with success, and he was made the instrument of leading two of his brothers to Christ. They both lived and died good men.

"Soon after his marriage he removed into the town of Bethlehem, N. Y., where he spent thirty-three years. In the same neighborhood he once asked a hotel-keeper if he would close his bar the next Sabbath, and allow them to hold a prayer-meeting in his ball chamber? The hotel-keeper assented. Hundreds came, a revival spread through the town, and Robert lived to see that small class become a large and flourishing society.

APPENDIX.

"R. C. moved to the town of Gilderland, in 1836. For seventy-five years he was an active member of the church and held responsible positions as class-leader and steward."—*Communicated*.

NOTE XV.

"GARRETSON LYON CARHART, M. D., entered the Albany Academy in 1844, and commenced the study of medicine in 1845, with Dr. James P. Boyd, of Albany. Attended the Albany Medical College, and was graduated in Feb., 1848. Removed to Wyoming Co., N. Y., 1850, where he married. Removed to Mt. Vernon, Iowa, in 1855. Practiced medicine until the war of the Rebellion, and was commissioned surgeon of the 31st Regt. of Iowa Volunteers, Oct. 13, 1862. Remained in the service over two years, as Operating Surgeon of the Division. Had charge of the General Hospital, at Marietta, Ga. Resigned on account of failing health, Dec. 1864, and returned to Mt. Vernon, Iowa. Since removed to Marion, Linn Co., Iowa."—*Communicated*.

NOTE XVI.

"LIEUT. GEORGE W. TALMAN was a student of Iowa College, when located at Davenport, and also, after removal, at Beloit. In the summer of 1863 he enlisted in Co. E. 20th Iowa Infantry. Was in the battle of Prairie Grove, Ark., where one third of his Company was either killed or wounded; was also at the seige of Vicksburg. In Nov. 1863, he was commissioned as 1st Lieut. in Co. I. 73 U. S. Infantry. During most of the next year Lieut. Talman was in charge at Baton Rouge. Having received an injury that unfitted him for service, he was reported in Washington for duty in the Invalid Corps. At the end of the war he returned to Gilman, Iowa, and settled on a farm."—*Communicated*.

NOTE XVII.

"MELISSA, daughter of JOHN and ANGELINE CARHART, died of hydrophobia, at her father's residence, Amity, Scott Co., Iowa, in the 12th year of her age.

"On the 5th of Nov. 1859, a large dog came to Mr. Carhart's, and as he pursued it to drive it away, Melissa opened the door and the dog rushed into the house. She attempted to drive him out, whereupon he seized her by the left arm, to which he held until her father came in, and with a pitchfork dispatched him, but not in time to save his child. Her arm was badly torn, but soon healed. Her parents and friends indulged a hope that the dog was not rabid, which hope nearly ripened into confidence: but on the 21st inst. some symptoms of an unfavorable character began to make their appearance. On the day following, there were unmistakable signs of hydrophobia. Upon seeing her parents' alarm and tears, she said, 'Don't feel bad; I do not want to see you cry.' She repeated the wish that they would not weep for her. Her father said to her, 'You are sick, and may not get well; I want you to examine the state of your soul, and then tell me how you feel.' She calmly replied, 'I am happy, and I am not afraid to die.' Finding her end approaching, she threw her arms around the necks of her parents, her sister and brothers, kissed and took an affectionate leave of each. On the 23d, at $5\frac{1}{2}$ o'clock, P. M., exhausted nature sank calmly into the sleep of death. From first to last she passed through this terrible scene, without a murmur or complaint."—*From Methodist Advocate and Journal.*

NOTE XVIII.

HACKALIAH[1] CARHART was the fifth son of Thomas[2] of Rye, who died in 1761, when this son was but six years old.

Before he reached the age of eighteen he had adopted the religious faith of the Quakers.

On the breaking out of the American Revolution, he professed allegiance to the Mother Country, though his religious scruples prevented him from voluntarily entering into warfare on either side. Notwithstanding this he was drafted into the American Army in his 19th year.

On learning this fact, he, with nine others of his own age, who had also been drafted, procured a boat and sought refuge on a British ship, commanded by Lord Howe, then lying in Long Island Sound.

On arriving on board, quite contrary to the expectations of inexperienced youth, they were required to enlist for the war. Seven of the number yielded after a short time, but the subject of this sketch and two others stubbornly refused, and were placed in irons in the hold of the ship on short allowance.

They remained in this situation until they were nearly starved, and had become covered with vermin; when Lieut. Carr, of the 17th Light Dragoons, became interested in their sufferings, and urged them to submit. Under his influence they yielded, and H. C. became his private secretary. After a few months he was transferred, and made Quartermaster of the "Queen's Rangers," under Col. R. G. Simcoe, and Brig. Gen. James De Lancy, "the famous partisan chief of the 'Neutral Ground,' and the ever active Col. of De Lancy's Light-Horse."

"The Queen's Rangers" were styled "The First American Regiment," and the officers ranked with those of the established army. They wore high caps, and were termed "Hussars."

On Friday, Nov. 13, 1779, the house of Col. Thomas Thomas, of Rye Woods, was surprised, and the Col. captured by a party of the "Rangers" under the command of Lieut. Col. Simcoe. During the attack, one man was killed, and another, Thomas Carpenter, came near losing his life, being stabbed in many places by the soldiers' bayonets while hidden under a bed. This man's life was saved by the interposition of Quartermaster Carhart, who accompanied the party of "Rangers," on this occasion.

He was also of the party who captured Gen. Silliman, at Stratford, Conn. The Federalists retaliated by capturing Judge Jones, of Hempstead, L. I., and an exchange was made in the middle of L. I. Sound opposite Huntington.

H. C. held the position of Quartermaster to the end of the war, and being disabled and lamed for life, by the falling of his horse upon him—the pummel of the saddle being pressed into his thigh—he was put upon the half-pay list for life.

The writer has heard him affirm many times that *he never drew a sword or fired a musket.*

He married in 1784, and took up his residence on King St., West Greenwich, Conn., about 3½ miles from Portchester, N. Y. Here he lived, reared a family, and died in 1837. Of the house in which he lived only a ragged outline of the foundation remains, marked by small heaps of stones, the standing remnants of two broad-based stone chimneys, pieces of broken window and door-frames, patches of plaster and scraps of iron.

The old home was built before the Revolution. It was an old style, double house, a broad hall in the centre, one story and a half high, and built of heavy oak timbers. It had an ample yard in front, shaded by rows of noble trees, and was altogether such a home as the great-grandfathers of this generation were proud to call their own.

H. C. was of fine personal appearance, being over six feet in height, of clear complexion, with brilliant hazel eyes, having a military carriage, and great dignity of manner. He was a great reader, and possessed of good intellectual ability, and though of limited education, one whose judgment and opinions were sought and valued by his friends and neighbors.

In the latter part of his life, he became very feeble from the effects of his wound, and the writer well remembers him, seated in his great arm-chair on the old stoop, with his Bible and books around him, seeking to render less tedious the weary days of age and feebleness.

He adhered through life to the faith of the Quakers, and was an uncompromising opposer of slavery.

He died in his eighty-third year, and was buried beside his mother and child Mary, the only one that did not survive him, in his own orchard, near the southern fence of Sherwood's road, and about 250 feet east from the line of King street.

Plain unmarked stones, as was the custom among Quakers, were placed at the graves. The next owner of the farm removed these stones, thus gaining a few more square feet of land for cultivation.

It is with pleasure that these facts are now recorded in such a way as to mark definitely a place still sacred in the memory of his descendants.

M. E. C. D.

NOTE XIX.

"ISAAC ANDERSON, came to Rye in 1707, and styled himself 'Mariner of New York.'

"In 1713 he bought lands in Will's Purchase and along Byrum river, and became one of the largest land owners in Rye. He built a mill on Byrum river, at Portchester, which is still standing and in use, 1879. His wife's name was Prudence.

"His will is dated 1722, and was admitted to Probate April, 9, 1723.

His son William is appointed administrator. On record at the Surrogate's Office, N. Y. *Book* 9., *p.* 425.

"I. A. had four sons, and perhaps others. His oldest, WILLIAM, was Treasurer and Sheriff of New York from 1703 to 1710, and one of the Vestry of Trinity Church from 1710 to 1717.

"In 1750 he bought lands upon the cross road between White Plains and Harrison." [This property remains in the possession of his descendants at the present day. Joseph H. Anderson, member of Congress about 1846, was of this family.]

[Another son was JEREMIAH, who died unmarried, Jan. 22, 1794, and who gave the deed for the Anderson Cemetery. Another son was ISAAC, who belonged to the British Navy, and in 1750 was an overseer in the Navy Yard at Antigua, W. Indies, where he died about 1776.]

[Another son was JAMES, who lived on the east side of King Street, West Greenwich, Conn., about four miles north of Portchester. His will is dated Aug. 27, 1782. The homestead was given to his son WILLIAM, and remains in the possession of his great-granddaughter, ELIZABETH ANDERSON, at the present day, 1879. Isaac, son of James, was the father of MARGARET, who married HACKALIAH[1] CARHART].

NOTE XX.

KING ST. was laid out in 1681, and called the "Kings's Road." It is about 12 miles long, extending from Portchester to Bedford, Westchester Co. It runs about midway of the plateau between Blind Brook and Byrum (old name Armonk) river, and crosses and recrosses the line between New York and Connecticut several times. The house of Hackaliah Carhart stood in Connecticut, but a part of his lawn and the entrance to it was in New York State.—*M. E. C. D.*

NOTE XXI.

THE ANDERSON CEMETERY is situated on the east side of King street, in Connecticut, about three miles from Portchester. It was deeded for a Cemetery for the Anderson family, and others connected by marriage, by JEREMIAH ANDERSON, brother to the above JAMES (see Note 19). The testator is buried alone in the extreme S. E. corner of the ground. He died Jan. 22, 1794, unmarried.—*M. E. C. D.*

NOTE XXII.

According to the "REDFIELD Pedigree" the name was originally "Redfin."

"WILLIAM REDFIN came from England and settled in Massachusetts early in the 17th century."

APPENDIX. 101

[SIMEON REDFIELD, of Portchester, N. Y., was son of JAMES, of Greenwich, who was son of JAMES, of Orange Co., N. Y., and grandson of JOHN, of Fairfield Co., Conn.]

Arms—Ar. on a fesse gu. three fleur de lis of the field.—*See Redfield Pedigree.*

NOTE XXIII.

"PETER, JOSEPH, and GILBERT TOTTEN, came from England early in the 18th century.

"PETER is mentioned in 1739 as living on west side of King St., Rye, W. C. Co., N. Y., about four miles north of Portchester."

[DAVID, son of Peter, b. about 1730, inherited his father's farm, which again descended to his son Samuel, who was the father of PHEBE TOTTEN, who married ALFRED CARHART.]

II. "JOSEPH TOTTEN engaged in mercantile pursuits in the city of New York. [John C. Totten, book publisher in the early part of this century, was his grandson.]

"Attached to the cause of the mother country, he left that city, on the breaking out of the American Revolution, for Annapolis, Nova Scotia, leaving behind him two sons, one of whom, PETER GILBERT, married, in 1787, GRACE MANSFIELD, of New Haven, who died leaving two children.

"1. GEN. JOSEPH GILBERT TOTTEN.

"2. SUSAN MARIA, who married COL. BEATTY, an English officer, and who was still living in 1865, a widow in London.

"JOSEPH GILBERT TOTTEN, entered the Academy at West Point and graduated in 1805. Was attached for many years to the U. S. coast survey, with the title of Gen. by Brevet. He died at Washington, D. C., April 22, 1864.

"PETER GILBERT TOTTEN, father of GEN. JOSEPH GILBERT TOTTEN, was appointed U. S. Consul at Santa Cruz. His son was left under the care of his maternal uncle, Jared Mansfield, a graduate of Yale College, and a learned mathematician. In 1802, his uncle was appointed Capt. of Engineers and teacher in the U. S. Military Academy at West Point.

"COMMODORE BENJAMIN J. TOTTEN was born in the West Indies, and entered the United States Navy, from Connecticut, on the 5th of March, 1823. In 1830 he was promoted to the rank of Passed Midshipman. In 1834 he attained the rank of Lieutenant. In 1855 he received his commission as Commander. In 1862 he received his commission as Commodore.

"COMMODORE TOTTEN was placed on the retired list under the Act of April 21, 1864, his services extending over more than 18 years. During the past few years he has resided at New Bedford, where he died, May 9th, 1877, aged 71 years.

"The English TEMPLES married into the American TOTTEN family, and young Totten, of the Army, so recently killed by the cars mutilating him, was a descendant of this family."

III. [GILBERT TOTTEN settled on the southern point of Staten Island, and founded TOTTENVILLE, where his descendants are living at the present date, 1879.]

NOTE XXIV.

"THE PECKS were found seated at Belton, Yorkshire, Eng., at a very early date. A branch settled at Wakefield, in Yorkshire, whose descendants removed to Beccles. Suffolk Co., and were the ancestors of Joseph, who came to Hingham, Mass., in 1638. He was a lineal descendant, in the 21st generation, from John Peck, Esq., of Belton, Yorkshire, and was baptized, April 30, 1587, being in the fiftieth year of his age. Samuel Peck, a lineal descendant of Joseph of Hingham, Mass., settled at Greenwich, Conn., and died there in 1746, aged 88 years. He had, Samuel, Jr., Jeremiah, Joseph, David, Nathaniel, Eliphelet, THEOPHILUS, Peter, and Robert.

"Samuel, Jr., had John and Samuel. The latter, a deacon at Greenwich, in 1793, had Calvin, of Sharon, Conn.

"THEOPHILUS had a grandson David, a Baptist minister, and ROBERT, a deacon, who died in 1828, aged 85 years. [The latter was the grandfather of ROBERT, the father of ANNIE, who married ALFRED CARHART.]

"The name has been spelt, Pek, Peck, Pecke, Peke, Peak, and Peake. The Pedigree may be found in the British Museum."

Arms—Ar. on a chevron, engrailed, gu. three crosses formée of the first.—*See Peck Genealogy.*

NOTE XXV.

"PRICE OF BRYN-Y-PAYS, Co. Flint, Wales. The LLOYDS OF GLEN GRILLY, now represented by the family of PRICE, were in direct descent from RHODRI MAWR, KING OF WALES."

Arms of Price, of Flintshire, Wales—Ar. three cocks, gu. two and one, armed, crested and jilloped, or.—*Burke's Heraldry.*

NOTE XXVI.

"GROVE FARM, on Spicer's and Brocket's Necks, on the southwestern extremity of Throckmorton's Neck, Westchester Co., N. Y., was patented by Gov. Nichols, to THOMAS HUNT, in 1667. These Necks are on the North shore of Long Island Sound, near New Rochelle.

"HUNT'S POINT, has been occupied by the HUNT family, for nearly one hundred and sixty years.

"The burial place of the Hunt family is near the entrance of the Point. The following inscriptions are copied from two of the monuments in this yard."

'In memory of THOMAS HUNT, who departed this life, July 4, 1808, in the 80th year of his age.

'He possessed the cardinal virtues, in an eminent degree. He was temperate, brave, patient and just.

APPENDIX.

The other is,

> The solid rock shall sink beneath
> The iron hand of time,
> But virtue dwells with
> Immortality.
>
> Sacred to the memory
> of
> JOSEPH RODMAN DRAKE, M. D.,
> who died, Sept. 21st,
> 1825,
> aged 25 years.
>
> *Bolton's History of Westchester.*

Arms of Hunt—Per pale, ar. and sa. a saltier, counterchanged.
Crest—A lion's head erased, per pale, ar. and sa. collared gu. lined and ringed, or.

NOTE XXVII.

"The town of PELHAM is enclosed on the east and north by the township of New Rochelle, on the west by Hutchinson's river, which separates it from East Chester, and on the south by the Sound, and lies ten miles south of the village of White Plains.

"Prior to the Revolution, PELHAM formed a portion of the old Manor of that name, which originally combined nine thousand one hundred and sixty acres."

"The name is of Saxon origin, and compounded of the words PEL, (remote) and HAM, (mansion.)

"PELHAM is the name of a Lordship in Herefordshire, Eng., and recorded to have been part of the possessions of WALTER DE PELHAM, A. D., 1292.

"A grant from the Sachem Ann-hoock was confirmed to THOMAS PELL, ESQ., on the 6th day of Oct., 1666, by his Excellency Richard Nichols, and recorded in the Office of New York, Oct. 8. 1666.

"The PELLS boast a remote antiquity, tracing their descent from the ancient family of that name in Lincolnshire. The seal of JOHN PELL, ESQ., attached to the Patent of New Rochelle, is charged with the arms of this ancient family.

Er. on a canton, az. a pelican, or. vulned gules.

This coat seems to have been granted, Oct. 19, 1594.

"Of this family was JOHN PELL, ESQ., of the Co. of Norfolk, Steward and Master of the King's Cup, living in 1597.

"His eldest son was JOHN, in holy orders, Rector of Southwych, in Sussex Co., Eng., who died A. D. 1616.

"This individual was the father of two sons, THOMAS PELL, b. in Southwyck, in 1608, first proprietor of the Manor of Pelham, and the Rev. John Pell. D. D., Rector of Fobbington, Essex.

"DR. PELL entered Trinity College, Cambridge, Eng. He became an eminent mathematician. His Patron was the PRINCE of Orange, who presented him with the Professorship of Mathematics, at Breda, in Holland. In 1654, he received an appointment from Oliver Cromwell, as English Resident Ambassador, to the Swiss Cantons, and received his letter of recall, from the Protector, May 6, 1658, arriving at home just three weeks previous to the death of his Patron on the 3rd of Sept., 1658.

"By the will of THOMAS PELL, ESQ., he bequeathed all his 'lands and houses in any part of New England, or in the Territory of the Duke of York,' to his nephew John Pell living in Auld England, the only son of his brother John Pell, D. D. John Pell, the legatee, came to America in 1670, and married Rachel Pinckney of East Chester, N. Y."—*See Bolton's History of Westchester, N. Y.*

NOTE XXVIII.

"ABOUT the epoch of the Revocation of the Edict of Nantes (1685), JEAN LOUIS MERLE, of Nismes, who was a sincere Protestant, fled from his country, and took refuge in Switzerland, in order to enjoy the religious liberty which France, under the rule of Louis XIV., denied him.

"His son, FRANCIS MERLE, married, in the year 1743, Elizabeth, the daughter of a Protestant nobleman residing in Geneva, whose name was GEORGE D'AUBIGNÉ. Agreeable to a usage which exists in Geneva, and in many other portions of Switzerland, by which a gentleman adds the name of his wife to his own, in order to distinguish him from other persons of the same name, Mr. Francis Merle appended that of d'Aubigné to his own, and was known as FRANCIS MERLE D'AUBIGNÉ. Since his day, the family have retained the name of Merle d'Aubigné.

"GEORGE D'AUBIGNÉ, just mentioned, whose daughter Elizabeth became the wife of FRANCIS MERLE, was a descendant of Theodore Agrippa d'Aubigné, who left France, in the year 1620, on account of religious persecutions. Theodore Agrippa d'Aubigné was the son of John d'Aubigné, Lord of Brie, in Saintonge, and Catharine de l'Estang, and was born Feb. 8, 1550, O. S. The d'Aubigné pedigree may be traced from Savari d'Aubigné, commander of the castle of Chiron, in France, for the King of England—a descendant of the d'Aubignés of Anjou.

"This Theodore Agrippa d'Aubigné was no common man. The old chronicles called him 'a zealous Calvinist, if there ever was one.' He bought the domain of Lods, near Geneva, on which he built the Château of Crest, which still remains. The old Huguenot warrior handled the pen and the lyre, as well as the sword; and his '*Tragiques*,' a poem full of life and genius, drew a vivid picture of the court of the imbecile Henry III. of France, and his infamous mother Catharine de Medici.

"His '*Histoire Universelle de la fin du 16me Siècle*,' had the honor of being publicly burnt at Paris in the year 1620, by order of Louis XIII. He wrote also the '*Confession de Sancy*,' and several other works. At the age of eight years he knew well the Latin and the Greek languages. At fourteen, he went to Geneva to finish his studies at the University of that city. Having completed his course at that Institution, he returned to France; whence, as has been stated he was compelled to fly in the year 1620."—*Robert Baird.*

"He married first Mademoiselle de Lezey, of St. Gelais, who died in 1595. D'Aubigné left three children, Constant, his only son, (who was the father of Madame de Maintenon), and two daughters. The eldest daughter married the Seigneur d'Adets de Caumont ; the other, the Seigneur de Villette de Murfey. After the death of his first wife he became allied by marriage with the families of the Burlamachi and Calandrini, two of the most honorable families in the city of Geneva, both of Italian origin, for Geneva was the 'City of refuge' to persecuted and exiled Protestants of Italy, as well as of France. D'Aubigné died in 1630."—*Life of Theodore Agrippa d'Aubigné.*

"MARCHIONESS FRANCOISE D'AUBIGNÉ, second wife of Louis XIV. of France, was born in Niort, Nov. 27, 1635. She was the daughter of Constant d'Aubigné, and Jennie de Cardillac, and granddaughter of Theodore Agrippa d'Aubigné, the Huguenot historian of his time, and the friend and companion of Henry IV.

"Madame took the name of MAINTENON, from an estate at Versailles, which the King purchased for her. She was married privately at Versailles, Père la Chaise, in the presence of the Archbishop of Paris.

"FRANCIS MERLE D'AUBIGNÉ had many children, one of whom, AMIE ROBERT MERLE D'AUBIGNÉ, was born in 1755, and was the father of three sons. The oldest was GUILLAUME MERLE D'AUBIGNÉ, a merchant well known for forty years in New York city and Brooklyn.

"The second was the REV. DR. JOHN HENRI MERLE D'AUBIGNÉ, of Geneva, Switzerland, author of the 'History of the Reformation of the 16th Century.'

"The third was JOHN AMIE MERLE D'AUBIGNÉ, a merchant of New Orleans."

NOTE XXIX.

"REV. THOMAS NEWMAN, became a member of the M. E. Church, at the age of sixteen.

"In 1829, he was licensed to preach. He joined the N. Y. Conference in 1831, and afterwards received the following appointments : Saratoga, 1831-2, Chatham, N. Y., 1833, Marbletown, 1834-5, and subsequently, New Windsor, Sugar Loaf, Montgomery, New Paltz, Plattekill, Ellenville and Monroe, Orange Co., N. Y.

His health failing in 1856, he was obliged to retire from the active ministry.

"From 1855 to 1875 he lived in the city of Oswego and town of Granby Centre, N. Y., and one year before his death moved to Fulton, Oswego Co., N. Y.

"He was a good preacher, a faithful pastor, and a conscientious disciplinarian ; and is affectionately remembered by those who came within the circle of his labors.

"He endured the great suffering of his last illness with patience and fortitude. His end was peaceful and full of trust, and of him it may be said, 'He wrapped the drapery of his couch about him, and lay down to pleasant dreams.' "—*Methodist Advocate and Journal.*

NOTE XXX.

"Mary Fletcher Abbott, wife of Rev. Henry C. Abbott, of the Northern N. Y. Conference, and daughter of Rev. Thomas Newman, of the N. Y. Conference, died at Heuvelton, St. Lawrence Co., N. Y., Feb. 2, 1874. She was a woman of rare Christian worth, a cheerful worker in the Church, a devoted wife and mother, a true helpmate to her husband, sharing his anxieties, and helping to bear his burdens. She met with fortitude, and bore without complaint, the peculiar privations and hardships of the Methodist itinerancy. During the thirteen years of her married life, she was abundant in Christian labors.

"The last few months of her life were a season of special trial. During her brief illness she was most of the time delirious, but in her lucid moments, assured her attendants that 'She was going home.' During moments of severe suffering she would whisper that verse of Wesley's hymn,

> "Oh what are all my sufferings here,
> If, Lord, Thou count me meet?"

"Commending the dear children and the loved companion to the God in whom she trusted, she passed through the opened gates in triumph, and entered into rest."—*From the Methodist Advocate and Journal.*

NOTE XXXI.

"The Huguenots, or French Protestants of New Rochelle, came directly from England, and were a part of the 50,000 persecuted who fled into that country four years before the Revocation of the Edict of Nantes.

"This is confirmed by the charter of Trinity Church in New Rochelle, wherein they specify that they fled from France in 1681.

"The cruelties which they suffered in France are beyond anything of the kind on record, and in no age was there ever such a violation of all that is sacred either with relation to God or man; and when we consider the exalted virtues of that glorious band of brothers, we are amazed, while we are delighted with their fortitude and courage. Rather than renounce their Christian principles they endured outrages shocking to humanity, persecutions of unheard of enormity, and death in all its horrors.

"To be a Huguenot was enough to ensure condemnation. Whoever bore this name was imprisoned, arraigned for their lives, and, adhering to their profession, were condemned by merciless judges to the flames. Some of the name and character were murdered in cold blood and massacred without any legal forms of justice.

"On Sunday, Aug. 24, 1572, was perpetrated the massacre of St. Bartholomew. De Thou, a Popish historian, relates that 30,000 perished on this terrible occasion. Another estimates 100,000. In Paris alone they amounted to 10,000, and among the number 500 Huguenot lords, knights and military officers, with several thousand gentlemen.

APPENDIX.   107

"Some of the Huguenot families of New Rochelle, appear to have preserved the memory of that fatal day, by adopting it as a Christian name for their offspring.

"Under the promise of protection from King Charles II. of England, in 1681, the Huguenots of New Rochelle fled from France to England, aided in their escape by the English vessels that lay for some time off the Island of Rhé, opposite La Rochelle, in which they were conveyed to England. Tradition says they were subsequently transported to America in one of the King's ships.

"Bonnefois, or Bouffet's Point, on Davenport's Neck, on the north shore of Long Island Sound, was the spot where they first landed about 1689. Upon this spot the first house was erected, the remains of which are still visible.

"There is a tradition that one of the old Huguenots would daily repair to this place, 'and turning his eyes in the direction where he supposed France was situated, would sing one of Marot's hymns, and send to heaven his morning devotions.'

"The first church edifice of New Rochelle of which anything is known, was built by the Huguenots about 1692–3, upon the site of the present Episcopal Church."—*Bolton's Westchester.*

"Prior to the erection of this church, the devoted inhabitants of this town walked regularly every Sunday to New York, a distance by the road of 23 miles, to attend the Sabbath service of the old Church du St. Esprit, in Pine St., and returned in the evening to their homes. They invariably commenced their march on Sunday morning by singing one of the psalms of Clement Marot.

"Prior to their departure on Sunday, they collected the young children, and left them in the care of friends, while they set off early in the morning and walked to the city barefooted, carrying their shoes and stockings in their hands, stopping by the way to take rest and refreshments, and at a fresh water pond near the city, washing their feet and putting on their shoes and stockings, and then walking to the French Church. They continued to worship after this manner till the American Revolution broke out."—*Recollections of the late John Pintard, L.L.D.*

"The ancestor of the SYCARD or Secor family was AMBROISE SYCARD, who married JENNIE SERROT. They had Ambroise, DANIEL, and Jaques."—*Bolton's History Westchester.*

"DANIEL¹, had DANIEL², jr., whose wife was MARIE; and they had JOHNATHAN, b. Feb. 8, 1742, who married SARAH FLANDREAU, bap. Sept. 9, 1761, (dau. of James and Marie Flandreau). Their dau. MARY, b. March 1778, m. March, 1802, JESSE ADAMS, of Scarsdale, b. April, 1779, (son of Jesse Adams and Sarah Rogers, of White Plains, Westchester Co., N. Y.)

The first persons of the name of FLANDREAU, who came to America, were JACQUES FLANDREAU and his wife, who landed here about 1689. He is referred to as collector at New Rochelle, in 1710. His son JAMES FLANDREAU, b. about 1721, married MARIE —— and had SARAH, bap. Sept. 19, 1751, who married JOHNATHAN SECOR, and had MARY, b. March 1778, and married, March 1802, JESSE ADAMS, of Scarsdale, Westchester Co., N. Y."—*Family Records.*

[Mrs. Armenia Chesbro, of Nottingham, Ohio, oldest child of Jesse and Mary Secor Adams, relates the following tradition, descriptive of the embarkation of her great-great-grandparents, from Rochelle, France.]

"They were very pious Christians, and left France at the time of the persecutions of the Huguenots. They felt that they loved their religion more than they did the things of this world; and being so sadly persecuted and deprived of the enjoyment of it, they determined to leave Rochelle, and find freedom in America.

"A few hours before the time of sailing, they learned that a ship would leave Rochelle in the night. Without informing any of their neighbors of their intention they filled a chest with the best they had, of clothing and other valuables; and a friend, the only one in the secret, drove a dray to the back entrance of the house, upon which they placed the chest, and then loaded the dray to the top with hay, to avoid suspicion; and thus their little all was taken to the ship.

"Then they set the table as for supper, heated the oven, and placed bread therein, leaving the lid down, so that if any one came in they would suppose them to be absent but for a short time. Then, in their common clothes, they quietly walked to the shore, and were taken on board, thus leaving their native land with deep feelings of sadness, but looking forward with joyful anticipations of happiness and freedom in their new home."

[Mrs. Chesbro had the chest in her possession until recently, when she committed it to the care and keeping of her nephew, W. I. Adams, of Montclair, N. J.]

NOTE XXXII.

"Hon. GEORGE BRIGGS was born in Fulton, N. Y., in 1805, and removed with his parents to Vermont in 1812. In 1837, he was elected a member of the lower house of the Vermont Legislature, and served one term; at the end of which he removed to New York in 1838, where he engaged in the hardware business, in which he amassed a large fortune. He was elected as a Whig, to Congress, from New York, in 1849, serving until 1853. In 1858, he was again elected as a representative in the thirty-sixth Congress, and served as Chairman of the Committee on Revolutionary Claims."—*Congressional Reports.*

[As a citizen of New York, the Hon. George Briggs held a deservedly high position, and was much esteemed by all who knew him. He married Charlotte Sweet, daughter of Dr. Sweet, of Shaftsbury, Vt.]

NOTE XXXIII.

WILL *of* CORNELIUS[1] CARHART, *the son of* ROBERT,[1] *and grandson of* THOMAS.[1]

In the name of God, Amen, the eleventh day of February, in the year of our Lord one thousand eight hundred and six, I, Cornelius Carhart, Senr., of Mansfield, in the County of Sussex, and State of New Jersey, being of sound mind and memory, and calling to mind the mortality of my body, and knowing that it is appointed for all men once to die, do make and ordain this my last will and testament, that is to say, principally, and first of all, I give and recommend my soul into the hands of God, who gave it, and for my body, I recommend it to the earth to be buried in Christianlike and decent manner, at the discretion of my executors, nothing doubting, but at the resurrection I shall receive the same again, by the power of God ; and as touching such worldly estate, wherewith it hath pleased God to bless me in this life, I give, devise and dispose of the same in manner and form as following, viz. : In the first place I order that my funeral charges and just debts be paid, likewise, as soon after my decease as may be convenient, I order that my executors hereinafter named, do cause an inventory of all my movable estate to be taken, except such articles as will be hereafter named, and to dispose of them to the best advantage at vendue. And my will is, that the amount of the sales of such movables, after paying my funeral charges and my just debts, be divided amongst my children, and my dearly beloved wife, as undernamed, share and share alike, viz. :

Cornelius, Robert, Samuel and John Carhart, Mary, wife of Robert McShane, Sarah, wife of John Dusenbury, Lydia, wife of James Bowlby, Williamphy, wife of Benjamin Lacy, and Phebe, wife of John Coleman, and my wife, Williamphy. And likewise my will is, that my widow do live in the new house, on the homestead farm, and that my sons, Samuel Carhart and John Carhart, do pay or cause to be paid to my widow, five pounds each, yearly and each year during her natural life, and likewise I order that my son John Carhart do provide, or cause to be provided, everything necessary for my widow's maintenance, and that in a decent and genteel manner ; and likewise my will is, that my widow have for her own proper use, out of my movable estate as under : one feather bed and bedstead and bedding complete, one chest, the dresser, and what may go on it, three chairs, one table, half dozen knives and forks, and what linen or woollen yarn may be on hand at my decease. My will is that my widow have what she chooses for her own use, and likewise one cow, the choice of the flock, three sheep and large brass kettle. Likewise I give unto my son, Robert Carhart, a certain bond of fifty pounds, with what interest may be due thereon, which I have against Cornelius Carhart, Jr., due May the first, one thousand eight hundred and two. Likewise I give and bequeath to my two grandsons, John D. Carhart and Daniel Carhart, ten pounds each, to be paid out of my movable estate. Likewise I give and bequeath to my son John Carhart, one bay horse and young brown mare, wagon and harness for two horses, one plough and irons ; likewise two bonds and two notes, that I have against Cornelius Carhart, Jr., as under one bond of fifty pounds, due May first, one thousand eight hundred and one ; two notes of siz pounds five shillings each, due May first, one thousand eight hundred and three ; and one bond of five hundred dollars, due May first, one thousand eight hundred and six. My will is that the above obligations, principal and interest, are not to be paid to my executors, nor to any other, but that the whole be canceled and of no effect. I likewise give, devise and bequeath to my son John Carhart, my homestead plantation, to him, his heirs and assigns for ever. Likewise I give, devise and bequeath to my son Samuel Carhart, the tavern lot, to him, his heirs and assigns for ever. Likewise my will is that the two wood lots, one bought of Robert Shields, and the other bought of Thomas Bowlby, be equally divided ; and I do give and devise and bequeath to my son John Carhart, his heirs and assigns for ever, one equal half of said lots so divided ; and

110 APPENDIX.

I likewise give and devise and bequeath to my son Samuel Carhart, to him, his heirs and assigns for ever, the other equal half of each lot so divided. Likewise I give and devise and bequeath to my son Robert Carhart, and my daughters, as under named : Mary, wife of Robert McShane, Sarah, wife of John Dusenbury, Lydia, wife of James Bowlby, Williamphy, wife of Benjamin Lucy, Phebe, wife of John Coleman, to them, their heirs and assigns forever, all my lands lying and being in the State of Virginia, share and share alike. I do likewise constitute and appoint Samuel Sherwood and my son Samuel Carhart, to be my sole and lawful executors of this my last will and testament, as witness my hand and seal the date first above written. CORNELIUS CARHART, Sen.

Signed, sealed, published and pronounced and delivered, this to be my last will and testament, in the presence of ROBERT PIERSON.
WILLIAM MILLER.
JOHN SHERWOOD.

NOTE XXXIV.

"JOSEPH BEAVERS was Colonel of the 2nd Regiment, Hunterdon Co., Militia in 1776, and held the office during the Revolutionary War, according to records in the Adjt. General's office, Trenton, N. J. He was of Scotch-Irish descent, and settled in Hunterdon Co. before the war. He was for some time a Justice of the Peace, and remarkable for his love of right doing. His courts were more properly Chancery Courts, than Courts of Law. His judgments were seldom appealed from, and usually not with success. He was also, for some time, a Judge of the Common Pleas, for Hunterdon Co., carrying out his love of right in all his decisions. If the law agreed with his conception of justice, it was well; if not, he decided in accordance with his understanding of it, law or no law. He was a man of stern integrity, and feared no man, in doing what he considered to be his duty. Any one who deserved a reprimand from him, and received it, did not require another from the same source soon. He deprecated law-suits generally, and settled many in a friendly way, without costs. He contributed largely towards building the Presbyterian Church at Greenwich, N. J., in 1775, of which he was a member. One of the pews, of the ancient and orthodox style, was built and owned by Judge Beavers. He owned and managed a large farm, equal to two, at the present time. His family consisted of two sons and thirteen daughters. Joseph, the eldest, died young. George purchased an estate and became the proprietor of the Pattenburgh Mill, now known as Beaver's Mill, near Clinton, N. J. The remains of this Christian patriot were interred in the Cemetery of the Greenwich Church."—*Communicated.*

NOTE XXXV.

"GEORGE BEAVERS CARHART, of Hunterdon Co., N. J., passed many years in the Southern States, connected at times with a number of banking institutions, in different important cities of the South. He was as well, at other periods, engaged in commerce, and for several years President of the N. Y. and N. Haven R. R."—*Communicated.*

NOTE XXXVI.

"SIMRI ROSE, ESQ., born in 1799, at North Branford, Conn., died Dec. 12, 1868, at Macon, Ga. His first American ancestor was Robert Rose, who with Margery, his wife, and seven children, embarked at Ipswich, Co. of Suffolk, Eng., April, 1634, in the ship Francis, John Cutting, master, for the colonies.

"It is not clearly ascertained that this family settled at Watertown, Mass., as was supposed, but it is probable, as they came over in the same ship with several Watertown families, and belonged to the colony that went to settle Wethersfield. Robert Rose was sworn in constable at Wethersfield, Feb. 6, 1639. On the Nanbec farms he had an allottment of 312 acres. In 1644 part of the church at Wethersfield removed to Totokel (Branford) on account of difficulties with their minister, Rev. Henry Smith.

"Robert Rose was one of the eight individuals who purchased the Totokel grant from the first proprietors. He died at Branford, 1664–5, leaving a large estate. His eldest son, John, built the first house in that portion of the grant known now as North Branford, about 1680. According to tradition, he was succeeded by his eldest son, Capt. Johnathan Rose, who died in 1736. This latter left several children. From his second son, David, born 1700, died Sept. 1785, was descended, Simri, of Macon, Ga. It is stated in a church record that both 'David Rose, and Hannah his wife, died of old age.' The epitaph on the tomb of the latter is as follows:

> "From English tyranny she fled,
> And made a safe retreat.
> She now is free among the dead;
> Her soul immortal great."

"Simri Rose went to Macon, Ga., when it was but an unimportant, frontier town, and there made his home.

"He was Editor and Proprietor of a paper, called the 'Macon Messenger,' from the time of its foundation until his death. It is at the present day one of the influential papers of the State.

"Simri Rose was a public spirited and influential citizen; always taking an interest in every enterprise that tended towards the prosperity of Macon. It was due to his influence and personal exertions that the 'Rose Hill Cemetery' was founded, one of the finest in the State, and which still bears his name."—*Communicated.*

NOTE XXXVII.

"COL. EDMUND BLOUNT, of Sodington, Co. Worcester, England, emigrated with two brothers, to North Carolina, and lived near Plymouth.

"He was well known in that state, and was actively engaged with a military force, during the revolutionary struggle with England, quelling the disturbances of the Tories and preventing their inroads upon the farms and the families of those who had gone to the war.

APPENDIX.

"He was at times a Member of the Legislature, and, when at home, the general benefactor of the poor; his house being noted for the generous hospitality it afforded.

"COL. EDMUND BLOUNT, married a Miss Rhodes; and by her had issue. JAMES BLOUNT ESQ., who married ELIZABETH GREGOIRE DE ROULHAC, b. Oct. 4, 1786, daughter of PSALMET GREGOIRE DE ROULHAC, of the Hermitage, Beaufort, N. C.

"PSALMET GREGOIRE DE ROULHAC, was a member of the noble family of de Roulhac, of Limoges, France, and came to North Carolina, in 1777, as agent for a commercial house in France. He married in 1783, Miss Annie Maule, a lady of wealth, residing on the Pamlico river, in the vicinity of a little town called Washington.

"JAMES BLOUNT, ESQ., removed to Georgia in the early part of this century. His daughter, LAVINA HELEN ELIZABETH BLOUNT, married SIMRI ROSE of Macon, Ga., and their daughter, MARY E. ROSE, married GEORGE BEAVERS CARHART."—*Communicated.*

NOTE XXXVIII.

CHARLES[4] CARHART, son of JOHN, and great grandson of CORNELIUS[1], resides at Perryville, Hunterdon Co., N. J., and owns a large portion of the homestead of his grand-uncle, CORNELIUS[2]. He has been untiring in his exertions, and unsparing in liberality, in tracing the Carhart history.

I have permission to speak here of an affliction of which Charles Carhart has sustained the life-long and saddening trial; which is, that he has not heard the sound of the human voice since his twelfth year, having lost his hearing from scarlet fever. Notwithstanding this affliction, he has lived a most active life, and found enjoyment and happiness where many would have yielded to repinings and despair.—*M. E. C. D.*

NOTE XXXIX.

"MR. KENYON, is a practical machinist and manufacturer, at Raritan, N. J. He has made many valuable improvements in machinery for the manufacture of woolen goods, which have been introduced into the woolen manufactories of Massachusetts, New Hampshire, New York, New Jersey and Ohio, and his patented machines are in use in almost every country of the world.

"Mr. Kenyon is grand-nephew of the founder of Kenyon College, Ohio, and is descended from the N. Y. branch of the Kenyon family. He is a second cousin of Congressman Kenyon, of N. Y. state. He is connected, on his mother's side, with the Crane family, of Elizabeth, N. J., whose ancestors left England during the reign of Charles II., having been obliged to flee from religious persecution. Their ancestor was Stephen Crane, who came with a company of 113, in the ship Caledonia, which they had repaired and fitted out at their own expense. The vessel was wrecked off the coast of Amboy, N. J., but all reached the shore in safety. They were among the first settlers of Elizabeth, N. J., where many of their descendants still reside."—*Communicated.*

NOTE XL.

From the Clinton, N. J., Democrat.—"The announcement of the sudden death of Mr. JAMES D. CARHART, long a prominent merchant of New York, which occurred on the 23d ult., at the Albemarle Hotel, N. Y., was received with profound regret by his many friends in this vicinity. It seems by the Macon, Ga., papers, that the sad news also caused a severe shock in that city. We quote from The Macon Telegraph and Messenger of that city, the following sketch of deceased:

"Mr. Carhart was born on the 2d day of May, 1815, in Hunterdon county, New Jersey, and was consequently in the 63d year of his age. He came to Macon in 1831, and for a number of years was employed as clerk by Wm. B. Parker, at that time one of the leading merchants of Macon. His first lessons in business were received from Mr. Parker, who was an intelligent, honorable and high-toned gentleman, and an admirable model for the young men in his employ. When Mr. Parker retired from active business, Mr. Carhart formed a copartnership with the late Isaac Scott. After the dissolution of this firm, he associated his brother, William B. Carhart, and John B. Stow in business with him, under the firm name of Carhart, Bro. & Co., and, as a member of that firm, was for many years one of the most successful and influential merchants of our city. In February, 1852, Messrs. Carhart, Brother & Co., sold their business to Carhart & Roff, and on the 20th of May, 1852, removed to New York, to avail themselves of the facilities of that great city for the expansion of their business. On the day previous to their departure from Macon, a complimentary dinner was given them at the Lanier House, at which the honored James Rea, the Nestor of our merchants presided; and the account of the dinner which appears in the files of The Journal and Messenger, shows very clearly the high appreciation in which Mr. Carhart and his partner were held by the mercantile community of Macon. Upon the wider theater of action to which he removed he was as successful as he had been in this city and to the day of his death he was a model of method, regularity, promptness, devotion to his business, and fidelity to all his engagements.

"When the war between the States began, Mr. Carhart and his brother, William B. Carhart, came promptly to the South, and remained in Georgia until the surrender, sharing with its people the losses, the sacrifices, the privations, and the anxieties of that memorable struggle. Though doing business in New York, he has always regarded our city as in some sense his home, has made large investments in the State, and has kept up a constant and close intercourse with its business men. He was familiarly and intimately known to many of the oldest citizens, who will receive with profound sorrow and regret the announcement of his death. Mr. Carhart married Miss Sarah Curd, of this city, a daughter of Mrs. Sarah E. Curd, in 1846, who, with four children, survives him.

"He was an exemplary man in all the relations of life, and his career as a merchant was eminently honorable and successful. He was fortunate in his life and fortunate in his death, for his sun sank suddenly from its meridian, and he died in the full possession of all his powers."

NOTE XLI.

Cornelius[2] Carhart, son of Cornelius,[1] of Sussex Co., settled at what is now known as Perryville, Hunterdon Co., N. J.

The oldest real estate owned by the Carhart family in Hunterdon Co., is a property on the Old Post Road, between New Brunswick and Easton, Pa., being about fourteen miles from the latter place. This estate was purchased by Cornelius[2], great grandson of Thomas[1], about 1788-90, and then comprised about 200 acres. Here Cornelius built a good substantial house, and the necessary farm buildings, which are still in a good state of preservation, and here, as the years came and went, the lapse of time was marked by prosperity, and the family circle was enlarged to a goodly number. About 1812, Cornelius commenced building a hotel a short distance from his residence, for the better accommodation of wayfarers in a sparsely inhabited country. The house was situated on the Post Road, and is known at the present day as the Brick Hotel, and the place and surroundings, as Perryville. This name was adopted from the following facts and circumstances:—Soon after the building was finished news came of the victory of Perry on Lake Erie, and as the place was without a special name, and was fast becoming worthy of that honor, it was proposed to call it Perryville, thus commemorating the victory and the name of the hero.

Prosperity in wealth and increase in numbers seems to have prevailed with the Carharts of Perryville, and the grand-nephews of Cornelius now own about 2000 acres in the vicinity. A large portion, together with the family home, is owned by Charles Carhart, above mentioned as the patron of the Record (See Note 38).—*M. E. C. D.*

NOTE XLII.

Samuel Carhart, Superintendent of the temperance-incorporated borough of Ocean Beach, died of apoplexy at that place, on May 13, 1879, while waiting with some friends the arrival of the train of the Long Branch Division of the Central New Jersey R.R.

He was 44 years of age, and was apparently in his usual health until he was stricken with this disease.

He was a pioneer Surveyor on the Central R.R. line, along the seashore, and was engaged in the Civil Engineer Corps of the Central R.R. on the proposed new road from Sea Girt to Tom's River.

He had also been employed on different railroads in his professional capacity. He was President of Ocean Beach, and one of the founders of the prosperous young village wherein he had made his home.

On the breaking out of the late war, he was appointed Captain of the 31st N. J. Regiment. His service in this capacity having expired he was appointed Provost Marshal of Elizabeth; both of which positions he filled satisfactorily.

He was highly respected in the community in which he lived, and was one of the best known citizens of Monmouth Co. He was buried under Masonic direction.—*M. E. C. D.*

NOTE XLIII.

"John Carhart may be said to have founded the village of Zion, Md. When he took possession of this land it was in a most unpromising condition, worn out and overgrown with scrub pine and almost without fences. There was a log church (Methodist), called Zion Church, and two or three small houses. With the energy and perseverance of one determined to conquer, he commenced agricultural improvements. He put up good buildings and fences, underdrained wet lands, and by the free use of fertilizers, has made " the wilderness to blossom as the rose." He also built a store, which was conducted by himself and sons, and a substantial brick church, (Presbyterian) was erected on his land, under his supervision. Around this nucleus, a thriving village has sprung up. The farmers, one by one, have followed his example in cultivating and improving their lands, and now the country around, as far as the eye can reach, is dotted with comfortable houses, surrounded by fields of grain and other farm products, and enclosed by good fences. Much of this improvement can be traced to the influence of the moral force and physical energy of John Carhart, and his truly estimable wife and family. The sons, six in number, are prosperously engaged in mercantile pursuits, in Philadelphia and Oxford, Pa., and Zion, Md.

"J. C. is interested and active in all public enterprise, and has been a trustee in the Presbyterian Church for thirty years. Being in his 76th year he has lived to pass the fiftieth anniversary of his wedding day in health and prosperity."—*M. E. C. D.*

NOTE XLIV.

JOHN LARISON, a Danish nobleman, in the reign of Frederick III of Denmark, lost his estates by confiscation, and was obliged to flee from his country in consequence of political disturbances growing out of a conspiracy, in 1660, between the clergy and burghers, in the interest of the King, with the design of humbling the nobles by the imposition of taxes, from which they had previously been exempt.

The nobles were stubborn in their resistance, but were at last obliged to yield, and the most prominent leaders became liable to imprisonment or death.

John Larison fled to Scotland, and learning that a price was set upon his head, he came to America, about the year 1700, and purchased a large tract of land near Brooklyn, N. Y. He lived to an advanced age, and died at Chester, Morris Co., N. J. He had six sons, two of whom were killed by the Indians. The others were Roger, James, William and John.

Roger Larison, his son, settled in Pennsylvania.

William and John located at Chester, Morris Co., N. J. The estate of William, on the North bank of the Black River, opposite the Chester Depot, is still in possession of his descendants. In the centre of this tract of 300 acres, is a large burying-ground, in which once stood a Presbyterian church, (now removed to the village of Chester.) In this grave-yard are buried the Larison descendants of nearly two generations, as many marble stones bear witness.

William Larison d. at Chester, Sept. 1777, leaving three sons; Andrew James and David.

The late Wm. Larison, A. M., a Master in Chancery in Chicago, was a grandson of James. He was graduated at Oberlin College, Ohio, in 1847, and died in 1872.

J. Jay Larison, of Mecklenberg, Schuyler Co., N. Y., is a grandson of David.

JAMES LARISON, (son of John, of Denmark) b. about 1695, purchased 242 acres of land at Hopewell, Mercer Co., N. J., in 1740. He died there in 1792, aged 97 years. He had nine children, only three of whom left male descendants. These were, 1. ANDREW, 2. Roger, 3. David.

ANDREW LARISON, b. 1738, d. in 1800, and is buried in the Old Episcopal Churchyard, at Ringoes, N. J. His sons were, 1. GEORGE, 2. JAMES. 3. Andrew, 4. Benjamin.

1. GEORGE, married Catharine Lambert, dau. of Ex.-Gov. Lambert of N. J., and had LAVINA, who married SAMUEL CARHART.

2. Roger Larison, lived in Bethlehem Township, Hunterdon Co., N. J., and had James, Theodore and John. The Rev. John Larison, of Ridgbury, Bradford Co., Pa., is a son of Theodore.

3. David had two sons, Amos, and Johnathan, whose descendants reside near Cincinnatti.

2. JAMES LARISON, (son of ANDREW) b. Nov. 3, 1765, m. Kesiah Holcombe, (dau. of Jacob Holcombe). James d. July 25, 1848. Kesiah d. Oct. 23, 1854. They lived near Evartstown, Hunterdon Co., N. J., and had Lavina, b. July 25, 1788, who m. Samuel Britton. Rachel, b. Aug. 15, 1791, m. John Van Syckel. KESIAH, b. July 8, 1811, m. Sept. 25, 1829, JOHN CARHART.

4. Benjamin Larison, (son of ANDREW), b. Jan. 5, 1806, resides near Stockton, N. J. He has four sons.

1. George Larison, M. D. of Lambertsville, N. J. 2. Cornelius W. Larison, Prof. of Natural Science, in the University of Lewisburg, Pa. 3. Rev. Andrew B. Larison, Pastor of the Baptist Church at Ringoes, N. J., and Principal of the Seminary at that place. 4. John D. Larison, an extensive farmer at Stockton, N. J.—*Collated from History of Denmark, and Family Records.*

NOTE XLV.

To the patient labors of ELWOOD CARHART, many of the New Jersey branches owe the fact that their names appear in this record. But for him and his cousins, CHARLES and AMORY SIBLEY, the Carhart record would not have been published in its present comprehensive form; and many facts and traditions would probably have become confused or obliterated in the lapse of time, and the descendants have lost the knowledge of their origin.—*M. E. C. D.*

INDEX.

DESCENDANTS *by the name of* CARHART, *from* JOHN,[1] *of Rye, Westchester County, N. Y.*

	PAGE
Abraham, son of Sanford, of Gilderland, N. Y.,	42
Ada Newton, dau. of Robert,[3] of Gilderland, N. Y.,	42
Ada R., of Marion, Ohio,	28
Addie Sweet, dau. of Edwin M., of New Baltimore, N. Y.,	38
Adelia Cora, dau. of William Edgar, of Baltimore, Md.,	53
Adeline, m. Allen, dau. of Isaac A., of Binghamton, N. Y.,	52
Alanson, son of James, of Coeymans, N. Y.,	35
Albert Elijah, son of John, of Grinnell, Iowa,	44
Albert, son of John, of Newtown, L. I., N. Y.,	52
Alfred,[1] son of Hackaliah, of West Greenwich, Conn.,	48
Alfred, son of Ambrose, of Oxford, N. Y.,	30
Alfred, of Milwaukie, son of John Weed, of Chicago, Ill.,	27
Alfred, son of Levi, of Schodack, N. Y.,	40
Alfred Bangs, son of Rev. Lewis Henry, of Texas,	36
Alice Elizabeth, m. Ferro, dau. of Jeremiah, of N. Y.,	28
Almeda Matilda, m. Brown, of Marion, Ohio,	29
Amanda, m. Strong ; m. 2d, Davids, of Chicago, Ill.,	27
Ambrose, of Oxford, Chenango Co., N. Y.,	30
Andrew Rickey, son of Isaac D., of Trempealeau, Wis.,	36
Angeline B., m. Murray, dau. of Thomas D., of Albany, N. Y.,	43
Angie Electa, dau. of Peter S., of Collamer, N. Y.,	46
Ann Augusta, dau. of Fletcher, of Brooklyn, N. Y.,	41
Ann Eliza, m. Willson, dau. of Hackaliah,[2] of Conn.,	47
Ann Elizabeth, dau. of John, of Dutchess Co., N. Y.,	57
Anna Georgine, dau. of Lyman Beecher, of Peekskill, N. Y.,	49
Anna G., dau. of Leonard, of Coeymans, N. Y.,	41
Anna Maria, dau. of Peter, of Albany, N. Y.,	41
Annie, m. Cregier, dau. of Thomas,[3] of Bethlehem, N. Y.,	34
Annie, m. Gedney, dau. of Thomas,[2] of Rye, N. Y.,	31
Annie, m. Losee, dau. of Jordan, of Dutchess Co., N. Y.,	57
Annie, m. Owens, dau. of John,[3] of Oxford, N. Y.,	28
Annie, m. Titus, dau. of Daniel,[2] of Coeymans, N. Y.,	37
Annie, m. Utter, dau. of Daniel,[1] of Coeymans, N. Y.,	35
Annie, dau. of David Wood, of Berlin, Wis.,	27
Annie, dau. of George Henry, of Bedford, N. Y.,	47
Annie, dau. of Joshua,[1] of Washington, Dutchess County, N. Y.,	57
Annie, dau. of Robert, of Whitestown, N. Y.,	33
Annie, dau. of Solomon, of Coeymans, N. Y.,	39
Archibald McBean, son of Richard, of Chicago, Ill.,	41
Arlington, son of Elliott, of Macon City, Mo.,	29
Arthur L., son of Elliott, of Macon City, Mo.,	29
Barbara Ann, m. Huntley, dau. of Isaac, of Manlius, N. Y.,	45
Barbara, m. Rowe, dau. of Daniel,[1] of Coeymans, N. Y.,	46
Barbara, m. Terry, dau. of Daniel,[2] of Coeymans, N. Y.,	38

INDEX.

	PAGE
Barbara Lavinia, dau. of Daniel S., of Coeymans, N. Y.,	38
Benjamin Irving, son of Edwin M., of New Baltimore, N. Y.,	38
Bessie Merle, dau. of Lyman Beecher, of Peekskill, N. Y.,	49
Calvin, son of Daniel,[2] of Coeymans, N. Y.,	39
Calvin, son of Edward E., of New Baltimore, N. Y.,	39
Caroline, m. Post, dau. of John Weed, of Chicago, Ill.,	27
Caroline E., dau. of Calvin, of Coeymans, N. Y.,	39
Carrie, dau. of Wm. H., of New York city,	57
Carrington Elliott, son of Elliott, of Macon City, Mo.,	29
Carroll Kearns, son of William Edgar, of Baltimore, Md.,	53
Catharine, m. Armstrong, dau. of Hackaliah,[2] of Coeymans, N. Y.,	40
Catharine, dau. of Solomon[2], of New York city,	40
Catharine, m. Brasher, dau. of Elisha, of Albany, N. Y.,	43
Catharine, m. Leyden, dau. of Isaac, of Manlius, N. Y.,	45
Catharine, m. Tuttle, dau. of Solomon[1], of Coeymans, N. Y.,	39
Catharine, m. Van Vosberg, dau. of Levi, of Schodack, N. Y.,	40
Catharine Amanda, dau. of Hackaliah[2], of Conn.,	48
Catharine E., dau. of Thomas D., of Albany, N. Y.,	43
Catharine R., m. Hotaling, dau. of Daniel Sutton, of Coeymans, N. Y.,	37
Catharine R., m. Ward, dau. of Henry, of Gilderland, N. Y.,	37
Celia M., dau. of James Isaac, of New York city,	52
Charles, son of Ambrose, of Oxford, N. Y.,	30
Charles, son of Charles Burt, of Chicago, Ill.,	52
Charles, son of Fletcher, of Brooklyn, N. Y.,	41
Charles, son of Joshua[2], of Brooklyn, N. Y.,	53
Charles, son of Rev. John Wesley, of Oshkosh, Wis.,	38
Charles, son of Sanford, of Gilderland, N. Y.,	42
Charles Albert, son of Richard, of Chicago, Ill.,	41
Charles Burt, of Chicago, son of Isaac, of Binghamton, N. Y.,	52
Charles Hight, son of Daniel M., of Cleveland, Ohio,	51
Charles Lyman, son of Lyman Beecher, of Peekskill, N. Y.,	49
Charles Watkinson, son of William Edgar, of Baltimore, Md.,	53
Charlotte Ophelia, m. White, dau. of Isaac D., of Trempealeau, Wis.,	36
Charlotte, dau. of Daniel Matthews, of Cleveland, Ohio,	51
Charlotte, m. Vanderheyden, dau. of Nicholas, of Coeymans, N. Y.,	35
Charlotte, dau. of Daniel Matthews, of Cleveland, Ohio,	51
Clara, dau. of Lewis, of Dubuque, Iowa,	29
Clara, dau. of Stephen, of Columbus, Ohio,	29
Clara, m. Van Vosberg, dau. of Levi, of Schodack, N. Y.,	40
Clara Josephine, dau. of Isaac D., of Trempealeau, Wis.,	37
Clara Virginia, dau. of William Edgar, of Baltimore, Md.,	53
Claude Mortimer, son of William Edgar, of Baltimore, Md.,	53
Clorinia, m. Durie, dau. of Thomas,[3] of Bethlehem, N. Y.,	34
Cora B., dau. of Richard, of Chicago, Ill.,	41
Daniel[1], of Rye, and Coeymans, N. Y.,	34
Daniel[2], son of Daniel[1], of Coeymans, N. Y.,	35
Daniel, son of John[4], of Guilford Centre, N. Y.,	31
Daniel H., of Pleasant Plains, N. Y.,	56
Daniel Matthews, son of Isaac, of Binghamton, N. Y.,	51
Daniel Matthews, Jr., son of Daniel Matthews, of Cleveland, Ohio,	51
Daniel Sutton, son of Daniel[2], of Coeymans, N. Y.,	37
Darius, son of Henry, of Oxford, N. Y.,	29
David Wood, of Berlin, son of John Weed, of Chicago, Ill.,	27
Deborah, dau. of Daniel[2], of Coeymans, N. Y.,	38
Delia Huntley, dau. of Isaac D., of Trempealeau, Wis.,	36
Edith Adelaide, dau. of Elliott, of Macon City, Mo.,	29
Edward, son of Alanson, of Coeymans, N. Y.,	35

INDEX. 119

	PAGE
Edward E., son of Calvin, of Coeymans, N. Y.,	39
Edward, son of Solomon,[2] of New York city,	40
Edward Chesebro, son of John, of Grinnell, Iowa.	44
Edward E., son of Rev. John Wesley, of Oshkosh, Wis.,	38
Edward W., son of Daniel, of Pleasant Plains, N. Y.,	56
Edwin M., of New Baltimore, N. Y.,	38
Edwin, son of Fletcher, of Brooklyn, N. Y.,	41
Elenor, dau. of Stephen, son of Henry, of Oxford, N. Y.,	29
Elijah B., son of James, of Pontiac, Mich.,	33
Elisha, son of Thomas D., of Albany, N. Y.,	43
Eliza, m. Ball, dau. of James,[2] of Coeymans, N. Y.,	35
Eliza, m. Carhart, dau. of Robert, of Gilderland, N. Y.,	37 & 41
Eliza, m. Osgood, of Troy, N. Y.,	29
Eliza J., dau. of Elisha, of Albany, N. Y.,	43
Elizabeth, m. Adams, dau. of Hackaliah, of Conn.,	54
Elizabeth Ann, m. Clark, of Auburn, Mich.,	33
Elizabeth, m. Terry, dau. of Daniel,[2] of Coeymans, N. Y.,	37
Elizabeth, m. Tucker, of Oxford, N. Y.,	31
Elizabeth, m. Wilkins, of Cicero, N. Y.,	44
Elizabeth, dau. of Joshua,[1] of Dutchess Co., N. Y.,	57
Elizabeth, dau. of Hackaliah,[2] of Coeymans, N. Y.,	39
Elizabeth Ann, dau. of Lewis, of Dubuque, Iowa,	29
Ella Almeda, of Marion, Ohio,	28
Ella M., dau. of Leonard, of Coeymans, N. Y.,	41
Ellen, dau. of Robert B., of Grand Travers, Mich.,	33
Ellen D., dau. of James, of Oxford, N. Y.,	28
Elliott, of Macon City, Mo.,	29
Elma Maria, m. Cannon, dau. of Alfred,[1] of New York,	48
Elma, m. Redfield, dau. of Hackaliah,[1] of Connecticut,	48
Elma, m. Swaney, dau. of Peter, of Janesville, Wis.,	40
Elma, m. Weaver, dau. of Robert, of Gilderland, N. Y.,	42
Elmira C., m. Flagler, dau. of Elisha, of Albany, N. Y.,	43
Elmer Howard, son of Peter, of Collamer, N. Y.,	46
Eloise Ophelia, dau. of Lyman Beecher, of Peekskill, N. Y.,	49
Emily J., dau. of Edwin M., of New Baltimore, N. Y.,	38
Emma Frances, m. Allen, of Clarendon, Texas,	36
Emma, dau. of George W., M. D., of Jackson, Mich.,	33
Emma, dau. of William, of Albany, N. Y.,	42
Erastus, son of John,[4] of Guilford Centre, N. Y.,	31
Ernest McAlpine, son of William Edgar, of Baltimore, Md.,	53
Ervietta, dau. of Sylvanus, of Guilford, N. Y.,	31
Estelle, dau. of James, of Pontiac, Mich.,	33
Esther, m. Towne, dau. of James, of Waterford, N. Y.,	35
Everest L., son of Richard, of Chicago, Ill.,	41
Fanny L., m. Meadon, of Greenpoint, L. I.,	42
Fanny, dau. of Stephen, of Columbus, Ohio,	29
Fletcher, son of Solomon,[1] of Coeymans, N. Y.,	41
Frances, dau. of Solomon,[2] of New York city,	40
Frances Henrietta, m. Terry, dau. of Alfred,[1].	49
Frances Matilda, m. Ives, dau. of Erastus, of Guilford, N. Y.,	31
Frances Terry, dau. of Edward E., of New Baltimore, N. Y.,	39
Frank, son of Fletcher, of Brooklyn, N. Y.,	41
Frank Billops, son of William Edgar, of Baltimore, Md.,	53
Frederick, son of Daniel Matthews, of Cleveland, Ohio,	51
Frederick, son of Fletcher, of Brooklyn, N. Y.,	41
Frederick, son of John,[4] of Guilford Centre, N. Y.,	31
Frederick Mark, son of Charles Burt, of Chicago, Ill.,	52

INDEX.

	PAGE
Galileo, of Grand Travers, Mich.,	33
Garret, of Washington, D. C., son of Solomon[2], of New York,	40
Garretson Lyon, M. D., of Marion, Iowa,	42
Gedney, son of Henry Augustus, of Brooklyn, N. Y.,	52
George, son of Fletcher, of Brooklyn N. Y.,	41
George, son of George W., of Albany, N. Y.,	43
George, son of James, of Pontiac,	33
George, son of Joshua[2], of Brooklyn, N. Y.,	53
George Arthur, son of Alfred, of Milwaukie, Wis.,	27
George B., son of James, of Oxford, N. Y.,	28
George Bancroft, son of Dr. Garretson L., of Marion, Iowa,	42
George Escott, son of George Whitfield, of New York city,	27
George Henry, son of William H., of Brooklyn, N. Y.,	47
George Henry, Jr., of Bedford, N. Y.,	47
George N., son of Stephen, of Oxford, N. Y.,	30
George R., son of Daniel H., of Pleasant Plains, N. Y.,	56
George T., son of Richard, of Chicago, Ill.,	41
George W., son of William, of Albany, N. Y.,	43
George W., M. D., of Jackson, Mich.,	33
George Washington, son of Isaac, of Binghamton, N. Y.,	52
George Whitfield, son of John Weed, of Chicago, Ill.,	27
George Williams, of Marion, Ohio,	28
Georgianna, dau. of George N., of Oxford, N. Y.,	30
Gertrude, dau. of David Wood, of Berlin, Wis.,	27
Grace, dau. of John Weed, jr., of Appleton, Wis.,	27
Hackaliah, of Penn Yann, son of Solomon[1], of Coeymans, N. Y.,	40
Hackaliah[1], of West Greenwich, Conn., son of Thomas[2],	47
Hackaliah, son of Daniel[1], of Coeymans, N. Y.,	39
Hackaliah[2], son of Hackaliah[1],	47
Hackaliah, son of John[3], of Oxford, N. Y.,	27
Hallie, son of Rev. John Wesley, of Oshkosh, Wis.,	38
Hamilton B., of Grand Rapids, Mich.,	33
Hannah, dau. of James[2], of Coeymans, N. Y.,	35
Hannah, m. Hovey, of Lowell, Mass.,	27
Hannah, m. Van Cleft, dau. of Nicholas, of Coeymans, N. Y.,	35
Hannah A., dau. of James, of Oxford, N. Y.,	28
Hannah Anderson, m. Lyon, dau. of Hackaliah, of Conn.,	50
Hannah M., m. Mowrey, of Oxford, N. Y.,	30
Hannah M., m. Smith, of San Francisco, Cal.,	52
Hannah Maria, dau. of Isaac, of Manlius, N. Y.,	46
Harriet, m. Evander, dau. of James[2],	35
Harriet, m. Pipe, dau. of Hackaliah, of Coeymans, N. Y.,	40
Harriet L., dau. of James, of Pontiac, Mich.,	33
Harriet N., dau. of Stephen, of Oxford, N. Y.,	30
Harrison, son of Isaac, of Oxford, N. Y.,	28
Harrison, son of Lewis, of Dubuque, Iowa,	29
Harvey, son of Lewis, of Dubuque, Iowa,	29
Helen, dau. of Wm. H., of New York city,	57
Henrietta, m. Clark, dau. of Hackaliah, of Coeymans, N. Y.,	40
Henrietta, m. Smith, of Fox Lake, Wis.,	27
Henry, son of Daniel,[2] of Coeymans, N. Y.,	37
Henry, son of James, of Babylon, L. I.,	46
Henry, son of John[3], of Oxford, N. Y.,	28
Henry, son of Lewis, of Dubuque, Iowa,	29
Henry, son of Nicholas, of Coeymans, N. Y.,	35
Henry, son of Peter, of Janesville, N. Y.,	40
Henry Augustus, son of Joshua,[2] of Brooklyn,	52
Henry Dunstan, son of Isaac, of Manlius, N. Y.,	46

INDEX.

	PAGE
Henry Smith, Prof., of Evanston, Ill.,	38
Herbert, of Marion, Ohio,	29
Herbert Addison, son of Peter, of Collamer, N. Y.,	46
Hester, m. Furbeck, dau. of Isaac, of Manlius, N. Y.,	46
Hiram, son of Robert, of Whitestown, N. Y.,	33
Howard, son of George W., of Albany, N. Y.,	43
Huldah A., m. Hallenbeck, of Gilderland, N. Y.,	43
H. Wilber, son of Leonard, of Coeymans, N. Y.,	41
Ida, dau. of George Henry, of Bedford, N. Y.,	47
Ida, dau. of Stephen, of Columbus, Ohio,	29
Ida C., m. Gifford, of Oxford, N. Y.,	30
Ida May, of Warrensburg, Mo.,	29
Ira, son of Nicholas, of Coeymans, N. Y.,	35
Irene, dau. of Robert, of Gilderland, N. Y.,	42
Isaac, of Manlius, N. Y.,	43
Isaac, son of Henry, of Oxford, N. Y.,	28
Isaac, son of John,[3] of Oxford, N. Y.,	28
Isaac Anderson, son of Hackaliah, of Conn.,	51
Isaac Anderson, jr., son of Isaac A., of Binghamton, N. Y.,	52
Isaac D., son of Daniel,[2] of Coeymans, N. Y.,	36
Isaac Rowe, son of Isaac, of Manlius, N. Y.,	46
Isaac Whitfield, of Hot Springs, Ark.,	36
Jacob Edward, son of Elisha, of Albany, N. Y.,	43
Jacob Gurney, son of Edwin M., of New Baltimore, N. Y.,	38
James[1], of Babylon, L. I., N. Y.,	46
James, of Pontiac, Mich.,	33
James[2], son of Daniel[1], of Coeymans, N. Y.,	34
James, son of Henry Augustus,	52
James, son of John[3], of Oxford, N. Y.,	28
James, son of Nathan, of Bethlehem, N. Y.,	33
James, son of Richard, of Dutchess Co., N. Y.,	56
James Alfred, son of Alfred[1],	49
James Henry, son of James Isaac, of New York,	52
James Isaac, son of Isaac, of Binghamton, N. Y.,	52
James W., son of William, of Albany, N. Y.,	42
Jane, dau. of George Henry, of Bedford, N. Y.,	47
Jane, dau. of John, of Dutchess Co., N. Y.,	57
Jane, m. Waldron, of Waterford, N. Y.,	35
Jane Eliza, m. Terry, dau. of Solomon,[1] of Coeymans, N. Y.,	40
Jannette, m. Fisher, dau. of Joshua[2], of Brooklyn, N. Y.,	53
Jasper, of Boston, son of Solomon[2], of New York,	40
Jennie, dau. of Thomas[3], of Bethlehem, New York,	34
Jeremiah, son of Isaac, of Oxford, N. Y.,	28
Jerretta, dau. of Jeremiah, of New York,	28
Jesse F., son of Stephen, of Albany, N. Y.,	43
Jesse Peck, son of Rev. Lewis Henry, of Texas,	36
John[1], of Rye, N. Y.,	25
John[2], of Rye, N. Y.,	26
John[3], of Oxford, N. Y.,	26
John[4], of Guilford Centre, N. Y.,	31
John, of Grinnell, Iowa,	44
John, son of George W., M. D., of Jackson, Mich.,	33
John, son of Joshua[1], of Dutchess Co., N. Y.,	56
John, son of Joshua[2], of Brooklyn, N. Y.,	52
John, son of Richard of Dutchess Co., N. Y.,	56
John Burton, son of Arlington, Manchester, Iowa,	29
John Derbin, son of Isaac, of Binghamton, N. Y.,	52

122 INDEX.

	PAGE
John Melvin, son of Sylvanus, of Guilford Centre, N. Y.,	31
John McKendrie, son of Isaac D., of Trempealeau, Iowa,	36
John Weed, of Chicago, Ill.,	27
John Weed. jr., of Appleton, Wis.,	27
John Wesley, Rev., of Oshkosh, Wis.,	38
Jordan, son of Joshua[1], of Dutchess Co., N. Y.,	56
Joshua[1], son of Thomas[2], of Rye, N. Y.,	55
Joshua[2], son of Hackaliah[1], of Conn.,	52
Judith, m. Martin, of Ellington, Minn.,	40
Judson, son of James, of Pontiac, Mich.,	33
Julia S., dau. of Edwin M., of New Baltimore, N. Y.,	38
Kate, m. Balmer, dau. of Jeremiah, of New York,	28
Kate Louise, m. Cook, dau. of Isaac Rowe, of Manlius, N. Y.,	46
Katie Gertrude, dau. of Albert Elijah, of Iowa,	44
Lafayette, son of Robert, of Whitestown, N. Y.,	33
Lafayette J., son of James, of Pontiac, Mich.,	33
Laura A., dau. of Stephen, of Oxford, New York,	30
Lavinia A., m. Munson, dau. of Alfred[1],	49
Leila, dau. of Wm. H., of New York city,	57
Lena Bell, dau. of Elliott, of Macon city, Mo.,	29
Leonard, son of John, of Newtown, L. I.,	52
Leonard A., son of Solomon, of Coeymans, N. Y.,	41
Leonard Romaine, son of Leonard A.,	41
Lester Brown, of Hampton, Iowa,	45
Levi, of Schodack, N. Y.,	40
Lewis, of Dubuque, Iowa,	29
Lewis, jr., son of Lewis, of Dubuque,	29
Lewis, son of Nicholas, of Coeymans, N. Y.,	35
Lewis Henry, Rev., of Clarendon, Texas,	36
Lewis P., son of Richard, of Chicago, Ill.,	41
Lilly Ruth, dau. of Wm. Edgar, of Baltimore, Md.,	53
Lizzie Adeline, dau. of Charles Burt, of Chicago, Ill.,	52
Louise M., m. Caswell, of Coeymans, N. Y.,	35
Lucinda, dau. of Sylvanus, of Guilford Centre, N. Y.,	31
Lucius Alfred, of Marion, Ohio,	28
Lucretia, m. Brown, of Pontiac, Mich.,	33
Lucy, dau. of Alanson, of Coeymans, N. Y.,	35
Lyman Beecher, of Peekskill, N. Y.,	49
Margaret, dau. of John Weed, of Chicago, Ill.,	27
Margaret, m. Newman, of Fulton, N. Y.,	54
Margaret A., m. Hauxhurst, of Coeymans, N. Y.,	37
Margaret A., m. Squires, of Binghamton, N. Y.,	51
Margaret A., m. Vanderzee, of Albany, N. Y.,	41
Margaret L., m. Van Beuren, of Ellington, Minn.,	40
Margaret M., m. Butler, of Appleton, Wis.,	27
Margaret Sprague Soulé, dau. of Prof. Henry Smith,	38
Margaretta A., dau. of William, of Albany, N. Y.,	42
Maria, m. Mercer, of Lewis Centre, Del. Co., Ohio,	29
Maria, m. Stickney, of Whitestown, N. Y.,	33
Maria, m. Wooster, of Portchester, N. Y.,	48
Maria Louise, dau. of Alfred[4],	50
Maribah, dau. of Wm. H., of New York,	57
Martha Eunice, dau. of Dr. Garretson L.,	42
Mary, dau. of George W., of Albany, N. Y.,	43
Mary, dau. of Hackaliah[1],	47
Mary, dau. of Hackaliah[2], of Coeymans, N. Y.,	39

	PAGE
Mary, dau. of Robert B., of Grand Travers, Mich.,	33
Mary, m. Hall, m. Cunningham, m. Scott, of Ohio,	29
Mary, m. Haviland, dau. of Joshua[1],	57
Mary, m. Haviland, of Glen Falls, N. Y.,	57
Mary, m. Jerolomon, of Coeymans, N. Y.,	34
Mary, m. Kniffin, of Rye, N. Y.,	26
Mary, m. Reynolds, dau. of Daniel[2], of Coeymans, N. Y.	36
Mary Adeline, dau. of James Isaac, of New York,	52
Mary E., dau. of James, of Pontiac, Mich.,	33
Mary E., dau. of George N., of Oxford, N. Y.,	30
Mary E. m. Herron, of Albany, N. Y.,	42
Mary E. m. Rounds, of Oxford, N. Y.,	30
Mary Ella, m. Sherwood, of Portsmouth, Va.,	53
Mary Ellen, m. Fredendall, of Albany, N. Y.,	43
Mary Elizabeth, dau. of Joshua[2],	52
Mary Elizabeth, m. Dusenbury, dau. of Alfred[1],	48
Mary Lavinia, m. Manly, of Parkersburgh, Iowa,	36
Mary Therese, dau. of Rev. John Wesley, of Oshkosh, Wis.,	38
Mattie Randolph, dau. of Wm. E., of Baltimore, Md.,	53
Matilda, m. Ferris, of Guilford Centre, N. Y.,	31
Matilda E., dau. of Rev. John Wesley,	38
Melissa, dau. of John, of Grinnell, Iowa,	45
Moses Totton, son of Alfred,[1]	48
Nathan, son of Thomas[3], of Bethlehem, N. Y.,	33
Nathan H., son of Isaac, of Trempealeau, Iowa,	36
Nellie, m. Wyncoop, dau. of James, of Coeymans, N. Y.,	35
Nicholas, son of James, of Coeymans, N. Y.,	34
Nina Beach, dau. of Rev. John Wesley, of Oshkosh, Wis.,	38
Orletta Louise, dau. of Peter S., of Collamer, N. Y.,	46
Orville Eugene, of Marion O.,	29
Oscar, son of Ambrose, of Oxford, N. Y.,	30
Oscar, son of Stephen, of Oxford, N. Y.,	30
Paul, son of Geo. W. M. D., of Jackson, Mich.,	32
Perry Mead, son of Sanford, Gilderland, N. Y.,	42
Peter, son of Thomas[3], of Bethlehem, N. Y.,	34
Peter, of Albany, son of Robert,[2]	41
Peter, of Janesville, Wis., son of Solomon[1],	40
Peter, son of Alanson, of Coeymans, N. Y.,	35
Peter Sanford, son of Isaac, of Manlius, N. Y.	46
Phebe, dau. of John[3], of Oxford, N. Y.,	31
Phebe, m. Divine, dau. of Joshua[1], of Dutchess Co., N. Y.,	57
Phebe, m. Hall, dau. of James, of Pontiac, Mich.,	33
Phebe, A. m. Walker, of Oxford, N. Y.,	29
Phebe J., dau. of Richard, of Dutchess Co., N. Y.,	56
Rachel, dau. of Hackaliah[2], of Coeymans, N. Y.,	39
Rachel, m. Prior, of Jericho, L. I.,	56
Ralph, son of Stephen, of Columbus, Ohio,	29
Raymond Albert, son of Albert Elijah	44
Raymond Henry, son of Peter S., of Collamer, N. Y.,	46
Richard of Chicago, son of Peter, of Albany, N. Y.,	41
Richard, son of Joshua[1], of Dutchess Co., N. Y.,	56
Robert, son of Daniel[1], of Coeymans, N. Y.,	41
Robert, son of James[2], of Coeymans, N. Y.,	35
Robert, son of Thomas[3], of Bethlehem, N. Y.,	33
Robert, son of Sanford, of Gilderland, N. Y.,	42

INDEX.

	PAGE
Robert B., of Amhurst, Ohio[1],	33
Robert Benjamin, of Marion, Iowa,	42
Robert Nelson, son of Alfred[1],	48
Robert Seymour, son of Henry, of Gilderland, N. Y.,	37
Rose Ella, dau. of Elliott, of Macon City, Mo.,	29
Samuel, of Grand Travers, Mich.,	33
Samuel, son of Thomas D., of Albany, N. Y.,	43
Samantha Brush, m. Hotaling, of Cleveland, Ohio,[1]	51
Sanford, of Gilderland, Albany Co., N. Y.,	41
Sarah, dau. of Richard, of Dutchess Co., N. Y.,	56
Sarah, m. Robbins, of Babylon, L. I.,	56
Sarah Adelle, dau. of Wm. H., of New York city,	57
Sarah Anna, dau. of Stephen, of Albany, N. Y.,	43
Sarah Elizabeth, m. Terry, of Coeymans, N. Y.,	38
Sarah G., dau. of George N., of Oxford, N. Y.,	30
Sarah Helen, m. Ludlum, of Oyster Bay, L. I.,	57
Sarah Maria, m. Litchfield, of Washington, D. C.,	39
Solomon[1], son of Daniel[1], of Coeymans, N. Y.	39
Solomon[2], son of Solomon, of Coeymans, N. Y.,	40
Stephen, son of Henry, of Oxford, N. Y.,	28
Stephen, son of John[3], of Oxford, N. Y.,	29
Stephen, son of Thomas D., of Albany, N. Y.,	43
Susan, of Grand Travers, Mich.,	33
Susan, dau. of Joshua[2], of Brooklyn, N. Y.,	53
Susan, dau. of John, of Newtown, L. I.,	52
Susan, m. Pinckney, dau. of Thomas[3], of Bethlehem, N. Y.,	34
Susan, m. Talman, dau. of John, of Grinwell, Iowa,	44
Susan May, dau. of Charles Burt, of Chicago, Ill.,	52
Sylvanus, son of John[3], of Oxford, N. Y.,	31
Sylvanus[2], of Guilford, son of John,[4]	31
Sylvia, dau. of Isaac, of Oxford, N. Y.,	28
Thomas[1], of Staten Island, and Woodbridge, N. J.,	25
Thomas[2], of Rye, West Chester Co., N. Y.,	26
Thomas[3], of Bethlehem, Albany Co., N. Y.,	33
Thomas[4], of Troy, N. Y.,	33
Thomas[5], son of Robert, of Whitestown, N. Y.,	33
Thomas D., of Albany, son of Daniel[2], of Coeymans, N. Y.,	42
Thomas Newman, son of Isaac, of Binghamton, N. Y.,	52
Thomas S., son of Leonard, of Coeymans, N. Y.,	41
Urania Esther, m. Wren, Brooklyn, N. Y.,	53
William, of Green Bay, Wis.,	56
William, son of Fletcher, of Coeymans, N. Y.,	41
William, son of Joshua,[1] of Dutchess Co., N. Y.,	56
William, son of Thomas D., of Albany, N. Y.,	42
William, son of William H., of New York city,	57
William[2], son of William H., of New York city,	57
William Edgar, son of Joshua[2], of Brooklyn, N. Y.,	53
William Edgar, jr., son of William Edgar, of Baltimore, Md.,	53
William Garretson, son of Dr. Garretson, L. of Marion, Linn, Co., Iowa,	42
William H., adopted son of Jeremiah, of New York city,	28
William H., of New York city, son of John, of Dutchess Co., N. Y.,	57
William Henry, son of Hackaliah[2], of Conn.,	47
William Merle, son of Lyman Beecher, of Peekskill, N. Y.,	49
William S., of New Orleans, cannot be assigned,	14
William Taylor, son of Peter, of Albany, N. Y.,	41

DESCENDANTS *by the name of* CARHART, *from* ROBERT,[1] *of Monmouth County, N. J.*

	PAGE
Abraham, son of Daniel[1], of Elwood, N. J.,	66
Albert, of Oxford, Pa.,	72
Amory Sibley, of Brooklyn, N. Y.,	64
Annie, dau. of Robert[1], of Monmouth Co., N. J.,	61
Annie, dau. of William, of Phillipsburg, N. J.,	63
Annie, of Washington, N. J., dau. of John,	75
Arthur Ivans, son of Samuel J., of Newton, Buck's Co., Pa.,	71
Asa, of Clarksville, N. J.,	66
Austin Craig, of Zion, Cecil Co., Md.,	73
Bedford, of Clinton, son of John[5],	67
Bertrand, son of Robert, of Phillipsburg, N. J.,	63
Caroline, dau. of Charles[2], of Harmony, N. J.,	63
Carrie L., of Cecil Co., Md.,	67
Catharine, dau. of Cornelius[2],	73
Catharine, m. Wycoff, of Washington, N. J.,	74
Charles[5], of Annandale, N. J.,	66
Charles[2], of Harmony, son of Robert[2],	62
Charles, of Harmony, son of William,	62
Charles,[4] of Perryville, N. J.,	64
Charles[1], son of Cornelius[1], of Washington, N. J.,	64
Charles[3], son of Cornelius[3], of Perryville, N. J.,	67
Charles, son of James Larison,	72
Charles F., of Philadelphia, and Danville, Va.,	68
Charles Richards, son of Wm. E., of Brooklyn, N. Y.,	65
Charles Whitfield, of Maple Grove, Perryville, N. J.,	67
Christina m. Davis, of Bradford, Pa.,	70
Christina m. Dunham, of Clinton, N. J.,	67
Clarence of Clinton, N. J.,	66
Clarence M., of Maple Grove, Perryville, N. J.,	67
Cora of Galion, Ohio, dau. of Henry Clay,	74
Cornelius[1], of Washington, Sussex Co., N. J.,	62
Cornelius[2], of Perryville, N. J.,	67
Cornelius[3], of Washington, N. J.,	70
Cornelius[4], of Washington, N. J.,	74
Cornelius, of Matawan, son of Robert, of New Brunswick, N. J.,	76
Cornelius V., of Phillipsburgh, N. J.,	64
Daniel[1], of Elwood, Atlantic Co., N. J.,	66
Daniel[2], of Maple Grove, Perryville, N. J.,	70
Daniel[3], of Philadelphia and Danville, Va.,	68
Daniel D., of Washington, N. J.,	70
Deborah M. Van Pelt, m. 2nd. Wood, of Brooklyn, N. Y.,	76
Dewitt Clinton, of Oxford, Chester Co., Pa.,	72
Diana V., dau. of Cornelius[3], of Washington, N. J.,	70
Edmund of Phillipsburgh, N. J.,	64
Edmund H., of New York city,	63 & 64
Edward D., of Oxford, Chester Co., Pa.,	71
Edwina, dau. of Robert, of Phillipsburgh, N. J.,	63

INDEX.

	PAGE
Edwina M. Watts, of Brooklyn, N. Y.,	66
Elijah H., of Macon, Ga.,	66
Elizabeth, of Washington, N. J., dau. of John,	75
Elizabeth, m. Eckel, of Mount Pleasant, N. J.,	68
Elizabeth, m. Hoffman, of Clinton, N. J.,	67
Elizabeth, m. Oberly, dau. of Charles[2], of Harmony, N. J.,	62
Elizabeth, m. Vannetta,	74
Elizabeth, m. Youmans, of Washington, N. J.,	74
Ella, of Washington, dau. of John,	75
Ella, of Washington, dau. of Cornelius[3],	70
Ellen E., m. Dillon, of Philadelphia, Pa.,	63
Ella N., dau. of James Larison,	72
Elmer, of Phillipsburgh, N. J.,	75
Elmer E., of Elwood, N. J.,	67
Elmer Ellsworth, of Phillipsburg, N. J.,	64
Elmore C., of Phil.,	68
Elwood, of Oxford, Chester Co., Pa.,	72
Emily A., m. Crowe, of Nebraska,	70
Emma, of Washington, N. J., dau. of John,	75
Emma, dau. of William, of Phillipsburg, N. J.,	63
Emma L., m. Hagerman, of Trenton, N. J.,	63
Emma O., of Maple Grove, Perryville, N. J.,	67
Emma S., Oxford, Pa., dau. of Ellwood,	72
Fanny, of Phillipsburgh, N. J.,	75
Fanny A., of Zion, Cecil Co., Md.,	73
Francis L., of Auburn, N. Y.,	73
Frank Matthew, of Auburn, N. Y.,	73
George, of Clinton, N. J., son of John[5],	67
George, of Elwood, N. J., son of Joseph B.,	67
George B., of Philadelphia, son of Samuel,	75
George B., son of Charles[4], of Perryville, N. J.,	65
George Beavers, of Brooklyn, N. Y.,	64
George Beavers, son of Whitfield Dunham,	66
Helen, of Oxford, Pa., dau. of Albert,	72
Helen Josephine, of Phil.,	68
Helen Mar, m. Bonnell, of Clinton, N. J.,	71
Henrietta, m. Carhart, dau. of Samuel[3],	63
Henry, son of Robert, of Phillipsburgh, N. J.,	63
Henry Brigham, of Knoxville, Tenn.,	65
Henry Clay, of Galion, O.,	74
Henry E., of Auburn, N. Y.,	73
Henry S., son of Theodore, of Belvidere, N. J.,	63
Ida, of Washington, N. J., dau. of John,	75
Isabella, m. Rassenberg, of Martin's Creek, Pa.,	75
Isabella, m. Shine, of Ackermansville, Pa.,	75
Jacob, of Ackermansville, Pa.,	75
Jacob, son of Charles, of Harmony, N. J.,	62
James B., of Nebraska,	70
James Dunham, of Macon, Ga., Brooklyn, N. Y.,	65
James Dunham, jr., of Macon, Ga., and New York,	65
James Dunham, son of Charles[4], of Perryville, N. J.,	65
James Dunham, son of Whitfield Dunham,	66
James Larison, of Phil.,	72

	PAGE
James Sidney Rockwell, of Brooklyn, N. Y.,	65
Jennie, dau. of William[2], of Harmony, N. J.,	62
Jessie, dau. of William[2], of Harmony, N. J.,	62
Jessy, of Phillipsburgh, N. J.,	75
John[2], son of Charles[1] of Monongalia Co., Va.,	64
John, son of Charles, of Harmony, N. J.,	62
John, son of Cornelius[1], of Mansfield, N. J.,	75
John[1], son of Samuel[2], of Philadelphia, N. J.,	63
John[2], son of Samuel[2], of Philadelphia, N. J.,	63
John[6], of Clinton, N. J.,	67
John, of Zion, Cecil C., Md.,	71
John, of Washington, N. J., son of Samuel[1],	75
John B. Lamar, son of Whitfield Dunham,	66
John Britton, son of Samuel J., of Newtown, Bucks Co., Pa.,	71
John Bracken, of Auburn, N. Y.,	73
John Clayton, of Zion, Cecil Co., Md.,	73
John P., of Buffalo, N. Y.,	73
John Warren, son of Thomas F., of New York city,	63
Joseph, son of William, of Phillipsburgh, N. J.,	63
Joseph B., of Elwood, N. J.,	67
Joseph B., of Maple Grove, Perryville, N. J.,	67
Josephine, of Galion, Ohio, dau. of Henry Clay,	74
Josephine, dau. of Larison B.,	71
Kate, dau. of Dewitt C., of Oxford, Pa.,	72
Kate Rockwell, dau. of James Dunham, Jr.,	65
Kate L., m. Rutherford, of Oxford, Pa.,	72
Kesiah, dau. of Albert, of Oxford, Pa.,	72
Larison B., of Norton, Hunterdon Co., N. J.,	71
Laurence G., son of John Clayton, of Oxford Pa.,	73
Lavina, of Elwood, Atlantic Co., N. J.,	67
Lavina, m. Moore,	71
Lewis R., of Phillipsburgh, N. J.,	75
Lillie, of Whitehouse, Somersett Co., N. J.,	75
Lomson, of Whitehouse, Somersett Co., N. J.,	75
Lydia, dau. of Robert[1], of Matawan, N. J.,	75
Lydia, m. Bowlby, of Va.,	73
Lydia, m. Fitts, of Washington, N. J.,	75
Lydia, m. Phillips, of Port Murray, N. J.,	64
Lydia, m. Raub, of Harmony, N. J.,	63
Lydia, m. Van Buskirk, m. Bunn,	69
Lyndon A., of Washington, N. J.,	70
Maria L., dau. of Thomas F., of New York city,	63
Martha Beavers, m. Kells of Perryville, N. J.,	65
Matilda D., m. Wire, Belvidere, N. J.,	63
Mary, dau. of Robert[1], of Matawan, N. J.,	61
Mary, of Elwood, Atlantic Co., N. J.,	66
Mary, dau. of William, of Phillipsburgh, N. J.,	63
Mary A., dau. of Cornelius[3], of Washington, N. J.,	70
Mary Alice, of Galion, Ohio, dau. of Henry Clay,	74
Mary Damaris, dau. of Samuel J., of Newtown, Bucks Co., Pa.,	71
Mary Emma, dau. of Cornelius[3], of Washington, N. J.,	70
Mary Elizabeth, dau. of Charles[2], of Annandale, N. J.,	66
Mary F., of Hamilton, Cecil Co., Md.,	71
Mary S., dau. of Theodore, of Belvidere, N. J.,	63
Mary S., dau. of Samuel, of Phillipsburgh, N. J.,	64
Mary W., of Ackermansville, Pa.,	75

INDEX.

	PAGE
Mary, m. Cummins, of Vienna, Warren Co., N. J.,	74
Mary S., m. Evans, of Philadelphia, Pa.,	72
Mary V., m. Humphrey, of Philadelphia,	67
Mary, E., m. Kenyon, of Raritan, N. J.,	64
Mary Louise, m. Lewis, of Knoxville, Tenn.,	65
Mary, m. Marlow, dau. of Samuel³,	63
Mary, m. McShane, dau. of Cornelius¹,	62
Mary, m. Sigmon, of Warren Co., N. J.,	64
Mary, m. Van Syckel, of Milford, N. J.,	68
Mary E., m. Van Syckel, of Clinton, N. J.,	66
Mary H., m. Weller, of Warren Co., N. J.,	75
Nehemiah, of Auburn, N. Y.,	73
Oliver Allen, son of Samuel J., of Newtown, Bucks Co., Pa.,	71
Phebe, m. Coleman, of Sussex Co., N. J.,	74
Phineas M., of Wilksbarre, Pa.,	63
Rachel, m. Craig, of Pepack, N. J.,	71
Ralph, son of Thomas F., of New York city,	63
Richard, son of Samuel¹,	76
Robert¹, of Matawan, Monmouth Co., N. J.,	61
Robert², of Hampton, Hunterdon Co., N. J.,	62
Robert, son of William, of Phillipsburgh, N. J.,	63
Robert, of Galion, Ohio, son of Henry Clay,	74
Robert, of New Brunswick, son of Samuel¹,	76
Roderick, of Belvidere, N. J.,	64
Sallie of Phillipsburgh, dau. of Jessy,	75
Samuel¹, son of Robert¹, of Matawan, N. J.	75
Samuel², son of Cornelius¹, of Mansfield, N. J.,	74
Samuel³, of Phil., son of Robert², of Hampton, N. J.,	63
Samuel⁴, son of Samuel³,	63
Samuel, son of Robert, of New Brunswick, N. J.,	76
Samuel, of Phillipsburgh, son of William P.,	64
Samuel, Jr., of Phillipsburgh, son of Samuel,	64
Samuel, of Elwood, Atlantic Co., N. J.,	67
Samuel, of Ocean Beach, N. J.,	67
Samuel Louis, son of Samuel, of Ocean Beach, N. J.,	67
Samuel, of Zion, Cecil Co., Md.,	71
Samuel, of Philadelphia, son of William, of Mansfield, N. J.,	75
Samuel J., of Newtown, Bucks Co., Pa.,	71
Samuel, son of Cornelius²,	71
Samuel N., of Rochester, N. Y.,	73
Sanford, of Ogden City, Utah,	70
Sarah, of Annandale, N. J.,	66
Sarah A., of Auburn, N. Y.,	73
Sarah Virginia, dau. of Charles, of Perryville, N. J.,	65
Sarah L., m. Case, of Washington, N. J.,	75
Sarah, m. Dusenbury, dau. of Cornelius¹,	62
Sarah, m. Frittz, m. 2d Pitnord, of Ill.,	75
Sarah E., m. Parshall, of Oxford, Chester Co., Pa.,	72
Sarah, m. Runckel, m. Van Syckel,	70
Susan, of Whitehouse, Somersett Co., dau. of Lomson,	75
Susanna, m. Cline, of Harmony, N. J.,	63
Sylvester Leonard, of Auburn, N. Y.,	73

INDEX. 129

	PAGE
Tamson, m. Wycoff, of Washington, N. J.,	74
Theodore, of Belvidere, N. J.,	63
Theodore, son of William, of Phillipsburgh, N. J.,	63
Thomas F., of New York city and White Plains, N. Y.,	62
Thomas F., Jr., of White Plains, West Chester Co., N. Y.,	63
Virginia, dau. of Dewitt Clinton, of Oxford, Pa.,	72
Whitfield Dunham, of Clinton, N. J.,	66
Whitfield Dunham, Jr., of Clinton, N. J.,	66
Willimpia, m. Lacy, of Mansfield, N. J.,	74
William^2, son of John^2, of Harmony, N. J.,	62
William, son of Samuel, of Philadelphia, Pa.,	63
William, son of Samuel, of Philadelphia, Pa.,	75
William, of Phillipsburgh, N. J., son of William P.,	63
William, Jr., son of William, of Phillipsburgh, N. J.,	63
William, of Mansfield, son of Samuel,	74
William, of Clinton, son of Daniel^1, of Atlantic City, N. J.,	66
William Beavers, of Brooklyn, N. Y.,	65
William Beavers, of Clinton, N. J.,	66
William B., son of Whitfield Dunham,	66
William Edward, of Brooklyn, N. Y.,	65
William Edward, Jr.,	65
William P., of New Hampton, N. J.,	63
William S., son of Samuel, of Phillipsburgh, N. J.,	64

130   INDEX.

DESCENDANTS *by the name of* CARHART, *from* WILLIAM,[1] *of* PERTH
AMBOY, N. J.

	PAGE
Ada, dau. of Charles E., of Tuckerstown, N. J.,	80
Adelaide, of Burlington, dau. of Samuel,	82
Alfred, son of William, of Matawan,	81
Alfred, son of William, of Long Island, N. Y.,	82
Alice R., of Milltown, N. J.,	83
Amanda, m. Seely, of Port Murray, N. J.,	81
Ambrose, son of Richard, of Elizabeth, N. J.,	80
Amelia, dau. of John[5], of Keyport, N. J.,	82
Amelia, dau. of William. Res. unknown,	82
Angeline M. Case,	83
Annie, dau. of William, of Long Island, N. Y.,	82
Arthur, son of Gershom, of Bridgeboro, N. J.,	80
Augusta, dau. of Richard, of Elizabeth, N. J.,	80
Azeneth, of Keyport, N. J., dau. of John K.,	80
Benjamin, son of Cornelius, of Keyport, N. J.,	83
Bishop, of Keyport, N. J.,	80
Burnett, son of Gershom, of Bridgeboro, N. J.,	80
Caroline, dau. of Cornelius, of Keyport, N. J.,	83
Caroline, dau. of John S.,	80
Carrie, dau. of Nelson, of Port Monmouth, N. J.,	80
Carrie, dau. of William, of Matawan, N. J.,	81
Catharine, dau of William. Res. unknown,	82
Catharine, of Keyport, N. J.,	80
Catharine, m. Grisson, of Buffalo, N. Y.,	80
Catharine A., m. Holmes,	80
Charles, son of Richard, of Port Monmouth, N. J.,	81
Charles, son of Thomas P.,	82
Charles, son of Joseph, of Keyport, N. J.,	83
Charles E., of Tuckerstown, N. J.,	80
Charles Henry, son of George P.,	82
Charles W., of Keyport, N. J.,	81
Charlotte M., m. La Fumeé, of Brooklyn, N. Y.,	82
Clara, of Greenpoint, L. I., N. Y.,	80
Conover, son of Joseph, of Keyport, N. J.,	83
Cornelius[1], of Keyport, son of Thomas[3],	82
Cornelius[2], of Keyport, son of Cornelius[1],	82
Crawford, of Petersburgh, Va.,	83
Daniel, son of William. Res. unknown,	82
David B., son of William, of Port Monmouth, N. J.,	81
David Van Pelt, of Hightstown, N. J.,	83
David E., son of David Van Pelt,	83
Deborah, dau. of James, of Marlboro, N. J.,	81
Delinda, dau. of Thomas[4],	82
Edmond A., son of Richard, of Holmdell, N. J.,	81
Edson, of Bridgeboro,	80
Edwin, son of Joseph, of Keyport, N. J.,	83
Elenor, dau. of Richard A.,	83

INDEX. 131

	PAGE
Elizabeth, dau. of Thomas³,	83
Elizabeth, m. Gravatt, dau. of Joel,	83
Ella, of Greenpoint, L. I., N. Y.,	80
Elmer, son of Gershom, of Bridgeboro, N. J.,	80
Elmira, dau. of William. Res. unknown,	82
Elmira, dau. of Samuel, of Burlington, N. J.,	82
Elmira M., m. Wright,	83
Elwood, of Milltown, N. J.,	83
Emily, of Keyport, dau. of Samuel,	83
Emma, dau. of Thomas⁴,	82
Emma, dau. of Richard, of Port Monmouth, N. J.,	81
Emma, dau. of William. Res. unknown,	82
Emma V., m. Biddle,	83
Estella, of Keyport, dau. of Charles W.,	81
Eugene, son of Thomas P.,	82
Evelyn, dau. of Gershom, of Bridgeboro, N. J.,	80
George, son of Gershom, of Bridgeboro, N. J.,	80
George, of Port Monmouth, son of John³,	81
George, of Port Monmouth, son of Richard,	81
George P., of Brooklyn, N. Y.,	82
Gershom, of Bridgeboro, N. J.,	80
Hannah, of Keyport, N. J., dau. of John³,	81
Hannah, dau. of Thomas³,	82
Henrietta, dau. of Richard, of Port Monmouth, N. J.,	81
Henrietta, dau. of Cornelius, of Keyport, N. J.,	83
Henrietta, m. Williams,	83
Henry, of Bridgeboro, N. J.,	80
Holmes, of Petersburgh, Va.,	83
Ida, dau. of William, of Long Island, N. Y.,	82
Isabella, dau. of Richard A.,	83
Isaac, son of George¹, of Port Monmouth, N. J.,	81
Irwin, son of Charles W., of Keyport,	81
Jacob, son of Samuel, of Burlington, N. J.,	82
Jacob, son of William, of Perth Amboy, N. J.,	79
James, of Marlboro, N. J.,	81
James, of Long Island, N. Y.,	82
James N., of Bordentown, N. J.,	83
Jane L., of Hightstown, N. J., dau. of David V.,	83
Joel, of Keyport, son of Samuel,	83
Joel, of New Brunswick, N. J.,	83
John², of Keyport, son of William¹,	79
John³, of Keyport, son of John²,	79
John⁴, of Port Monmouth, son of John³,	79
John⁵, of Keyport, son of Thomas³,	82
John⁶, of Brooklyn, son of John⁵,	82
John, of Flemington, son of Thomas².	79
John Henry, of Keyport, N. J.,	83
John Joseph, of Green Castle, Ind.,	82
John K., of Keyport, N. J.,	79
John L., of Milltown,	83
John S., of Keyport, son of John K.,	80
Joseph, of Keyport, son of Samuel,	83
Joseph, son of George¹, of Port Monmouth, N. J.,	81
Joseph, of Brooklyn, son of John³,	81

132 INDEX.

	PAGE
Joseph, of Keyport, son of Thomas³,	83
Josephine, dau. of Gershom, of Bridgeboro, N. J.,	80
Josie Idell, dau. of David B., of Port Monmouth, N. J.,	81
Kate, m. Robinson, of Philadelphia, Pa.,	79
Laura, dau. of Cornelius, of Keyport, N. J.,	83
Leander, son of Thomas⁴,	82
Leila, dau. of Edmond A.,	81
Leroy, of Jersey City, N. J.,	80
Lillie, dau. of Edson, of Bridgeboro, N. J.,	80
Lina, dau. of Richard A.,	83
Lois, dau. of Thomas,⁴	82
Louise, dau. of Joseph, of Keyport, N. J.,	83
Lydia, dau. of Richard A.,	83
Lydia, of Keyport, N. J.,	80
Lydia, dau. of David B., of Port Monmouth, N. J.,	81
Lydia A., dau. of Joseph, of Port Monmouth, N. J.,	81
Lydia M. dau. of David V.,	83
Malcomb, son of Richard A.,	83
Margaret, of Bridgeboro, dau. of Gershom,	80
Maria, of Keyport, dau. of Cornelius,	83
Martha, of Keyport, N. J.,	80
Matilda, of Long Island, dau. of William,	82
Mary Ann, dau. of Joseph, of Brooklyn, N. Y.,	81
Mary A., m. Jones,	83
Mary E., m. Henry, of Port Monmouth, N. J.,	81
Mary, m. Walling, of Keyport, N. J.,	82
Mary E., dau. of Richard, of Elizabeth, N. J.,	80
Mary F., of Keyport, N. J.,	80
Mary, dau. of Joseph, of Keyport, N. J.,	83
Mary, dau. of John⁵, of Keyport, N. J.,	82
Melissa, dau. of Benjamin, of Keyport, N. J.,	83
Minnie, dau. of Nelson, of Port Monmouth, N. J.,	80
Minerva, dau. of Cornelius, of Keyport, N. J.,	83
Nelson, Capt., of Port Monmouth, N. J.,	80
Newell, son of Cornelius, of Keyport, N. J.,	83
Nicholas, son of James, of Marlboro, N. J.,	81
Oscar, son of Richard, of Elizabeth, N. J.,	80
Oscar, son of Thomas P.,	82
Phebe, of Bridgeboro, N. J.,	80
Philander, Capt., of Keyport, N. J.,	80
Ralph, of Keyport, N. J.,	80
Rebecca, dau. of Henry, of Bridgboro, N. J.,	80
Reuben, of Bridgeboro, N. J.,	80
Rhoda, dau. of Joseph, of Keyport, N. J.,	83
Richard, of Elizabeth, N. J.,	80
Richard, son of William¹, of Perth Amboy, N. J.,	79
Richard, of Holmdell, Monmouth Co., N. J.,	81
Richard A., son of Joseph, of Keyport, N. J.,	83
Richard, son of Richard, of Port Monmouth, N. J.,	81
Richard, son of George¹,	81
Samuel, of Keyport, son Thomas³,	83
Samuel, of Keyport, son of Samuel,	83

INDEX.

	PAGE
Samuel, of Burlington, N. J.,	82
Samuel, of Trenton, N. J.,	83
Sarah, dau. of Cornelius, of Keyport, N. J.,	83
Sarah, dau. of Samuel, of Keyport, N. J.,	83
Sarah J., of Hightstown, N. J.,	83
Stephen E., of Greenpoint, L. I., N. Y.,	80
Sylvanus of Greenpoint, L. I., N. Y.,	80
Taylor, son of Edmond A.,	81
Theodore, son of Nelson, of Port Monmouth, N. J.,	80
Theodore, son of William, of L. I.,	82
Timothy, son of Samuel, of Keyport, N. J.,	83
Thomas^2, of Flemington, N. J.,	79
Thomas, of Flemington, son of Thomas^2,	79
Thomas, son of William^1,	79
Thomas^3, of Keyport, son of John^2,	82
Thomas^4, son of Thomas^3,	82
Thomas, son of William^2. Res. unknown,	81
Thomas, son of Richard, of Port Monmouth, N. J.,	81
Thomas, of Keyport, son of Samuel,	83
Thomas, of Keyport, son of John K.,	80
Thomas P., son of William. Res unknown,	82
Virginia, of Keyport, N. J.,	80
Virginia, dau. of John Henry,	83
Wilbur A., of Philadelphia, Pa.,	83
Wilbur F., of Philadelphia,	83
William^1, of Perth Amboy, N. J.,	79
William^2, of Keyport, son of John^3,	81
Wililiam^3, of Port Monmouth, son of John^4,	80
William, son William^2,	81
William, of Tuckerstown, son of Charles E.,	80
William of Bridgeboro, son of Henry,	80
William, D., of Port Monmouth, son of David B.,	81
William, of Matawan, N. J.,	81
William, Rev., of Baltimore, Md.,	80
William, of Keyport, son of Thomas^2,	82
William, of Long Island, N. Y.,	82
William, V. of Port Monmouth, N. J.,	81
Zackariah, son of David, V.,.	83

DESCENDANTS FROM FEMALE BRANCHES

BY OTHER NAMES.

		PAGE			PAGE
ABBOTT	Grace Mary.	54	BURTELL	Lucy; Sanford; Agnes	36
	George Irving	54	BUTLER	Maggie Carhart.	27
	Anna Laura	54	CANNON	Alfred Spencer.	48
	Grace Mary.	54		Henry Lyman	48
ADAMS	W. Irving.	55	CASE	Dewitt; Elizabeth.	69
	Elizabeth Armenia	55		Lucy.	69
	Margaret Emily.	55	CLARK	Orville L.; Walter E.	45
	Mary Louise	55		Edward R.	45
	Elma Maria.	55	COOK	George R.	46
ADAMS	Briggs Booth	55		Charles Carhart.	46
	Charlotte Elizabeth	55		Henry Lansing.	46
	W. Irving Lincoln.	55		Florence Lucy.	46
	Mary Wilson.	55		Mabel Louise	46
ALPAUGH	James; Caroline	69	COOLEY	James; Elizabeth.	68
	William; Lambert.	69		Samuel; Mahlon	68
	Edward; Mary.	69	COTTIER	Claude Van Beuren	40
APGAR	M. Virginia.	69	CRAIG	Rev. Austin; Emily.	71
	Jane E.	69	CRAIG	Lucretia; Adelaide	71
	Cornelius V.	69		Moses.	71
	Emily C.	69	CROWE	Milton.	70
	Wm. Henry.	69	CUMMINS	Carhart L.	74
	Edwin	69		Jacob P.	74
BALL	David; Charles.	35		Theodore; George	74
BESSON	Elbridge V. S.	70	DAVIDS	Jennie; James B.	27
	Josephine; Louise	70	DAVIS	Rose E.	70
	James; Charles	70	DIVINE	Phebe A.	57
BIRD	Lewis E.	65	DUNHAM	Mary Elizabeth	67
BIRD	Walter; James K.	65		Charles C.	67
BONNEL	Amy H.	71		Catharine H.	67
	Alexander.	71		Helen Mar	67
	Lillie; Charles	71	DUSENBURY	Mary Josephine.	48
	Elmer E.; Josephine C.	71	ECKEL	Samuel Carhart	68
	Alexander Carhart.	71		Sarah Dunham.	68
BOWLBY	Willimpia.	73		Hannah Baker	68
BRASHER	Ellen C.	43		Selinda; Amanda.	68
BROWNE	George W.; Ann Eliza	32		John Jordan.	68
BROWNE	Louise; Charlotte	32		Joseph Henry	68
	Richard Dominick.	32		Elizabeth	68
	Sarah A. Gedney	32	ECKEL	Stanford J.	68
BROWN	Edith B.; Bertha	33		C. Virginia.	68
	Lulu.	33		Martha J.	68
BRUCKNER	Rudolph Eglin	40		Albert S.	68
BUNN	Henry E.; Caroline	69		Hannah E.	68
	Isabelle D.	69	ECKEL	Paul H.	69
	Paul H. Provost.	69		Stewart; M. Belle	69
	Melinda	69	EVANS	Elsie	72
BURTELL	Edwin	36		J. Lacy Hough	72
	John Wesley.	36	FERRIS	Clarance D.	31

INDEX. 135

		PAGE			PAGE
FISHER	Sarah Augusta	53	KENYON	Minnie Matilda	65
	Lucy; Clara	53		Angeline Dales	65
FLAGLER	Henry C.	43		Charles Carhart	65
	Hattie B.	43	KNAPP	Katie Estelle	50
FOLLETT	William Irving	55		Burras Frank	50
FREDENDALL	George; Edward	43	LA FUMÉE	Edwin Forrest	82
FRISBEE	Alanson	37		Frances Angeline	82
	Ellen Louise	37		Charlotte Louise	82
FITTS	Samuel	75		Josephine Clements	82
	Julia; John	75	LEWIS	John Walker	65
	Enoch; Joseph	75	LEYDEN	Maurice; Frank M.	45
	Mary; Sarah	75		Isaac H.; Hart C.	45
	Ada; Henry	75		Hester A.; Mary E.	45
	Thyrza; Margaret	75		Eliza J.; Barbara M.	45
	Rosa; Jessie	75		Ella Louise	45
FURBECK	Duane L.; George	46		Catharine; Edwin C.	45
GEDNEY	Robert; Sybil	32		Lucy F.	45
GEDNEY	Sarah Ann	32	LITCHFIELD	Hiram Sanford	39
	Emeline Amanda	32		Edward Henry	39
	Mary Eliza	32		Jane Ann	39
	Pauline	32		Hannah Maria	39
	George W. Browne	32		Solomon Carhart	39
	Robert Laurence	32		William Elbert	39
HALLENBECK	Luella Minerva	43		James Allen	39
	Ernest A.; Mary C.	43		John Van Beuren	39
HAUXHURST	Osman Baker	38	LUDLUM	Helen	57
HAVILAND	Clarence Floyd	54		James Henry	57
HERRON	Fanny; George	42		Lillie; Frederick	57
	Ada; William	42		Louise Carhart	57
	Jane; Esther	42	LYON	Nathan Emory	50
	Charles; James	42		Gilbert; Albert	50
HOFFMAN	Christina	67		William Edwin	50
	Sarah	67		Addison; Margaret	50
HOLBROOK	Isaac; Nancy	36		Warren; Elmira	50
HOLLY	Frances Glover	47	LYON	Sarah Maria	50
	Alice Maud	47		Emory Garretson	50
	Mary Charlotte	47		Emma E.; Mary Jane	50
	Carrie Renshaw	47		Andrew Simpson	50
HOTALING	Frank H.	37		Charles Benjamin	50
	Edwin Olin	37		William Warren	50
	William B.	37	LYON	Calvin Augustus	50
	Henry L.	37		William Edwin	50
HOTALING	Herbert Eugene	51		Albert Edward	50
	Emily; Henry	51		George Nelson	50
HOUGH	Jane; H. Page	70		Lizzie Sanford	50
HOVEY	Frances R.	27		Edwin Anderson	50
	Henrietta Failing	27		Harry Gedney	50
	Harriet C.	27		Wilbur Carhart	50
JEROLOMON	William; Nathan	34		Hattie Frances	50
	Nicholas; David	34	LYON	Ella Frances	50
	Nellie; Mary	34		William Edwin	50
	Ann Eliza	34		Margaret Jane	50
JEROLOMON	Lansing; Martin	34		Charles Warren	50
	Egbert; David	34		Irving	50
	Olin	34		James Newman	50
KELLS	Mary Catharine	65		Minnie Estelle	50
	Georgianna	65		Lillie	50
	William Whitfield	65	LYON	Olivia Augusta	51
KELLS	Henry C.	65		Leonora; Emma	51

INDEX.

		PAGE			PAGE
LYON	Mary Augusta	51	REYNOLDS	Levi; Isaac	36
LYON	Nathan Emory	50	REYNOLDS	Mary Ann	36
	Emma Augusta	50	REYNOLDS	George	36
	Ella Elizabeth	50		Christopher	36
	Emma Mary	50		William; Edward	36
LYON	Charles Emory	50		Alanson; Sarah Ann	36
	Alice Mary	50		Mary; Katie; Jacob	36
	Ida Luella	50	REYNOLDS	Edward; Richard	36
MARTIN	Maria Louise	40		Hiram; David	36
	Ada C.; Helen C.	40		Stephen; Sarah E.	36
MATTISON	Samuel	68		Frank; William	36
MEADON	Ada; Howard	42		Annie; Georgianna	36
	George; Mary	42	REYNOLDS	Albert; Eva	36
METTLER	Mary V.; Carrie C.	68	REYNOLDS	Carrie	36
MOORE	Mary; George L.	71	ROBBINS	William B.	56
MOWRY	Lydia M.	30		Sarah C.	56
	Narissa	30		Edward; Walter. W.	56
	Andrew Franklin	30		Phebe Ann; John	56
	Phila A.	30	ROOKE	Theodore Augustus	51
	Washington Everett	30		Frank Adylott	51
MOWRY	Laura H.; Ira A.	30		Ida Jean	51
MUNSON	Frank Beecher	49		Jessie; Carrie	51
	Grace	49		Warren Augustus	51
	Mary Josephine	49	ROUNDS	Minnie	30
	Louise Weed	49	RUNCKEL	Charles; Virginia	70
NEGUS	Robert P.	69	RUNCKEL	George; Sarah	70
	Susan E.; James E.	69		Nelson; Almira W.	70
	William S.	69		John C.	70
NEWMAN	Sarah Elma	54	RUNCKEL	Helen; Philip H.	70
	Enoch George	54	RUTHERFORD	Allen	32
	Mary Fletcher	54		Robert Gedney	32
	Henrietta Bancroft	54	RUTHERFORD	Kate L.	72
	Grace Beverage	54	RYAN	Sarah	35
NEWMAN	Eva Myra	54	SHAPLEIGH	Frances Hovey	27
	George Nathan	54	SEELEY	Annie Belle	30
	Mary Emma	54		Hattie May	30
OWENS	Ambrose; Eunice	28		George Ray	30
	James; Isaac	28	SHERWOOD	Mabel Randolph	53
	Phebe; Alanson	28		Mary Virginia	53
	Hannah; Sylvanus	28	SMITH	Henrietta; Regina	27
PARRY	Edward; Rev. Samuel	69	SMITH	Lydia; James B.	73
PARRY	Rachel	71		Rebecca; Lucinda	73
PINCKNEY	Maria; Clara	34		Mary A.; Matilda	73
	Lydia	34		Henry Clay; Alvin B.	73
	John Townsend	34		Elmore Y.	73
	Thomas Carhart	34	SQUIRES	Richard	51
PINCKNEY	Mary Augusta	34		Charles	51
	Julia Victoria	34		Margaret Adeline	51
	Louise Matilda	34		Isaac Carhart	51
	J. H. Hobart	34		William Theodore	51
	Thomas Coatsworth	34	STRONG	Nathan	27
POST	Frederick	27	TALMAN	Grace Melissa	44
	John Carhart	27		Ida M.; Angeline	44
PRICE	Harry Irving	55		Clara Mabel	44
	Oscar Benson	55		George Albert	44
	George Briggs	55		Susan; Lucy Maria	44
PRIOR	William H	56	TERRY	Washington Carhart	40
REYNOLDS	Daniel; Peter	36	TERRY	Alfred Carhart	49
	Ann; John	36		Marvin Bartlett	49

INDEX. 137

		PAGE			PAGE
TERRY	Mary; James	40	VAN SYCKEL	Sanford; Horatio D.	68
	Peter Lansing	40		Albert; Gustavus A.	68
	Emma E.; Frank	40		Virginia	68
	Ida; Malvina	40	VAN SYCKEL	Daniel	68
	Sidney	40		George; Holloway	68
TITUS	Isaac Henry	37		Eoline	68
	David	37	VAN SYCKEL	Mary Isabella	68
	Mary Elizabeth	37		Fannie; John E.	68
TITUS	William H.	37	VAN SYCKEL	Jacob B.	69
	David Allen	37		Lydia E.	69
	Charles Jefferson	37		J. Augusta	69
TITUS	Elizabeth; Ann	37		George H.	69
TITUS	Elma Margaret	54	VAN SYCKEL	Elbridge	69
	Frank Willis	54		Catharine	69
	Edmund James	54		Mary; Isabelle	69
	William Smith	54		Nehemiah	69
	Eleanor Edith	54	WALDRON	Margaret	35
THOMAS	Isabelle	69		Susan; Peter	35
	Fannie; Howard	69		James; Asa	35
TOWNE	Emma E.	35		Eliza	35
	Frances L.	35	WALKER	Christina V.	29
TURNER	Everett P.; Richard	29		James L.; Clarence D.	29
TUTTLE	Levi Carter	39		Sarah E.; Frederick C.	29
	Charlotte Ann	39		Laura A.	29
	Mary; Henrietta	39	WALKER	Frederick A.	30
	Catharine	39	WALLING	Mary	82
UNGAR	Mary Ernestine	55	WARD	Frank Arthur	40
	Ferdinand Adams	55		Zettie; Alberto	40
UTTER	Daniel; Isaac	35		Hattie Julia	40
	Palmer; Robert	35	WEAVER	Catharine; Anna	42
	Lavinia; Sarah	35	WHEELER	Eleanor May	30
	Elizabeth; Barbara	35	WILKINS	Lucy; Augustine	44
VAN BEUREN	Henrietta	40		Lettie A.; George H.	44
	Ida Louise	40	WILLSON	Mortimer; Adeline	47
	Estelle	40		Jotham S.; Mary Haight	47
	Adelle Bertha	40	WILLSON	Edith	47
	Grace Evelyn	40	WOOSTER	Adeline; Frank	48
VANBUSKIRK	Cornelius V.	69	WREN	Dollie Louise	53
	Sarah Ann	69		Jessie; Charles	53
VANBUSKIRK	John M.	69		William Cuthbert	53
	William D.	69		Amy	53
VANDERZEE	Elizabeth	41		Emma Josephine	53
	Catharine	41	WYCOFF	Jacob R.	74
VAN SYCKEL	John H.	66		Mary C.; Edith	74
	George C.	66	WYCOFF	Julia A.; Sarah C.	74
	Chester; William C.	66		Daniel M.	74
	Lamar; Mary E.	66	WYNCOOP	Peter	35
VAN SYCKEL	Holloway W.	68		Ann Eliza; John	35
	Isabella D.	68		Henrietta; Elizabeth	35
	Selinda; Elbridge	68	YOUMANS	Hugh; Tamson	74

INTERMARRIED NAMES.

	PAGE		PAGE
Abbott, Rev. Henry	54	Brady, Jane	27
Adams, B. Scureman	54	Brandt, Nancy	36
Adams, Sarah	47	Brasher, Walter	43
Albertson, Emma	32	Briggs, C. C.	56
Albright, Rachel	63	Briggs, Marion Lydia	55
Allen, Francis Isabella	65	Britton, Fanny	71
Allen, George	52	Brooks, Amanda	44
Allen, Rev. Richard W.	36	Brown, George	29
Aller, Isaac	68	Brown, Jennie L.	27
Allshouse, Rebecca	62	Brown, Robert	33
Alpaugh, William B.	68	Browne, Thomas	32
Alpaugh, William C.	69	Bruckner, Carl H.	49
Anderson, Julia	30	Buck, Sarah	33
Anderson, Margaret	47	Bunn, Jacob	69
Anderson, Mary	52	Burrows, Sarah	31
Anderson, Marion G.	30	Burt, Susan Wooley	51
Andrews, Catharine	56	Burtell, John	36
Apgar, William M.	69	Bush, Mary	28
Armstrong, George	40	Butler, Mr.	27
Armstrong, Phebe	33		
Atkins, Lucy	51	Cannon, M. D. Henry Rutgers	48
Austin, Rosanna	42	Carle, Catharine Halfe	36
Aumack, Catharine	81	Carter, Sarah B.	33
		Castera, Louise	62
Baker, Phebe	55	Case, John R.	83
Ball, Charles	35	Case, Levi	69
Ballard, Minnie	27	Case, Mr.	75
Balmer, Charles	28	Caswell, Henry	35
Bancroft, Martha Boylan	42	Cathers, Louise	71
Bangs, Nancy	36	Chambers, Lydia	83
Beavers, Mary	64	Chesbro, Angeline	44
Beebe, Alanson	35	Chichester, Helen	70
Beebe, Ellen S.	43	Churchill, Adelaide	71
Benedict, Elmira	28	Clark, Edwin R.	45
Besson, Jacob	70	Clark, George	40
Beyer, Susan	67	Clark, John	33
Biddle, Richard	83	Cline, Jacob	63
Billops, Virginia Lilly	53	Coles, Catharine	50
Bird, Christina	70	Coles, Oscar	32
Bird, Elizabeth	70	Coles, Peter Sheldon	50
Bird, M. D. Joseph	65	Coleman, John	74
Bird, Joseph B.	65	Coleman, Willimpia	62
Bixby, Albert H.	51	Compton Lydia	80
Blankman, Mary	33	Cook, George R.	46
Blodgett, Elizabeth	34	Cooly, James B.	68
Bloomer, Elizabeth	34	Coonly, Ellen	40
Bloomer, Jennie M.	39	Cottier, John B.	40
Bonnell, Elizabeth	66	Coyle, Mary	82
Bonnell, Samuel L.	71	Craig, Moses	71
Bowers Elizabeth	28	Cregier, Mr.	34
Bowlby, James	73	Crowe, Allen	70
Boyce, Catharine	36	Cummins, Simon	74

INDEX. 139

Name	Page	Name	Page
Cunningham, Wilson	29	Gano, Lucinda	71
Curd, Sarah V.	65	Gardyne, Elizabeth	69
		Garver, William A.	40
Dale, Cornelia	73	Garrett, Ann	39
Davids, James B.	27	Garruguz, Margaret L.	45
Davis, Dwight	70	Gascoygne, Elizabeth	37
D'Aubigné, Ophelia Merle	49	Gedney, Joshua	31
Dickinson, Nancy Maria	47	Gifford, Ruth	73
Dillon, James	63	Gillies, Josie	36
Divine, Joshua	57	Goodfellow, Samuel	46
Dosh, Maggie	44	Gordon, Mary	30
Duckworth, Mary	68	Gose, Nellie	52
Driscoll, Ellen G.	33	Gravatt, Ezekiel	82
Duncan, M. D. Wm. F.	47	Greene, Armenia	56
Dunham, Bethany	69	Greenwood, Sophia	81
Dunham, James	67	Grissom, Mr.	80
Dunham, Mary E.	64	Groat, Gertrude M.	43
Dunham, Sarah	67	Gurney, Emily J.	38
Dunham, Whitfield	67		
Durfey, George	40	Hagerman, William	63
Durie, John	34	Hall, Henderson	29
Dusenbury, John	62	Hall, John	33
Dusenbury, Mary E.	47	Hallenbeck, Albert C.	43
Dusenbury, Thomas Gilcrist	48	Hallenbeck, Jacob	34
		Hamilton, Damana C.	71
Eckel, John	68	Hart, Nellie A.	45
Eckel, Samuel V.	69	Hauxhurst, Rev. Jotham H.	37
Eddum, Sarah	69	Hauxhurst, Louise	52
Ellison, Mrs. Mary	27	Haverly, Sylvanus	35
Emory, Christian G.	67	Haviland, Grant	57
Emory, Mercy G.	67	Haviland, Joseph	57
Ennis, Sarah	52	Haviland, M. D.; Norman G.	54
Evander, George	35	Helm, Elizabeth	63
Evans, Theodore	72	Henry, George F.	81
Everett, Clara	28	Herron, Edward	42
Everett, Sarah	29	Hewett, Elijah	68
		Hewlett, Mary E.	56
Fergerson, Mary A.	51	Hickman, Margaret	36
Ferris, Alanson	31	Hight, Charlotte A.	51
Ferro, Edward	28	Hoff, Catharine H.	81
Fires, Catharine	39	Hoffman, Louise J.	67
Fish, Abagail	30	Hoffman, William F.	67
Fisher, George	53	Hogle, Peter	35
Fisher, Jannette	53	Holbrook, Peter	36
Fisher, Maria	69	Holmes, John	80
Fitts, John W.	75	Holly, M. D.; Francis Manton	47
Flagler, Henry E.	43	Horton, Mary	50
Flansberg, Elizabeth	39	Hotaling, Henry E.	51
Fluellen, Mary	47	Hotaling, Hester	40
Follett, Oscar	55	Hotaling, Maggie	37
Foot, Annie E.	30	Hotaling, Tunis G.	37
Francisco, Reed	30	Hough, M. D. Dewitt	70
Fredendall, Levi	43	Hovey, William	27
Frisbie, William	37	How, Adelia	29
Fritz, Ellen	74	Hubbs, Richard C.	56
Fritz, Rev. Jessy	75	Hubbard, Eber Granville	54
Fuller, Edwin C.	55	Hulsizer, Margaret	75
Furbeck, Henry	46	Humphrey, William	67
Furman, Eliza	52	Huntly, George W.	45

INDEX

	PAGE
Huntly, L. G.	36
Hulbert, Lucy	46
Hutchings, Joseph	32
Hyer, George	76
Irwin, Sarah	81
Ives, Samuel A.	31
Jacobson, Margaret	43
Jerolomon, Isaac	34
Jerolomon, Susan	34
Jerrold, Miss	28
Jones, Girard	83
Jones, William L.	82
Kells, James Scott	65
Kenyon, Randolph	65
King, Lizzie McK.	32
Knapp, Halsey W.	50
Kniffin, Caleb	26
Lacy, Benjamin	74
La Fumée, Joseph	82
Landis, Lizzie	29
Lane, Margaret	31
Langdon, Caroline	52
Lambert, Minnie E.	72
Laqueer, Jane	70
Larison, Amanda	67
Larison, Kesiah	71
Larison, Lavinia	71
Lattin, Miss	34
Layton, Helen	56
Leddings, Jane	36
Leonard, Cornelia	73
Leonard, Mr.	28
Lewis, Julius Walker	65
Lewis, Mary W.	50
Leyden, Michael	45
Litchfield, Elizabeth	34
Litchfield, Hiram Tompkins	39
Lomson, Julia A.	74
Lomson Lizzie	62
Lomson, Margaret	74
Long, Minnie	45
Lord, Mary	25
Losee, Mr.	56
Lowe, Mary E.	83
Ludlum, James M.	57
Lully, Clara H.	36
Lutz, Belinda	66
Lyon, F. Garretson	50
Manly, N. T.	36
Marchant, Ann Elizabeth	28
Marlow, William C.	63
Marshall, Mirabah	57
Martin, George	40
Martin, Margaret	37

	PAGE
Matthews, Eliza	51
Mattison Emily	64
Mattison, Mahlon	68
Mayberry, Elizabeth	69
McShane Robert	62
Mead Sophia	41
Meadon, Thomas	42
Mercer, Dr.	29
Merritt, Hannah	26
Merritt, Mary	33
Mettler, Isaac S.	68
Metz, Elizabeth	62
Mond, Mary	63
Moore, Gershom	71
Morris, Lucy A.	46
Morris, Mary E.	81
Morgan, Mary A.	50
Moul, Luella S.	37
Mowry, Andrew	30
Mull, Annie M.	83
Mumford, Theresa A.	38
Munson, Stephen T.	49
Murrey, George	43
Negus, James E.	68
Newman, Rev. Thomas	54
Nowland, Margaret	81
Oberly Anthony	62
Onderdonk, William	34
Opdyke, Holcomb	68
Osgood, Jared	29
Osman, Carrie M.	37
Owens, Abner	28
Palen, Frederick D.	40
Parry, M. D. Edward	71
Parry, Samuel	69
Parshall, E.	72
Parter, Sarah	35
Patty, Sarah	73
Peck, Anna	48
Peckham, Roxanan	28
Pell, Miss	34
Pettitt, Margaret	29
Phillips, Mr.	64
Pierce, Matilda	70
Pierson, Nancy	29
Pinckney, Joshua	34
Pipe, James	40
Pitnord, Mr.	75
Platt, Mr.	51
Platt, Bleecker	34
Post, Eliza	32
Post, William S.	27
Potter, Catharine	33
Pray, Mr.	46
Price, Henry M.	46
Prior, James	56

INDEX. 141

Name	PAGE	Name	PAGE
Purdy, Elizabeth	26	Smith, Stephen	73
		Snyder, Samuel	35
Rairack, Lucy	35	Soulé, Ellen M.	38
Rairack, Miss	34	Spearman, Eliza Dickson	42
Rassenberg, Mr.	75	Springstead, Catharine	40
Raub, Levi	63	Squires, Richard M.	51
Ray, Hannah	39	Stevens, Cornelia M.	34
Redfield, Mary Kellogg	64	Stevens, M. D. Lloyd	34
Redfield, Simeon	48	Steadwell, Susan	47
Reynolds, Christopher	36	Stickney, William	33
Reynolds, Margaret Ann	27	Stiger, Matilda	64
Richards, Augusta	65	Story, Josephine	68
Riley, Cordelia	30	Strong, Nathan H.	27
Robbins, John	56	Strong, Cornelia	56
Robbinson, Mr.	79	Sutton, Katie	35
Roberts, Edward E.	34	Sutton, Rebecca	35
Rockwell, Fanny	65	Swany, William	40
Rockafeller, Mary E.	66		
Rooke, Matthew R.	51	Talman, George W.	44
Rose, Mary E.	64	Taylor, Abigail	41
Rowe, Catharine	41	Terry, Daniel W.	49
Rowe, Hannah	43	Terry, Francis	38
Rowe, Stephen	46	Terry, James	40
Rounds, Reuben	30	Terry, Washington Carhart	38
Rudolphy, Charles	70	Terrill, Elizabeth	35
Runckel, Philip	70	Thomas, Edward	69
Russel, Julia A.	30	Thompson, Catharine Ann	46
Rutherford, Robert	32	Thompson, James	32
Rutherford, William	72	Titus, Alansen M.	37
Ryan, John	35	Titus, Rev. W. Smith	54
		Tomlinson, Mary F.	36
Sammis, Mary A.	57	Torrey, Amanda	38
Scott, Thomas	26	Totten, Mary	42
Scott, Julia	36	Totten, Phebe	48
Schermerhorn, Nancy	43	Towne, Lewis	35
Seamon, Thomas J.	56	Trace, Mary A.	71
Seely, Capt. Hiram	81	Tucker, William	31
Seely, Adelbert	30	Turner, R. M.	29
Shapleigh, William F.	27	Tuttle, William	39
Sharbraum, Miss	35		
Shepherdson, John	40	Ungar, Ferdinand	55
Sherman, Eliza	35	Utter, Elijah	35
Sherwood, Calder Smith	53		
Shine, Joseph D.	75	Van Antwerp, Margaret	35
Shultz, Elizabeth	40	Van Buskirk, John	69
Sigmon, Mr.	64	Van Beuren, John	40
Sloat, Jane	50	Van Brunt, Lydia	28
Smith, Caroline	34	Van Cleef, William	35
Smith, Eliza M.	31	Van Denberg, Francis R.	43
Smith, Elizabeth	71	Van Derbilt, Elizabeth	46
Smith, Elizabeth	41	Van Derheyden, Staats	35
Smith, Gilbert H.	34	Van Derpool, Caroline Amanda	38
Smith, Harvey	52	Van Derzee, Cornelius	41
Smith, M. D. J. T.	27	Van Eyck, Barent	35
Smith, Kate	72	Vannatta, Mr.	74
Smith, Lewis	35	Van Pelt, Mary A.	83
Smith, Lucinda A.	41	Van Pelt, Peter	76
Smith, Margery A.	72	Van Syckel, Daniel	68
Smith, Selinda E.	56	Van Syckel, Furman	68

	PAGE		PAGE
Van Syckel, George H.	69	White Benjamin F.	36
Van Syckel, M. D. Sylvester	66	White, Ellsworth	50
Van Zandt, John	34	White Elizabeth J.	74
Van Zyle, Harriet Newell	50	White Martha	35
Van Vosberg, William	40	Whitbeck, Phebe Ann	34
Van Vosberg Willard	40	Whitson, Martha	56
Vedder, Catherine	41	Wilcox, Jane	68
Vine, Kate	42	Wilkins, Leonard	44
Vine, Elizabeth	42	Williams, Andrew	32
Voorhes, Sarah	70	Williams, H.	83
Voorhes, Sarah	64	Willson, John B.	47
Voorhes, Emeline	69	Wiltsie, Elizabeth	35
Vredenberg, Esther Ann	53	Wiley, Lefa Jane	33
		Winchel, Laura A.	54
Wager, Benjamin	35	Wire, E. G.	63
Wakely, Major Charles W.	28	Wood, M. D. Barney	41
Waldron, Garret	35	Wood, Mr.	76
Walker, James	29	Woodruff, Elmira	66
Wallace, Phebe Ann	34	Woodruff, George	82
Walling, John	82	Wooster, Asbury	48
Warne, Thomas	25	Wren, William Cuthbert	53
Ward, William	37	Wright, Addie W.	45
Ward, David	40	Wright, Harriet	27
Watts, Henry D.	66	Wright, Miriam	31
Weaver, Charles	42	Wright, Wellington W.	83
Webb, Avery T.	27	Wycoff, George P.	74
Webster, Fanny	29	Wycoff, John H.	74
Weeks, Jane	41	Wyncoop, Jacob	35
Weller, Joseph	75		
Wetmore, James	26	Youngblood, William	34
Wheeler Hannah	31	Youmans, Mary	75
Wheeler, Julius	30	Youmans, Simon	74

THE END.

Milton Keynes UK
Ingram Content Group UK Ltd.
UKHW010309170224
437973UK00007B/736